TO RAISE A FALLEN PEOPLE

To Raise a Fallen People

THE NINETEENTH-CENTURY ORIGINS OF INDIAN VIEWS ON INTERNATIONAL POLITICS

Edited by Rahul Sagar

Columbia University Press
New York

Columbia University Press
Publishers Since 1893
New York   Chichester, West Sussex
cup.columbia.edu
Copyright © 2022 Columbia University Press
All rights reserved

Library of Congress Cataloging-in-Publication Data
Names: Sagar, Rahul, editor.
Title: To raise a fallen people : the nineteenth century origins of Indian views of the world /
[edited by Rahul Sagar].
Description: [New York, New York] : Columbia University Press, [2022] |
Includes bibliographical references and index.
Identifiers: LCCN 2021048824 (print) | LCCN 2021048825 (ebook) |
ISBN 9780231206440 (hardback) | ISBN 9780231206457 (trade paperback) |
ISBN 9780231556484 (ebook)
Subjects: LCSH: India—Foreign relations—1765–1857. | India—Foreign relations—1857–1919. |
India—Politics and government—19th century. | India—Intellectual life—19th century.
Classification: LCC DS447 .T63 2022 (print) | LCC DS447 (ebook) |
DDC 320.954—dc23/eng/20220114
LC record available at https://lccn.loc.gov/2021048824
LC ebook record available at https://lccn.loc.gov/2021048825

Cover design: Gavin Morris
Cover image: Shaykh Muhammad Amir, *Palanquin Carriers, 1820–1850.*
Courtesy of the Peabody Essex Museum, Salem, Massachusetts.

For Mia and Sophie

Peoples always feel the effects of their origins. The circumstances that accompanied their birth and served to develop them influence the entire course of the rest of their lives. If it were possible for us to go back to the origins of societies and to examine the first monuments of their history, I doubt not that we could discover in them the first cause of prejudices, habits, dominant passions, of all that finally composes what is called national character. . . . Thus would be explained the destiny of certain peoples that an unknown force seems to carry them along toward. . . . But until now the facts have been wanting for such study; the spirit of analysis has come to nations only as they aged, and when at last they thought of contemplating their cradle, time had already enveloped it in a cloud, ignorance and pride had surrounded it with fables behind which the truth lies hidden.

—ALEXIS DE TOCQUEVILLE, *DEMOCRACY IN AMERICA*, 1.1.2

CONTENTS

CONTENTS

PREFACE

This volume has been nearly two decades in the making. Its origin lies in the curious vitality that India began to exhibit toward the close of the twentieth century. A remarkable series of events—the liberalization of the economy, the development of nuclear weapons, the forging of new diplomatic relationships, the embrace of globalization—appeared to herald a revolution. The renunciatory ideals of recent decades were being displaced, observers declared, by a more pragmatic worldview. But, before long, the very same observers were expressing frustration at signs of continued inwardness and apathy. From this uneven experience arose a question of some importance: Should we expect a rising India to behave as great powers do—by concertedly developing its capabilities and advancing its national interests—or not? Seeking to understand the sources of India's conduct, I set out to investigate what role Indians thought their country should play on the world stage.

How to conduct such an investigation was not obvious. Whom exactly to study? In which time period? What documents to examine? Little had been published on the role of ideas since Bimal Prasad's pioneering *The Origins of Indian Foreign Policy*, which appeared in 1962. Archives seemed the natural starting point. But government documents on "grand strategy" were classified, and I was told, more than once, that debate on this subject was conducted in person and not on paper. Therefore, I began interviewing bureaucrats and ministers with a view to identifying ideas important to them. But busy officials and wary retirees were not always willing or able to speak candidly. Those who did volunteer their views struggled to elaborate them at length. The generalities they voiced suggested that they were influenced not by some precise doctrine but by ideas in the wider milieu. Hence, I began trying to discern broad intellectual currents in public life. This was not a straightforward process either. I searched for polls or surveys, but sources like these were hard to come by at the time. The little data available was unreliable and topical rather than conceptual. It did not, therefore, illuminate the ideas informing public attitudes.

At an impasse, I discussed the matter with J. N. Dixit, the cerebral former foreign secretary (and later national security advisor). He suggested examining what leading figures immediately before and after Independence had said about international politics (which later became the subject of his *Makers of India's Foreign Policy*, a valuable collection of short biographies). I was reassured by his stress on the impact that ideas had had on decision-makers, but felt unsure about focusing on a few prominent figures, especially those from the Congress era. The churning unleashed by the "million mutinies" underway suggested that India's future political leadership would emerge from new and varied segments of society. A close study of the *grandees* of recent decades would shed light on their doings, but it would not illuminate what had come before or what was to come after.

Still mulling over the problem, I spoke with Jairam Ramesh, then in his avatar as a celebrated technocrat. A voracious reader, he happened to be in the middle of Walter Russell Mead's *Special Providence*, which outlined the competing "traditions"—Hamiltonian, Jeffersonian, Jacksonian, and Wilsonian—that had shaped American foreign policy. Why not do something similar in the Indian context, he suggested. I found the proposition appealing, but I was not persuaded by the "personification" of ideals because leaders typically only channel streams of thought that long precede them. As I searched for a way to trace these broader currents, Kanti Bajpai published his groundbreaking essay "India's Strategic Culture," which outlined the "schools of thought" he saw as shaping Indian conduct. Inspired by Bajpai's example, but differing from him on the characterization of the dominant ideals of the era, I eventually wrote my first essay on the subject, "State of Mind: What Kind of Power Will India Be?"

Often when preparing a publication, one learns how much one does *not* know. By the time my first essay was complete in 2008, I felt I had made an error in focusing solely on the post-Independence period. In effect, I had assumed that Indians only began thinking about international politics after 1947. This was in line with the prevailing view, voiced by George Tanham in his influential *Indian Strategic Thought*, and seconded by colossuses like K. Subrahmanyam and Jaswant Singh, that there was "little evidence" that Indians had previously "thought coherently and systematically about national strategy." As Subrahmanyam observed in *Shedding Shibboleths*, "When Tanham put forward his thesis in a seminar . . . in Delhi in February 1994 to an audience comprising a large number of retired defence and civilian officials and academics, the majority contested his thesis. 'Did not India have Chanakya as a strategic thinker?,' they asked. True indeed, but Chanakya lived some twenty-three centuries ago. What of the centuries after him?"

Contrary to Tanham, I was already starting to see signs that we would find, buried in the archives, many rich debates about international relations. I soon had a chance to make my case. In 2010, Kanti Bajpai invited me to a landmark conference, "Grand Strategic Thought." I presented there an essay detailing the hitherto-ignored corpus produced by Hindu nationalists in the early twentieth century. The reaction from the audience was all the encouragement I needed. A sabbatical at the National University of Singapore's Asia Research Institute (ARI) in 2011, for which I am indebted to Prasenjit Duara, allowed me to polish the essay (subsequently published as "'Jiski Lathi, Uski Bhains': The Hindu Nationalist View of International Politics"). It also gave me the chance to prepare an overview of the materials I had found (later published as "Before Midnight: Views on International Relations, 1857–1947").

After these essays started circulating, Devesh Kapur, that selfless mentor to generations of scholars, invited me to participate in a grant application to the Smith Richardson Foundation. Thanks to Allan Song, who saw merit in the proposal, the grant was approved and I could begin truly plumbing the archives. Initially, I focused on locating books. The going was slow because these materials were widely dispersed and oftentimes missing. Still, encouraged by Kanti Bajpai and C. Raja Mohan, I kept up the slog. Then, following a thought-provoking conversation with Pratap

Bhanu Mehta, I began to search more widely, trawling through periodicals and newspapers. I soon realized that owing to the costliness of printing and circulating books, the great bulk of public debate in colonial India had actually occurred in these periodicals and newspapers, which contained hundreds of essays, reports, and book reviews on international politics. This literature showed that, far from being mute subjects as Tanham had been led to believe, colonial-era Indians had given international relations much thought. In particular, when confronted with great power politics, they had reacted unevenly, with some embracing it and others fiercely decrying it. This history shed invaluable light on the question I had set out to investigate. It suggested that India's unsteady conduct does not stem from pragmatism being a new or inchoate phenomenon. Rather, it reflects lingering disagreement over the relevance and appeal of great power politics.

What remained was to thoroughly excavate the materials I had discovered. But there was a significant challenge: the periodicals in question were scattered around the globe, making them difficult and expensive to collect. Then I had another stroke of luck. In 2013 I moved to the National University of Singapore (NUS). The leaders of three institutions there were persuaded of the importance of what I had found and extended invaluable support: Kishore Mahbubani at the Lee Kuan Yew School of Public Policy, Pericles Lewis at Yale-NUS College, and Tan Tai Yong at the Institute of South Asian Studies (ISAS). As a consequence, I was able to build a team of research assistants to help me collect these far-flung periodicals. Subsequently, in 2015 I was recruited to NYU Abu Dhabi, where Hervé Crès, the dean of Social Sciences, and Fabio Piano, the provost, did everything possible to help me cross the finishing line. This volume is a direct outcome of the immense support they provided. I do not have words enough to thank them for their faith in my research.

So far, I have detailed the individuals and institutions that made this book possible. Along the way I also benefited greatly from colleagues that invited me to present the material in this volume or made illuminating observations on the themes developed in it. They include C. Raja Mohan, Ashley Tellis, Milan Vaishnav, and Constantino Xavier at Carnegie Endowment; Nicolas Blarel at Leiden University, Sunil Khilnani at SAIS, Johns Hopkins University; Rajesh Basrur, Sumitha Kutty, Anit Mukherjee, and xvii

PREFACE

Pascal Vennesson at RSIS, Nanyang Technological University; John Don-
aldson and James Tang at SOSS, Singapore Management University; Rahul
Mukherji at SAS, National University of Singapore; Rani Mullen, Ronojoy
Sen, and Sinderpal Singh at ISAS, National University of Singapore; Harsh
Pant at Observer Research Foundation; V. Krishnappa at the Institute for
Defense Studies and Analyses; Amit Ahuja, Dhruva Jaishankar, Devesh
Kapur, Siddharth Mohandas, Manjari Miller, Anit Mukherjee, Rohan
Mukherjee, Vipin Narang, Avinash Paliwal, Ankit Panda, Manjeet
Pardesi, Srinath Raghavan, Paul Staniland, W. P. S. Sidhu, and Shivaji Son-
dhi at the Annual Security Studies Workshop at CASI, University of Penn-
sylvania. I am also very grateful to Manu Bhagavan, David Malone, and
Ashley Tellis for opportunities to publish in volumes they edited, and to
Jonathan Fulton, N. Janardhan, Parag Khanna, Karthik Muralidharan,
David Sloan, and Vivek Sondhi for valuable discussions. Finally, I am
indebted to a number of retired officials for insightful off-the-record
discussions.

For the publication of this volume, I am deeply grateful to my editor,
Caelyn Cobb, for warmly supporting my book proposal, and to Susan
Pensak for shepherding the manuscript through the press. My sincere
thanks also to the anonymous reviewers, who took time in the midst of an
unsettling pandemic to evaluate the manuscript and provide valuable suggestions. My thanks equally to Sravya Darbhamulla and Arunava Sinha for
enriching the volume with their elegant translations, to Sebastian Ballard
for the helpful map, and to Gavin Morris for the gorgeous cover. These
invaluable additions were made possible by generous support from NYU
Abu Dhabi Grants for Publication Program. I am especially indebted to
Meghna Basu, Christian Fastenrath, Sanchi Rai, Khushi Singh Rathore, and
Nidhi Shukla. I would not have been able to complete the manuscript without their invaluable, untiring, and good-natured research assistance. This
manuscript was brought to a close during my Global Network University
Fellowship at NYU Shanghai. For this unique opportunity, and for their
warmth and support, I am very grateful to Joanna Waley-Cohen, the provost, Maria Montoya, the dean of Arts and Sciences, and Zvi Ben-Dor
Benite, the associate vice chancellor for Global Network Faculty Planning.
My greatest debts are to colleagues who have urged this manuscript along,
even when they have not always agreed with the conclusions I have drawn:

Kanti Bajpai, Hervé Crès, Devesh Kapur, Pratap Bhanu Mehta, C. Raja Mohan, and especially Anit Mukherjee and Rohan Mukherjee, who have soldiered through more drafts than they would like to remember.

Finally, on a personal note, I want to thank my family, Jyoti, Prema, Una, Simran, Isabella, and Kitty, for their love and support, without which I would have little to show for myself. Above all else, I am grateful to my daughters, Mia and Sophie, for their love, joyfulness, and brilliance. I cherish them more than words can say, and I thank them for making my life utterly happy and complete. I dedicate this work to them: may they be bridges; may they cross divides and advance international understanding.

August 15, 2021

The original essays have been edited for length. Deletions are indicated by ellipses. Spellings have been modernized where possible. Insertions are marked with square brackets.

TO RAISE A FALLEN PEOPLE

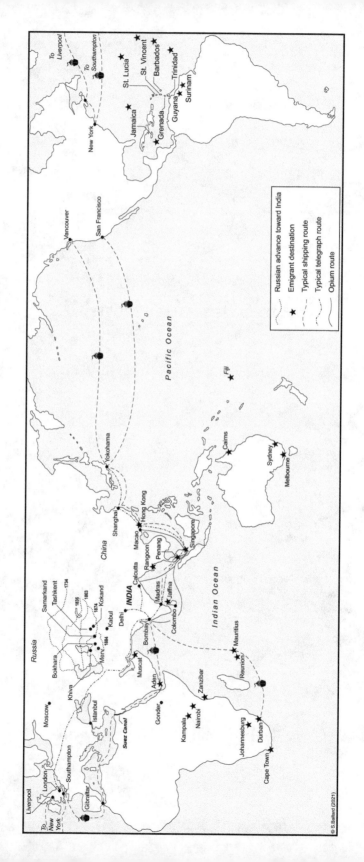

Russian advance toward India

★ Emigrant destination

Typical shipping route

Typical telegraph route

Opium route

To Liverpool

To Southampton

St. Lucia

St. Vincent

Barbados

Trinidad

Surinam

Grenada

Guyana

Jamaica

New York

Vancouver

San Francisco

Pacific Ocean

Fiji

Yokohama

Cairns

Sydney

Melbourne

Shanghai

Macao

Hong Kong

Rangoon

Penang

Singapore

China

Calcutta

Madras

Jaffna

Colombo

INDIA

Delhi

Kabul

Kokand

Samarkand

Tashkent

1734

1868

1863

1874

Merv

1884

Bokhara

Russia

Khiva

Bombay

Muscat

Aden

Zanzibar

Reunion

Mauritius

Indian Ocean

Moscow

Istanbul

Suez Canal

Gonder

Nairobi

Kampala

Johannesburg

Durban

Cape Town

Liverpool

London

Southampton

Gibraltar

To New York

INTRODUCTION

As its economic power, military strength, and cultural influence expands, India is becoming an ever more important actor on the world stage. The course of world events is also deepening its significance. China's extraordinary rise has prompted discussion in the West about whether it can employ India as a counterweight.[1] Consequently, there is growing interest in understanding Indian worldviews.[2] In particular, what do its decision-makers consider the nature of international relations to be, and what role do they think India ought to play in it?

When it comes to charting contemporary views, we are spoiled for choice. A slew of excellent books by officials[3] and scholars[4] have shed much light on India's foreign relations and the personalities[5] at the helm. Drawing on personal experience, public records, and private papers, these books have greatly advanced our understanding of Indian foreign relations since 1947.[6] Far less has been written, however, about ideas and debates on foreign relations that occurred *before* 1947.[7] This lacuna deserves to be rectified. As important as it is to study what leaders and citizens say and do today, we ought to also attend to what they have thought in the past. This is because a political community is informed by the ideals it inherits; its trials and tribulations create memories and sentiments that "can be inhibiting as well as inspiring."[8] These memories and sentiments fade or ferment quietly in recesses, and then forcefully reemerge when circumstances change.[9] It is important, therefore, to step back from contemporary personalities and current events and to search for deep sources of conduct—the "national ideas" that serve as "building blocks of international life."[10]

Until recently, there was some doubt as to whether Indians have thought about international relations in a "systematic and sustained way."[11] A number of observers worried that culture, geography, and history had fostered a lack of interest in foreign relations and thereby led to a culture of ad hoc policymaking.[12] These fears were put to rest by pioneering scholarship outlining the worldviews held by India's political and bureaucratic elites.[13] The doctrines of nonviolence and nonalignment championed by Mohandas Gandhi and Jawaharlal Nehru received particular attention in this regard. But barely had commentators begun to map the terrain than Indian decision-makers started distancing themselves from the renunciatory ideals associated with their predecessors. Decisions to openly develop nuclear weapons, invite foreign investment, and forge strategic partnerships, especially with the United States and Israel, constituted notable departures from previous ideological commitments.[14]

Thus arose the question that observers continue to debate today: Is India's incipient pragmatism a new, perhaps fragile, impulse, or is it the expression of deeper, more durable, beliefs? Put another way, we want to know whether India will henceforth behave like a traditional great power by concertedly developing its capabilities and advancing its national interests. A number of commentators answer this question in the affirmative. Pragmatism, they argue, is far from new or unusual in the Indian context: it is entirely in keeping with deep-seated civilizational beliefs about the nature and purpose of politics. As evidence, they cite texts and examples from when kingdoms in the Indian subcontinent commanded great power and influence, including classical treatises like the *Brihaspati Sutra, Manu Smriti, Arthashastra, Tirukkural, Agni Purana,* and *Nitisara*; literary wonders like the *Mahabharata* and the *Hitopadesa*; the examples set by ancient empires, especially the Mauryas and Cholas; and the medieval and early modern empires of the Pandyas, Vijayanagara, the Mughals, the Sikhs, and the Marathas.[15]

This revival of interest in ancient and early modern Indian statecraft is a welcome development. But can these striking examples truly be the source of contemporary conduct? Such a claim can be challenged on two fronts. First, the further back in history we delve, the more uncertain becomes the contemporary relevance of what we find. Present-day political institutions, moral values, social order, technological abilities, and economic engagements are entirely unlike those of the ancient Mauryans or even the early modern Marathas. This makes it difficult to draw anything like a straight line from their ideals to the current era. Second, if contemporary India is in fact deeply shaped by a centuries-old tradition of political realism, then there ought to be broad agreement on the ruthless nature of international politics and a corresponding willingness to do what is necessary. In practice, however, contemporary India openly neglects policies that would allow it to marshal resources and compete more effectively in the international sphere. Neither changes in political leadership nor institutional reform, despairing observers note, seem to make much of a difference.[16] Such widespread apathy cannot be an inheritance from the empire-building Mauryas or Marathas, surely.

Here then is the puzzle we confront when we search for the deeper sources of Indian conduct: the ideals of the *recent* past cannot explain the pragmatism of the present day; the ideals of the *distant* past cannot explain the half-heartedness of the present day. This puzzle seems to favor the skeptical opinion that Indian worldviews boil down to little more than "cautious prudence"—a "predominantly defensive" stance that does not spring from any sustained reflection on the nature of international relations.[17] But there is another possibility: What if scholars and commentators have not searched in the right place?

To Raise a Fallen People shows that India's perplexing behavior can be deciphered by changing *where* we look for evidence. If we want to understand how the past influences the present, then we need a fuller account of *modern* India's intellectual history. This history commenced in the *nineteenth century* when divided or distant communities came to see themselves as members of an overarching nation. This was the period when educated and capable public figures sought to influence colonial authorities as well as their compatriots through argumentation rather than agitation. The political forces these elites birthed became central in the post-Independence period. This makes what they previously read and wrote about international politics of continuing relevance to those seeking to understand contemporary India.

Upon first glance there would appear to be no evidence that nineteenth-century India bore witness to insightful debate on foreign relations. Only one book, the venerable *Sources of Indian Tradition*, has marshaled some of the available materials.[18] However, as its focus is on domestic politics, the extracts it contains touch on international politics only in passing. To compound matters, these extracts come from figures separated by decades, making it hard to discern something like sustained national conversations on foreign relations. Given such fragmentary evidence, scholars have naturally assumed that the nineteenth century was the era of domestic awakening, and that concerted engagement with international politics really only began a little before 1947.

To Raise a Fallen People overturns this conventional wisdom. It does so by drawing attention to the English-language literature that emerged and flourished in the nineteenth century, principally in the form of periodicals.[19] Though some of these periodicals have been used to good effect by historians, they have been overlooked by scholars of India's foreign relations. This owes, no doubt, to the wide dispersal of these periodicals and the woeful condition of libraries and archives in India. At any rate, the oversight deserves to be rectified. The emergence of English as the lingua franca and the growth of the post and the rail, which made long-distance communication viable, helped newspapers and periodicals do for India what the café did for Europe and the town hall did for America. In these fora, public figures developed and debated ideals that shaped India's subsequent trajectory. Thus, if we want to comprehend enduring patterns in Indian thinking about international politics, it is essential to examine what was said in the nineteenth century—the Age of the Page. By virtue of a decade of archival research, *To Raise a Fallen People* provides the bird's-eye view that we have thus far been lacking. It contains essays that permit us to rise above eccentric personalities and singular events and to instead witness broader national conversations on international politics.

Inevitably, only a very limited selection can be presented here. The interested reader will find a much larger sample in the section entitled "Further Reading" and in a new online archive.[20] And there is still more to be done. The focus on English-language sources means that we have before us the views of the metropolitan elite, especially of "eminent" Indians, as they were termed at the time. This focus is not unreasonable, seeing as this class of persons had, through the press and the dais, extraordinary and enduring influence on their compatriots' understanding of world events. But a still-wider sample, drawing on regional languages, will greatly deepen our knowledge of the ideas circulating in this era. Hopefully, scholars with relevant linguistic abilities will take up this challenge.[21] Regrettably, the archives revealed relatively little in the way of English-language publications on international (as opposed to domestic) politics by marginalized groups such as women and Dalits.[22] These perspectives appear in far greater numbers after the turn of the century, when increased access to education expanded the public sphere, and opportunities for travel as well as the upheaval produced by the Great War stimulated wider discussion on international questions. A forthcoming sequel to this volume that focuses on the first half of the twentieth century will incorporate and shed light on these valuable viewpoints.

So, what do the essays unearthed here show? Arguably, they reveal the foundations of India's half-hearted approach to great power politics. The pragmatism of India's metropolitan elite comes to life in chapters 1, 2, and 8, which trace historic debates on the necessity of pursuing modern education, traveling overseas, and adopting Western norms. The essays challenge narratives that depict Indians as powerless colonial subjects. For example, critics of colonialism depict the arrival of English education in India as an imposition founded on disdain for indigenous culture. They often angrily cite Thomas Babington Macaulay's remark that "a single shelf of a good European library was worth the whole native literature of India."[23] But Macaulay's bluster does not explain why *Indians* hastened to study English. *They* eagerly sought modern education because they realized that modern knowledge holds the key to power. Consider what Madhava Rao, who would go on to become a celebrated "native" statesman, had to say to his compatriots in 1846. Only by learning European arts and sciences, he urged, could they hope "to raise a fallen people high in the scale of nations."[24] There was no reason to shy away from the demands of the age. To the contrary, a true patriot would encourage the acquisition of Western knowledge because

> When once these advantages will be attained, the Hindoos will not rest satisfied with a mere perusal of the English works of science and literature; they will not rest contented with treading a beaten path; but now and then some towering genius may rise, and exploring some unknown track, make discoveries which may not fall short of those of Watt, or Newton, or any other illustrious ornament that English annals can boast of.[25]

At the same time, chapters 3 to 7 trace the growing disillusionment of India's metropolitan elite when England repeatedly betrayed the liberal ideals it publicly professed. This unhappiness opened the door to the reactionary ideas and movements, detailed in chapter 9, that gained influence in the closing decades of the nineteenth century. Prior to this moment, Indians had thought it incumbent upon rulers to preserve society from threats; their ancient treatises on statecraft warned them that international politics was governed by *matsya-nyaya*, or the "law of fishes," where the strong feed on the weak.[26] But in the final quarter of the nineteenth century, a contrary idea—that international politics was sordid and self-destructive—gained currency. This abrupt change owed much to European scholars of Indian civilization. Seeking to justify their arcane scholarship to European audiences that had an increasingly dim view of the peoples they ruled over, these "Orientalists" insisted that "materialist" Europe had much to learn from India's "spiritual" civilization. This endorsement thrilled Hindu revivalists in India, who employed it to balm their compatriots' wounded pride. And so, by the close of the century, it became routine to hear, as the crusading Theosophist Annie Besant declared in Calcutta's Town Hall in 1894: "Let lesser nations and lesser men fight for conquest, for place and for power; these gimcracks are toys for children, and the children should be left to quarrel over them. . . . In India's hand is laid the sacred charge of keeping alight the torch of spirit amid the fogs and storms of increasing materialism."[27]

Championed by charismatic figures and religious societies, the notion that "spiritual greatness" was India's "mission" became commonplace in the following decades. Thus, we find Gandhi depicting nonviolence as the quintessential Indian value, Rabindranath Tagore proclaiming India the embodiment of humanity, and Nehru promising that India would forge a new order characterized by peaceful coexistence. Though bitter experience has diminished the appeal of these ideals, they remain a potent force in contemporary India, taking the form of pacifism on the Left and spiritualism on the Right. A clearer sense of the origin of these ideals may help us understand their longevity. Born out of "the inflamed desire of the insufficiently regarded to count for something among the cultures of the world,"[28] these ideals are likely to remain alive so long as Indians feel the need to prove that they are morally superior to those more powerful than themselves.

Another insight from the essays in this volume is that many present-day controversies over foreign policy have a longer history than is commonly realized. Consider, for instance, the ideal of *swadeshi*, which calls for the boycotting of foreign products. This ideal, which resurfaces every so often, is widely believed to have originated with the Indian National Congress and is popularly associated with Gandhi's *charkha* (spinning wheel). In fact, as chapter 5 shows, the ideal emerged before the Congress even existed, and it originated not in romanticism or chauvinism but in anger at British India's unwillingness to protect "infant" domestic industry from foreign competition. Though legitimate, this grievance did not escape criticism from Indians themselves. Even in the nineteenth century we find statesmen pointing out that, the colonial authorities' indifference notwithstanding, there was much that Indians could do to make domestic industry more competitive. The example set by Japan, whose industries had clawed their way into world markets, was never far from their minds. Note, for instance, what Romesh Chunder Dutt had to say in his popular travelogue *Three Years in Europe*. Passing through the recently opened Suez Canal, Dutt observed in 1886:

> Among the steamers that we passed by in the Canal, I will mention one. It was a Japanese Man-of-War, entirely manned and officered by the Japanese. Among all the nations of Asia the Japanese are the only people who are keeping abreast of European civilization; and they are doing so by their energy and honest work, and by their freely adopting whatever is good and great in modern civilization.[29]

Consider another current controversy, namely, whether India ought to enter into alliances. To adopt a policy of this kind, it is sometimes said, would mean shedding a purportedly age-old policy of neutrality. This claim does not hold up to historical scrutiny, however. Chapter 3 shows that when the Great Game in Central Asia intensified, English-educated Indians publicly advocated for Britain and strongly opposed Russia—on ideological grounds. We should not conclude from this, however, that ties of language and culture made Britons and Indians "natural allies." For when Britain greedily pursued hegemony in Asia, and condoned racial discrimination against Indian migrants, the very same English-educated Indians grew disenchanted, creating a rift whose effects still linger. This is a precedent that contemporary observers in the West would do well to reflect upon.

To Raise a Fallen People has immediate relevance in another sense too. It reminds contemporary observers that India has long been home to vigorous debate about ends and means in international politics. As such, it disproves the notion that there is a singular, traditional "Indian" view of the world. Instead, we witness deep disagreement with views ranging from pacific cosmopolitanism to militant nationalism. Notice what this implies. It has become commonplace to depict contemporary India as being in the midst of an intellectual revolution, as an erstwhile saintliness is cast aside in favor of a new, unbecoming muscularity.[30] The essays recovered here cast doubt on this narrative by showing that 'New India,' as it has come to be termed, has deeper foundations than is commonly acknowledged. Muscularity may be more advertised today, but its importance has long been admitted in modern India. Consider, for example, this salutary warning in Bankim Chandra Chatterjee's masterpiece *Dharmatattva* (1888):

> The people who are strong will rob the weaker people. I am not speaking of the barbarians: this is the custom of civilized Europe. Today France is robbing Germany, next day Germany is robbing France. . . . Just as dogs in the rural markets snatch morsels from one another, peoples whether they are civilized or not are despoiling one another's property. A strong people is always ready to fall upon the weaker ones.[31]

ENGLISH EDUCATION

Let us now briefly survey the contents of this volume, proceeding chapter by chapter. The earliest evidence of sustained reflection on the nature of international relations comes from public discussions on the importance of modern education. The zeal with which nineteenth-century Indians sought out such education is well known. But the reasoning behind this collective decision is not nearly as well known. An examination is instructive because it reveals the striking pragmatism of India's metropolitan elite. Having realized how much power and prestige in the modern era depended on knowledge, they explicitly endorsed "European" education in order to raise India's standing. Thus, they flocked to private academies and charitable missionary schools and donated generously to create private institutions like Hindu College in Calcutta and Elphinstone College in Bombay.

Through associations like the Native Education Society in Bombay and the Hindu Literary Society in Madras, they also beseeched the British as well as their compatriots to fund such education.

"Knowledge Is Power," the first essay in this collection, sheds light on the thinking behind these endeavors. In it, the celebrated polymath Bal Gangadhar Shastri Jambhekar, then the "native secretary" to the Native Education Society in Bombay, urged his readers to "gain every acquisition, which has rendered European nations superior to Asiatics." Writing in the *Bombay Durpun*, which he had recently founded, Jambhekar, who was only twenty at the time, approvingly cited Prasanna Kumar Tagore's observation that England's "vast superiority" over India was due entirely to her "cultivation of the arts and sciences." The need of the hour, these figures agreed, was for wealthy natives to support modern education "as far as their circumstances will permit."[32]

This line of thought was developed at greater length in "On Native Education," an essay from the pen of an eighteen year old by the name of Madhava Rao, who would go on to become successively the dewan (or prime minister) of the Native States of Travancore, Indore, and Baroda. One of the earliest graduates of the Madras High School, which was launched in 1841 after some seventy thousand "Native Inhabitants" of Madras petitioned for the establishment of "Collegiate Institutions" for their "mental improvement," Rao wrote "On Native Education" in 1846 for a school competition.[33] The essay caused such a sensation that it led to questions about its genuineness, compelling the school to publish a statement confirming that it had indeed been written by "a Native youth."[34]

In his essay, Rao blamed India's having fallen "so low in the scale of nations" on her intellectual stagnation. The only way to raise her from "her prostrate condition," he declared, was to acquire the learning of "the first nation on the face of the earth"—specifically a "liberal education" in the arts and sciences. To this end, Rao urged his countrymen to support "English Seminaries" and to foster "an inextinguishable thirst for knowledge." If this were done, India would "gradually rise to eminence" and the "astonished nations of Europe" would, Rao promised, "behold a rival gloriously rising in the east, capable of coping with them for superiority." These claims were no "idle reveries of a deranged imagination," Rao insisted, because the "pages of History" showed that "the spread of enlightenment" inevitably brought about "complete moral and political regeneration."[35]

A major step toward the realization of this vision came in 1854, when universities were established in Calcutta, Madras, and Bombay. Within two decades the number of those educated in English grew from lonely hundreds to many thousands, with roughly five thousand heading every year into the professions alone. Initially, this development was extolled for producing "young people radiant with hope and ambition."[36] By the end of the 1870s, however, the euphoria was gradually being replaced by anxiety as an insurmountable breach appeared between those who were "for all intents and purposes, Englishmen" and those who, lacking such education, expected conformity with traditional norms.[37] *High Education in India*, an address by Chandranath Basu, official translator to the Government of Bengal, captured the dilemma perfectly.

Speaking at the Bethune Society, the preeminent learned society in Calcutta, Basu conceded that English education had "produced a schism in Hindu society, a schism in the Hindu family, a schism in the Hindu heart." But there was, he warned, no choice but to bear the "infinite misery" caused by this "revolution," as India could not return to that "isolated and inactive position which she was able to occupy in ancient times." Having been "introduced" to Europe, it was now "absolutely necessary" that she should "study Europe" in order to equal the latter in material terms. Otherwise, she risked ending up "absolutely without a position in the world." As he put it, "In plain prose, England has introduced India into the great comity of nations—has drawn India into the scheme of material life. . . . India is now, in fact, a country of Europe, not of Asia. . . . To be able to maintain this new position, to be able to fulfil this new destiny, India must receive that high scientific education which has resulted in modern Europe."[38] The need of the hour, then, was for India to "accept science as a duty and a necessity." It would not be easy to introduce "an atmosphere of practical thought" into the country, but without this, he warned, India would have little or no success in the emergent "industrial economy."

In spite of such exhortations, over the next two decades many Indians became *less* sanguine about the benefits of embracing English education. No one made the point more acutely than the England-educated liberal Bishan Narayan Dar, who would go on to preside over the Indian National Congress in 1911. Anachronisms were not easily eradicated, Dar pointed out in his essay "Some Characteristics of Indian English-Educated Youths" (1886), because "ideas change sooner and more easily than feelings." As he put it, "Our present instincts and tendencies are the resultant of forces that have been co-operating for ages; and no sudden change in our outward surroundings, such as the introduction of a European element into India, can change them. Centuries must pass away before new instincts and habits can be formed." There was a still deeper point. Indians were not the primitive and disorganized peoples that the Romans or the Arabs had conquered in their day. Even English-educated Indians felt that Hindu society had withstood the test of time because its mores and laws had much to commend in them. As Dar reminded his peers:

An Englishman thinks of his ancestors as barbarians, rude, illiterate, and the like ... and has no particular reason to be proud of being a descendant of Hengist and Horsa, or William the Conqueror. In fact, he considers the progress of European society to be hampered to a great extent by the customs and traditions of feudalism surviving up to this day. But can an Indian contemplate the course of Indian history with the same feeling? No. That there once existed a mighty civilisation in India, nobody can deny; and though in a great many respects it is not suited to the present age, yet it developed to their full extent certain qualities and faculties of the human mind, without which there can be no completeness in our progress, and which it will be ill for us to lose.

The impracticality of bridging "indigenous" and "modern" civilization meant, Dar observed that in practice the two worlds—the vernacular with its venerable traditions and the English with its newfangled notions—simply coexisted uneasily. From this extraordinary circumstance would emerge a lasting divide between the reverent and the radical, "the one sighing for the unreturning past, and the other pushing forward to realise the dim and distant future."[39] This divide would grow stronger in the following century, leading to sharply contrasting views on the kind of relationship India ought to have with the West, a subject we will return to later in this introduction.

CROSSING THE SEAS

If the clamor for modern education reveals the pragmatism of India's metropolitan elites, equally telling was their discarding of the peculiar taboo against overseas travel. Memory of this taboo has all but vanished today, but prior to the twentieth century, it posed a genuine barrier to knowledge of the outside world. This was especially true for upper-caste Hindus, but it was a concern for Muslim gentry as well.[40] In both cases, travel overseas was seen as "denationalising" as it made it difficult to adhere to (or to prove that one had adhered to) rules about diet and personal conduct. As the century wore on, however, Indians began publicly questioning this taboo on grounds of national advancement.

An early critique came from the pen of Bholanath Chandra, one of the first graduates of Hindu College, and an esteemed member of the emergent English-educated intelligentsia. Chandra's essay "Vindication of the Hindoos as a Travelling Nation" (1867) challenged the "common opinion" that "Hindoos have never been a travelling people." "Ancient Hindoos," he pointed out, had left "ample" evidence of their wide and varied travels. The contemporary "antipathy" to travel likely stemmed, he speculated, from Hindus' descent into an "effeminate" nation that feared competition. "It is always a policy of the weak against the strong, to avoid disastrous collisions— the contact of the earthen pot with a brass pot," he surmised. Fortunately, change was afoot. The "necessity for a more enterprising spirit than has hitherto distinguished the natives" was now "beginning to be felt."[41] The success that the first batch of native students of law and medicine had found upon their return from England in the late 1840s and early 1850s was encouraging "others to follow in a similar path."[42] Then there was the impetus generated by an emergent nationalism. As Chandra appealed to his countrymen:

> At present no enlightened Hindoo thinks of anything so much as to see his countrymen take a place amongst the nations of the world. . . . A widely diffused enterprising spirit is always the antecedent to that widely diffused national prosperity, by means of which alone can our nation ever hope to occupy a conspicuous position in the eyes of mankind. Such was the state of India once, such ought to be the state of India again.[43]

Over the next two decades the debate over crossing the seas became ever more acute as the number of Hindus venturing overseas started to swell. The question then became whether these emigrants ought to be received back into society upon their return. The orthodox held travelers to be "irretrievably forfeiting caste and religion," while reformists pled that they were entitled to be reincorporated on pain of "penances."[44] Perhaps the most remarkable individual to run the gauntlet was Anandibai Joshi, who decided in 1882 to obtain a medical degree from the Women's Medical College in Philadelphia. The prospect of Joshi's departure for the United States caused a furor in Serampore, where her husband was the postmaster. Christians in Serampore "did not wish her to go abroad unless she would submit to baptism before she went," whereas Brahmins "reviled her for even entertaining the intention" of traveling abroad. Both groups insisted that she was "liable to go astray." Joshi was undeterred, however, telling her supporters, who numbered "one or two in a thousand," that she wondered only about the "scruples" and the "timidity" of those attacking her. Still, when the bitter criticism transformed into public protests, Joshi was compelled to make "a public statement." This she did through a forthright lecture, delivered extempore, at Serampore College in February 1883. The lecture, reprinted here as "My Future Visit to America," was remarkable, coming at a time when it was a "grave misdemeanor" for a woman to appear, much less speak, at a public forum. It was also admirably succinct and logical. Her compatriots ought to support her, Joshi argued, because the efforts of individuals like her would help India "stand on her own feet." As she put it,

> The knowledge of history as well as other places is not to be neglected. The present state of things is the consequence of the former, and it is natural to enquire what were the sources of the good that we enjoy or the evils we suffer. . . . Ignorance when voluntary is criminal, and one may perfectly be charged with evils who refused to learn how he might prevent it. When the eyes and imagination are struck with any uncommon work, the next transition of an active mind is to the means by which it was performed. Here begins the true use of seeing other countries. We enlarge our comprehension by new ideas and perhaps recover some arts lost by us, or learn what is imperfectly known in our country.

As to the threat of excommunication, Joshi added, she did not "fear it in the least," because she would "make no change in my customs and manners, food or dress," stressing that she intended to "go as a Hindu, and come back here to live here as a Hindu." In the event, "why should I be cast out," she asked, "when I have determined to live there exactly as I do here?"[45]

Not everyone was as brave as Joshi. Unable to detain their ambitious progeny, but fearing social sanctions, Hindu elites eventually began pressing for assurance that travelers would not be excommunicated upon their return. In Calcutta, the controversy led to the formation of a "Sea Voyage Movement" that declared itself "the tangible expression of a natural desire felt by the Hindu community to supplement its growing knowledge by travel in foreign countries, and to add to its resources by the expansion of its commerce." Its leaders declared their intent to proceed along "orthodox lines" by seeking to "ascertain" from a range of eminent *pandits* (priests) "whether sea voyage and residence in foreign countries are permissible on the part of Hindus" so long as the requisite rules are followed. They left little doubt about what they expected to find, declaring, "The elasticity of the Hindu system is indeed its most remarkable characteristic. Its wonderful vitality is due to the readiness with which it recognises the pressure of external circumstances, and the ease with which it falls in with them."[46] Southern India did not lag behind in debating the question. "May Hindus Cross the Ocean?" by S. E. Gopalacharu in 1894 was one of many essays that attacked "narrow minded Pandits."[47] As Gopalacharu saw it, India's prosperity depended on acquiring "foreign methods":

> On every account it is necessary that some of our more intellectual men should visit England and other European countries in order to find out what means may be taken for the improvement of the condition of this country. We should remember the example of the Russian Emperor Peter the Great, who went to England and worked in a shipyard, and then went back to teach his own people how to work.

Like his contemporaries in Bengal, Gopalacharu was certain that an "exhaustive review" of the *shastras* (classical treatises) would show that Hindus were entitled to "arrange our duties according to the condition of the circumstance of the country, of the people, and of the time."[48] In practice, however, orthodox Hindus were not persuaded by what appeared to them a suspiciously convenient change in doctrine. Consider the experience of

Narendra Nath Datta—better known as Swami Vivekananda—whose voyage to America in 1893 gave him the opportunity to deliver his famous speeches before the World Parliament of Religions. As Vivekananda recounted in a letter to his associates in Madras:

> Remember one evening [in] Pondicherry—we were discussing the matter of sea-voyage with a Pandit, and I shall always remember his brutal gestures and his *Kadapi Na* (never)! They do not know that India is a very small part of the world, and the whole world looks down with contempt upon the three hundred millions of earthworms crawling upon the fair soil of India and trying to oppress each other.[49]

In the end, the question of whether Hindus may travel abroad was settled by deeds rather than words. No one pointed this out more clearly than the *litterateur* Bankim Chandra Chatterjee. The committee appointed by the Sea Voyage Movement had written to Chatterjee, "the apostle of Hinduism,"[50] seeking his views on whether the *shastras* permitted sea voyage. Chatterjee replied by questioning the utility of doctrinal validation. It was "doubtful," he wrote, whether following the *shastras*, with their many anachronistic rules, would really result in "social welfare." Hindu society traditionally had "cast off" elements of the *shastras* when "necessity" so demanded. On this basis, "Sea-voyages are conformable to religion because they tend to the general good. Therefore, whatever the *Dharma Sastras* may say, sea-voyages are conformable to the Hindu religion." Besides, increasingly what really mattered, Bankim claimed, was whether individuals had "the necessary means" to undertake the journey—when they did, tradition was simply ignored.[51] This was somewhat of an exaggeration, as travelers clearly remained fearful of social sanctions.[52] But Chatterjee was correct in discerning that the ground was shifting. Increasing numbers—thousands of traders and professionals, and tens of thousands of indentured laborers from varying castes— were emigrating and thriving overseas.[53] Meanwhile, the number of Hindu "gentlemen" traveling to England every year rose from less than a dozen in the early 1860s to more than 180 by the end of the century.[54] Then there were prominent examples of successful disobedience, none more widely reported than that of the celebrated Vivekananda. As the Sea Voyage Movement gleefully observed, far from being regarded as an "apostate," Vivekananda's accomplishments in the West led him to "being welcomed back warmly and looked up to as a prince of Hindoos and the pride of Hinduism."[55]

THE GREAT GAME

We have seen that the conviction that England owed her preeminence to her arts and sciences prompted Indians to study her literature and to travel to her shores. This education and contact had a striking effect on their outlook: though it prompted Indians to increasingly contest the English *in* India, it also gave rise to an ideological bond between English-educated Indians and Britain. This bond was evidenced most clearly in the former's support for "liberal" Britain in her test of wills with "despotic" Russia during the so-called Great Game.

From the early nineteenth century onward Russia began probing, and then expanding, southward into Central Asia. Convinced that Russia's ultimate objective was to challenge their rule in India, British strategists split into two camps. The so-called "masterly inactivity" school recommended waiting until the Russians reached the Indus, where their supply lines would be vulnerable and unruly Afghans would distract them, whereas the "forward" school proposed meeting Russia in Afghanistan, lest the Russians bribe the Afghans to turn on India. Initially, the "forward" school had the upper hand, prompting the First Anglo-Afghan War, which started in 1838 with the British seeking to impose a pliable ruler, and concluded with a revolt by the Afghans in 1842 and the decimation of retreating British contingents. Chastened, the British then moved in the direction of "masterly inactivity," focusing instead on securing the subcontinent, annexing Sind in 1843 and Punjab in 1849.

The Russians did not sit still in the interim. In spite of earlier attempts to penetrate Central Asia having ended badly, they persevered. By the middle of the nineteenth century, they had subdued the Kazakhs, and then, contrary to the expectations of the "masterly inactivity" school, they successfully traversed the barren Kazakh steppe and reached the frontiers of the Khanates of Kokand, Bokhara, and Khiva. In 1863 Russia publicly announced her intention to colonize Central Asia, and over the following decade she gained control over a number of important cities, including Tashkent in 1865 and Samarkand in 1868.

Since these developments implicated India and occurred at a time when her elites were schooling themselves in English, Indians naturally began following, and then contributing to, heated debates as to whether British India ought to accommodate or contain Russia's imperial ambitions. At first many Indians were swayed by British liberals who believed that Russia had little support in India since Hindus saw the English as stewards of much-desired reform and Muslims viewed Russia as their "inveterate foe." The adoption of a "forward" policy would imperil this favorable situation, British liberals argued, because Indian elites believed that conflict with Russia would divert funds to securing Britain's interests abroad and lead to "a suspension of those measures of development, on the success of which the advancement of this country depends" such as "the construction of new lines of railways, canals, and roads." British liberals also played down the threat Russia posed. Her capabilities, they insisted, were not as frightful as "Russophobists" claimed. They emphasized the challenge of projecting power in the region, especially in light of Russia's constrained finances. Should the Russians be foolish enough to intervene in Afghanistan, they declared, she would "only plunge into a sea of difficulties which will cost them men and money, without any material benefit from an unruly and wild race." At the same time, they expected Russia's militarism to be blunted by Tsar Alexander II's policies encouraging international commerce—that "great pacificator of nations." There was even the hope that, should Russia succeed in "subduing" Central Asia's "wild and lawless tribes," and perhaps even convert them to Christianity, she would turn the region into a "high road for pacific intercourse and civilization."[56]

In 1873 the Russians took Khiva, and then began pressing on Kokand, which they subsequently colonized in 1875. With Russia now in control of the vast swathes of territory that make up modern-day Kazakhstan and Uzbekistan, the belief that her ambitions would be thwarted by the harsh environs of Central Asia began to appear naive. As Russia began pressing down on Merv, an oasis town in modern-day Turkmenistan, the "forward" school revived under the aegis of Benjamin Disraeli's conservative administration. The consequence was the Second Anglo-Afghan War, which began in 1878 with another dethronement and concluded in 1880 with another retreat.

It was in the midst of this war, as the British Indian Army was struggling to hold Kabul and Kandahar, that "England and Russia" appeared in 1879 under the signature "India" in the Calcutta-based *Oriental Miscellany*. The writer rapped British liberals for their poor judgment, observing that

> English liberals consider the great deserts of Central Asia to be a crushing obstacle in the way of Russia. But foreign invaders of India from Alexander the Great to Ahmed Shah Abdali have proved that arguments based upon mountains and deserts do not and cannot possess overpowering force. Human power has accomplished feats more difficult and daring than Russia's march to India over the deserts of Central Asia and the mountains of Afghanistan would in all likelihood be.

British liberals, "India" argued, had also badly misread Russian intentions. For the foreseeable future, Russia's rapid development would arguably make her *more* rather than less war-like. This was because, like "all powers that are rising," Russia was "giving birth to great minds," particularly in the field of soldiery, where her ambitious military governors were "full of that buccaneering spirit which . . . produces restless activity." Where better to direct their ambitions than India, which represented "in a million-fold form the commerce of all the Central Asian khanates taken together"? Owing to these "strange tendencies working in her foremost minds," an invasion by Russia "at some future time is not an absolute impossibility—nay rather, is something like a moral certainty." A Russian invasion was a frightening prospect, "India" continued, because the British Indian Army's struggles in Afghanistan suggested that they lacked manpower. Nor was there much hope that their numbers could be quickly bolstered, since the imported troops British India relied on were hard to come, the English being unwilling to submit to compulsory military service. The deeper problem then was a civilizational mismatch: "the long reign of English industrialism" had "weakened the military instincts of the English people," whereas Russia retained the militarism of a less developed but hardy race. It would now take great statesmanship to make England "retrace her steps, cultivate the military instinct, and become the first-class military power" that she had been in the past.[57]

Soon after "India" had his say, the Liberal party returned to office under William Gladstone and reverted to the policy of "masterly inactivity." The Russians, as "India" had predicted, remained on the offensive. Undeterred by Britain's difficulties in Afghanistan, they rolled on, occupying Merv in

1884 and in 1885 Pandjeh, an Afghan border town between Merv and Herat. This was a momentous development as Herat had long been viewed as a crucial staging post on the marching route that led, via Kandahar and Kabul, to India. With the Russians now only a few hundred miles from British India, and with rumors of an impending invasion circulating in the bazaars, Indian elites urgently sought to rally public opinion in favor of Britain.

One prominent intervention was a pamphlet, "Why Do Indians Prefer British to Russian Rule?," jointly published and circulated by the most important political associations of the era, including the British Indian Association, the Indian Association, and the Poona Sarvajanik Sabha. The pamphlet expressed admiration for the English, who were "the freest and the most liberty-loving people in the world," whereas Russians were "slaves of a military caste." Its focus, however, was on stressing the comparative virtues of British rule. The "deepest and the firmest conviction of every educated Indian," it declared, was that, in spite of the "serious defects of its rule," Britain was "the friend and sympathizer" of subject nations like India, whom it was seeking to "elevate and educate," whereas Russia's "iron yoke" was "crushing not only to the races it has conquered" but also "to the mass of its own subjects." Hence, Indians had no interest, it concluded, in exchanging the "good things" associated with Pax Britannica for "the Russian system."[58]

Lesser-known figures also made their voices heard, including the Parsi writer Dinshah Ardeshir Taleyarkhan, the municipal commissioner of Baroda and erstwhile editor of the Gujarati daily *Guzerat Mitra*. Taleyarkhan offered what amounted to the Native States' view on Anglo-Russian relations. In an article written in July 1885, three months after the Russian occupation of Pandjeh and five months before the much-anticipated inaugural meeting of the Indian National Congress, Taleyarkhan assailed his compatriots for their misplaced priorities. So focused were they on getting "a handful of natives of India admitted into the civil service" that they had not "been able even to perceive the sources of such probable dangers to India as might someday make short work of the lesser aspirations by which they are now so entirely controlled." The real problem confronting India, he contended, was that "party differences" in England had led to a "temporising foreign policy" and delayed preparations that would "enable India to hurl irresistible and overwhelming armies against any foes which dared to invade her." This shortcoming had to be corrected, Taleyarkhan pleaded. Under English tutelage India could "fairly hope to be a free country at some future day." But it could bid "adieu to this bright hope—which Great Britain has lighted in our breasts—if ever India was trampled under the iron heels of the hungry and wily Cossacks." The need of the hour, then, was that "India must somehow or other be made capable of punishing her wrongdoer herself." Here Taleyarkhan could not resist expressing his distaste for Congress-wallahs, whose petitions and pleas had long demanded a curtailment of military expenditure. To prevent a cataclysm, he warned, Indians had to be willing to "pinch themselves a little more than now with financial burdens." But this was not all. British India too needed to adopt a fresh perspective. It could offset Russia's advantage in the field, he advised, by expanding the native component of the British Indian Army, and by drawing on the Native States' forces, such that "every member and every community of the Indian Empire may patriotically contribute to our fighting strength."[59]

By the middle of the decade, with Merv and Pandjeh now in Russian hands, and with the Burmese flirting with the French, Britain decided to beef up the British Indian Army. In 1885 the decision was made to fortify India's frontiers and to increase the size of the British Indian Army by some thirty thousand troops, which cost an additional two million rupees per annum.[60] This decision provoked intense public debate in India since these new troops were partly to be imported from Britain and partly recruited from "extra-Indian" territories, and the requisite funds were to be raised through a combination of domestic retrenchment, taxation, and expensive loans. Subsequently, two distinct critiques took shape. One side accepted that Russia posed a threat but demanded that British India respond by expanding the native element of the British Indian Army, in part by drawing on the Native States' military resources. The other side, by contrast, argued that British India would be better served by eschewing a confrontational foreign policy and focusing instead on domestic welfare.

Ganesh Vyankatesh Joshi's "The Native Indian Army" (1886) exemplified the former position. Joshi, the secretary of the illustrious Poona Sarvajanik Sabha, contended that the policy of "arithmetical addition" adopted by the British Indian Army did not "furnish any solid or safe basis" on which to address the "military difficulty" facing India. This was because the British were meeting their recruitment goals by importing expensive English troops and enlisting "foreign mercenaries." The mortality rates of the former and the uncertain loyalty of the latter raised serious questions about the army's steadfastness in the event of an invasion, and hence lowered national morale. This dangerous situation was compounded by the absence of military reserves or a national militia to fall back upon in the event of an emergency—a condition "without example in the modern world," Joshi protested. "We cannot believe that, in a serious struggle on the [North Western] or on the Eastern frontiers, with a formidable military power, we can safely count on obtaining needful supplies of drilled or seasoned men from across ten thousand miles of sea," he added. To make matters worse, rather than remedying this vulnerability, the British were "demartialising" the natives, with the Arms Act of 1878 having prohibited them from bearing or even possessing weapons.

These deficiencies, Joshi went on to argue, could be rectified in three steps. Most immediately, by offering commissions the British could increase recruitment from the native community, particularly from the upper echelons of Indian society, whose interests were firmly tied to the land. Furthermore, rather than suspecting and routinely threatening to abolish the militaries of the Native States, the British could convert these resources into a national reserve. It made no sense, said Joshi, to ignore "such splendid material as these armies of our native states can easily be turned into." Finally, the British could repeal the Arms Act and permit natives to volunteer, thereby laying the foundation for a national militia.

Joshi backed up his proposal with sharp complaint. The British, he warned, confronted an inescapable financial truth, namely, that India's military expenditure was "ruinous." Between 1865 and 1885, India's annual military expenditure had increased from 15.5 million to 21.5 million rupees per annum, which was more than any European country, France aside, spent on defense. Yet, even after "unmurmuringly" supporting this "maximum outlay" India enjoyed only "a minimum of effective forces," with the British Indian Army being less than two hundred thousand in number, which was a quarter of the size of the Russian Army. If financial considerations were given "due weight," Joshi lamented, his proposed reforms were "the only alternative open to Government."[61]

Critiques of the kind voiced by Joshi meant that at practically every session of the Indian National Congress between 1885 and 1900, delegates called for improvements in military preparedness via the establishment of military colleges where natives "may be educated and trained for a military career," the organization of a "system of militia service," and the promotion of "a widespread system of volunteering."[62] But even as these proposals gained support, a different perspective was becoming far more prominent. Joshi had questioned *how* the British Indian Army ought to be expanded, whereas a second critique questioned *whether* such expansion was necessary at all, especially when Russia's focus gradually shifted from Central Asia to the Far East.

An early exponent of this latter position was Dadabhai Naoroji, whose essay "Expenses of the Abyssinian War" (1868) criticized Britain for declining to cover the cost of utilizing the British Indian Army in Abyssinia. When the British replied that there was no loss to India from merely "lending" her troops, Naoroji responded that "if the troops are required for [India's] security, then it is unfair that India should be deprived of that security," and if the troops were not required for India's security then "the army should be reduced by so much."[63] Naoroji extended this critique in his essay "The Moral Poverty of India" (1880), where he pointed out that India's public debt had grown by leaps and bounds because of "English wars abroad in the name of India." A more affordable route to security, he contended, was for England to earn the trust of her subjects by investing in their development. "If the people of India be satisfied," he declared, England could "defy a dozen Russias."[64]

Between 1880 and 1885 this complaint became routine. In 1881, the East India Association memorialized against imposing the costs of the Second Anglo-Afghan War on the Indian exchequer, as it was an "Imperial" war, undertaken not to defend India but rather to fulfill England's desire "to dominate the affairs of Afghanistan."[65] In 1883, the same association petitioned against imposing the costs of the Anglo-Egyptian War on the Indian exchequer, once again observing that the war "was entered upon in pursuance of a European policy and mainly for the protection and advancement of European interests."[66] In 1885 such complaints were addressed directly to the English electorate then in the midst of a fiercely contested general election. The leading Indian associations of the era published leaflets pleading with British electors to condemn the "appalling enormity of Military Expenditure in India."[67]

After its founding in 1885, the Congress led the charge. Among the very first resolutions it ever passed was the declaration that "the proposed increase in the military expenditure of the empire is unnecessary, and regard being had to the revenues of the empire and the existing circumstances of the country, excessive." The Congress reaffirmed this stance at its meetings in 1889 and 1890, declaring "the necessity for the reduction of, instead of the continual increase to, the military expenditure of the country."[68] Behind these resolutions was extensive research by the Bombay liberal Dinshaw Edulji Wacha, who delivered at the 1891 Congress a scathing and widely cited assessment of British Indian military expenditure.

Invited to address the Congress on the factors behind India's continued poverty, Wacha laid the blame squarely on increased military spending, which left little room in the budget for developmental projects. By 1891 this expenditure included not only the additional two million rupees per annum necessitated by increased troop levels but also an additional sixteen million rupees on "special defense works" and "strategical railways" in the North West and ten million rupees on annexing Burma. These expenditures, Wacha insisted, were not truly necessary. Rather, "it is the policy of England in her relations with the politics of Central and Eastern Europe . . . which unhappily leads to military activity or military 'preparedness' . . . entailing crores of wasteful expenditure." A defensive posture in the vein of "masterly inactivity" was, Wacha argued, the only reasonable policy: "To go beyond our natural line of defence, gentlemen, is to court defeat. We expose ourselves needlessly and fritter away the resources and strength which we ought to conserve for the defence from within our impregnable boundaries whenever the dreaded external attack becomes a real one which, I think, is still a remote contingency." The expenditure necessitated by a "forward" policy was especially galling in view of the opportunity cost for an impoverished India, which had a "crying want" for "productive commercial railways and irrigation canals" that could "arrest the growth of that gaunt famine" stalking the land. "Think for a moment, gentlemen," Wacha lamented, "how contented, how prosperous, how progressive India might have been today had she been saved this huge extraordinary extra expenditure." The willingness of the British to "waste" money in this way, Wacha continued, suggested that the real menace that India confronted was not Russia, which only "idly threatens us," but "military tax eaters" who did not "leave a stone unturned" to find some "pretext" by which to obtain "promotions, decorations, and kudos."[69]

Such sentiments meant that from 1891 onward it became routine for the Congress to call for Britain to reduce or at least share India's military burdens, and for it to emphasize that recent "abnormal increases" were "principally owing to the military activity . . . in pursuance of the imperial policy of Great Britain." These criticisms became especially vocal as famine plagued the land. In 1897, the Congress condemned British India's frontier policy as "aggressive" and "injurious," and an "extravagance" in the face of widespread want, and in 1898 it attributed the "practical starvation of the civil administration" to Britain's unwillingness to return to the "only safe policy," which was to stay within India's "natural limits."[70]

THE EASTERN QUESTION

We have seen that Indians, particularly those associated with the Congress, sided with Britain against Russia but disagreed on the question of how the subcontinent might best be secured. This alliance received a further blow when Britain began to question its alliance with the declining Ottoman Empire, which had proven unable to honor its debts or to protect its Christian minorities from violence. This development prompted complaints from English-educated Indian Muslim elites. According to them, Britain's foreign policy ought to be predicated not on whether Turkey reformed itself but rather on the religious sentiments of Indian Muslims, who wished to see the Caliph preserved.

The steady decline of the Ottoman Empire gave rise in the latter half of the nineteenth century to the question of how the Great Powers ought to manage or absorb its splinters. For Anglo-Indians,[71] the vital issue in this so-called Eastern Question was whether Russia ought to be allowed to take control of Ottoman territories in Asia Minor, especially Turkey. Reverend James Long's essay "The Position of Turkey in Relation to British Interests in India" (1875) outlined the dilemma sharply. Long was uniquely positioned to comment on the topic, having made extended visits to Turkey and Russia following three decades in and around Calcutta, where he was active in public life, being a close confidant of Reverend Krishna Mohan Banerjee, one of the most influential native converts to Christianity.

Like a number of his Anglo-Indian contemporaries, Long operated on the premise that the Eastern Question and the Great Game were linked. Russian expansion into Central Asia was a product of her defeat in the Crimean War, which had prompted her to search for new avenues of expansion. Hence, writing in the wake of Russia's steady progress through

Central Asia, Long declared that Britain's only hope of averting expensive and destabilizing conflict at India's border was to "divert" Russia's energies back toward the more "natural" channel—that is, to accommodate her in Asia Minor. Besides, he doubted that Turkey could be placed on a stronger footing, as much-vaunted reforms to modernize her finances and liberalize her treatment of minorities had proven "little better than shams." Since she was unlikely to serve as a reliable bulwark against Russia's advances in Europe, there was, he thought, little point propping her up at the expense of British India. "Is it not safer for England to have Russia in force on the Mediterranean," Long asked, "than on the Hindu Kush and frontiers of Afghanistan?"

The principal objection to allowing Russia to annex Turkey was the fear, voiced by the Conservatives, that Britain's acquiescence would inflame India's Muslims. Long played down this prospect on the grounds that "ignorance and sectarian bitterness isolate[d] the Indian Moslems from the Turks," leading him to predict that the "fall of the Sultan" would have "little effect in India." And even if the Sultan's predicament riled them, this was not an undesirable outcome, he urged, because the "fall of the Crescent" could serve to temper their "pride and fanaticism." "The crumbling of Moslem power in Constantinople, Ispahan, Delhi, and Samarkand are signs of the times to the Indian Moslem," said Long.[72]

By 1877 Long had altered his view. In "The Eastern Question in Its Anglo-Indian Aspect," he conceded that "some" Indian Muslims did indeed "look up to the Sultan as the Caliph." Following the recent outbreak of the Russo-Turkish War, Muslims in India had raised a large sum of money "in aid of Turkey, and Russia has been publicly cursed in all the mosques." These Muslims, Long now conceded, would "doubtless . . . look on the expulsion of the Turks from Constantinople as a terrible disaster and disgrace." Though he correctly sensed that "the Moslem mind is waking up and beginning to feel that all is at stake with their religion," Long declined to change his conclusion. Were Britain to appease Indian Muslims' concerns about Turkey, he warned, they would still endanger their position in India because the majority—two hundred million Hindus—had "little sympathy for Turkey." Imagine how they would react, he warned, if Britain's continued support for Turkey goaded Russia into invading India. Hence, the question Britain had to ask itself was whether it wanted to "sacrifice the substance for the shadow."[73]

The emergent pan-Islamism Long had noted only grew stronger over the following decade. Few did more to kindle the flame than Jamaluddin Afghani, the Iranian pan-Islamist who found refuge in Hyderabad following his expulsion from Egypt in 1879. Arriving as a "cult of Turkey"[74] was taking hold among Indian Muslims, Afghani gave sermons on the "large idea" of "Mohammedan unity" that stirred important figures, including Hyderabad's prime minister, Salar Jung.[75] Afghani subsequently summarized his ideas in "Letter on Hindustan," which was published in the radical French newspaper *L'Intransigeant*, shortly after he had fled India in 1882. In this essay, Afghani warned the British that the "veneration" that Indian Muslims felt for "the reigning Caliph" meant that "the Sultan pushed to his limits would be a precious ally for the adversaries of the English in the Indies, by doing nothing more than preaching at the Mecca and sending to Hindustan a manifesto bearing his name by some Sheik authorized to speak in his name." And even if the Sultan could be prevented from acting in this way, he added, Britain's attempts to seize control of Ottoman possessions in the Middle East, "the cradle and citadel of Islamism," would be "enough to persuade Indian Muslims to now make common cause with any power that will invade English India."[76] The British, Afghani insisted, thought they could "oppose Indian Muslims to their compatriots belonging to other religions." But they were, he insisted, "strangely mistaken" because "all Indian inhabitants" had "the same degree of hatred of foreign oppressors."[77]

Afghani's expectation or hope of an anti-British alliance between Indian Muslims and Hindu "idolators"[78] had little chance of being realized. The former were beginning to espouse the separatism that would lead to the formation of the Muslim League, while the latter were, as Long had rightly surmised, unsympathetic to the Russian cause. Afghani's paeans to pan-Islamism had great impact, however. For a taste consider "Europe Revisited," an essay by Salar Jung II, son and short-lived successor to Salar Jung. Though he tactfully described Afghani, whom he knew the British intensely distrusted, as a "firebrand," Jung II shared the pan-Islamist's "intense love" for Turkey.[79] He visited Constantinople in June 1887, where he witnessed Britain and Turkey spar over the future of Egypt, which the former had occupied in 1882. Reflecting on the event in "Europe Revisited," Jung warned that Turkey could "no longer rely blindly" on Britain, as the latter now had a "modern school of politicians" who asserted that, "come what may, no nation which would preserve its self-respect can any longer

remain allied to the Porte." To these politicians Jung offered a stern warning. "England has in India some 50,000,000 of Mussulman subjects,
including in their mass the most warlike of the native races, the races
upon whom England must chiefly rely to roll back the tide of Russian
aggression." Should the Caliph come under assault, said Jung, these subjects might prove ungovernable. As he put it,

> I am aware that in the Western world the religious sentiment of nations is
> no longer considered an important factor in politics, but it would not be wise
> to regard any such maxim as applicable to the East. The myriads who today
> in the hottest regions in the world keep for an entire month each year the
> fast of Ramadan—entire abstinence from all food and water between sun-
> rise and sunset while continuing their full daily toil—the religious zeal that
> has endured this trial steadfastly for more than a thousand years at the bid-
> ding of the Prophet, is not likely to look on unmoved when his shrine at
> Mecca and his tomb at Medina have become the objective points of foreign
> aggression.

Liberals in Britain, Jung noted, were confident that Indian Muslims could
never support Russia. But they had misread the situation. "The strength
and the determination of our objection to any further Russian growth in
the direction of India" did not stem from "our dislike to exchange a constitutional for a despotic rule," he stressed, since his coreligionists attached
"but little importance to mere theories of representative government." What
animated the "Mahommedan millions" in India was the "alliance between
our Queen and our Caliph, between the temporal power in India and the
spiritual power that radiates from the Bosphorus." Should this alliance
crumble, then so too might resistance to Russia, for if Indian Muslims
were "destined to see Russia on the Bosphorus and the shrine of Mecca in
her possession," then where else could "the faithful look to find the
defender of their faith?"[80]

In the following decade, such polite threats were replaced with an overtly
confrontational stance. The precipitating factor was the severe criticism that
British liberals—led by Gladstone—were directing at the Ottomans in the
wake of the massacre of Armenian Christians in 1894–95. Ghulam-us-
Saqlain's "The Mussalmans of India and the Armenian Question" was among
the important replies. A product of the Mohammedan Anglo-Oriental

College, the principal venue at which Indian Muslims engaged with English education after 1875, Ghulam-us-Saqlain took the position that his coreligionists were newly relevant because, empowered by English education, they were better organized than their predecessors. As a consequence, "such an important portion of Her Majesty's subjects must never be omitted from the consideration of English statesmen," he warned. And when it came to "the political feelings of the Mussalmans of India," he stressed, "perhaps the most firmly seated is an attachment to the Mussalman Powers that still exist in the world," with Turkey being "the most important." Indian Muslims were agitated about Turkey, Ghulam-us-Saqlain wrote, because of a "campaign of reckless abuse, led by prominent English politicians," that seemed to be motivated by "racial and religious prejudices" rather than "secular politics." The question they asked themselves was whether "the abuses complained of in Turkey were such as exist in no other part of the world." For instance, "the alleged cruelties in Armenia do not exceed what is said and written about the cruelties suffered by the Siberian prisoners," Ghulam-us-Saqlain complained, "yet all the eloquence of a great English party and a great press is exhausted in depicting the unnameable Turkish horrors." Such considerations, he wrote, led the Indian Muslims to view English "professions of philanthropy and human sympathy as hypocritical pretensions," intended to provide cover for a modern-day "crusade."[81]

This unapologetic stance on Armenia deepened the rift between English liberals and English-educated Muslims. Relations further deteriorated in 1897, when the Christian majority in Crete, an Ottoman possession, appealed to Greece for assistance. When Britain responded to Greece's subsequent military intervention by proposing autonomy for Crete, newspapers like the Calcutta-based *Moslem Chronicle* bristled with anger. Their denunciations of British diplomacy prompted "The Musulmans of India and the Sultan" (1897), an essay by Malcolm MacColl, a Scottish clergyman closely associated with Gladstone and prominent defender of Christian minorities in the Ottoman Empire. Like Long, MacColl scorned the "ascending scale of protest" as the "vaporing" of a few "semi-Europeanised Musulmans." Still, he knew from personal experience that Indian pan-Islamists had "made some impression" in England.[82] One such figure was Rafiuddin Ahmad, a graduate of Deccan College, who passed through the Middle Temple before being called to the Bar in 1892. Ahmed gained enough support among Conservatives to become in 1895 the first Muslim to be nominated for a ticket (though concerns about Rafiuddin's sympathy for Turkey meant the ticket was eventually given to Mancherjee Bhownagree).[83] Rafiuddin even had access to Queen Victoria via his friendship with her servant, Abdul Karim, which had led her to propose, to the astonishment of her ministers, that he be appointed an attaché in Turkey.[84] To counter those swayed by pan-Islamists like Rafiuddin, MacColl stressed Long's earlier warning that "those who bid us beware of the anger of Indian Muslims forget that the Musulmans are not our only subjects in India. To the Hindus alone they stand in the proportion of one in four, and we are not likely to make the Hindus more loyal by truckling to the ignorant or manufactured prejudices of their vanquished oppressors." MacColl particularly challenged the idea that Indian Muslims were "entitled to dictate" how Britain ought to act "towards foreign countries." Its proponents, he angrily declared, would never have dared say the same in the Mughal era: "It is lucky for the little coterie of Indian Musulmans who claim a right to control the policy of this country in its relations with the Sultan, that they live under the tolerant rule of a Christian Queen. Any of their own past Sovereigns would have made a speedy end of themselves and their pretensions."[85] Denunciations of this kind only increased when Turkey's victory in the Greco-Turkish War of 1897 prompted celebrations among Indian pan-Islamists, including the giving of banquets.[86] This public snub to Britain alarmed pro-establishment Indian Muslims led by Syed Ahmed Khan, the modernizing figure behind the Mohammedan Anglo-Oriental College, who viewed the British as the guardians of Indian Muslims' interests. In "The Caliphate," which was published in the *Aligarh Institute Gazette* in September 1897, Khan tried to stem the tide by arguing that the history and law of their religion showed that "no Mahomedan sovereign is Caliph for those Mahomedans who do not live in his dominions." The upshot was that Indians Muslims were "not the subjects of Sultan Abdul Hamid nor does he possess any authority over us or over our country." Furthermore, since the British freely granted Indian Muslims "all freedom in religious matters," the latter had a "religious duty," Khan urged, "to remain faithful to and well-wishers of the English Government and not to do or say anything practically or theoretically inconsistent with our loyalty and goodwill to that government."[87]

Khan's reasoning was incomplete, however. Even if Abdul Hamid were not Caliph to Indian Muslims, Khan himself admitted that "we sympathize

with him as Mahomedans—happy for his happiness and grieved at his troubles."[88] In the event, were not pan-Islamists entitled to agitate on Abdul
Hamid's behalf?[89] The dilemma created by this "dual loyalty"[90] was captured by Rafiuddin's essay "A Moslem's View of the Pan-Islamic Revival"
(1897). The immediate stimulus for Ahmed's essay was unhappiness at the
Great Powers' decision following the war over Crete that "the Turk should
not be allowed to retain any portion of the land once occupied by Christians which he had conquered." Britain's role in this decision had prompted
Indian Muslims, who had "always believed that England is the friend and
Russia the enemy of the Sultan of Islam," to think that the two sides had
"changed places," he complained. The turn of events placed pan-Islamists
like Rafiuddin in a serious quandary. To continue to support Turkey exposed
them to the charge of disloyalty leveled by figures like MacColl. Yet they
were loath to give up pan-Islamism, as it allowed them to punch above
their weight in British India. Squeezed, Rafiuddin therefore pressed Britain and Turkey to "re-establish cordial relations." It was not "sentimental
love" but "interests" that underwrote their relationship, he stressed. Given
the threat that Russia posed to both sides, "England could not afford to
dispense with the sympathy of Islam; neither can the Muslim world afford
the permanent hostility of England."[91]

Following the turn of the century, the tensions exposed by the Eastern
Question would transform into action. Khan's views would be "bitterly
repudiated" by a new generation, which, influenced by Afghani's ideals,
would take the view that "political loyalty was due" to the Ottoman Caliph
and that "*jihad* was obligatory" to "reconquer any territory" taken from
him.[92] Following the Ottoman Empire's defeat in World War I, this worldview would lead Indian pan-Islamists to launch the Khilafat movement (as
it came to be termed) to preserve the Caliph.[93] The embarrassing rejection
of the Ottoman Caliph by the Young Turks would not be the end of pan-
Islamism in India. The founding of Israel would become the next front line,
bringing Indian pan-Islamists into renewed conflict with the West.[94]

FREE TRADE

For much of the nineteenth century, as we have seen, Indian elites accepted
British imperialism as a precursor to civilizational advancement, and therefore supported England against Russia. As the century progressed, however,

they became increasingly unhappy with Britain's perceived violations of liberal values in pursuit of hegemony in Central Asia and Eastern Europe. A further cause of disillusionment was British India's unfair trade policies, which gave rise to demands that Indian "infant" industry be protected against foreign competition. Ironically, this critique, which only sought a level playing field for domestic industry, would go on to generate wider disenchantment with international trade, setting the stage for Gandhians and socialists to subsequently demand autarky.

Shortly after consolidating its position in the subcontinent, the East India Company established a tariff policy whereby British manufactures were imported into India duty free or charged nominal duties of 2.5 percent, rising to 3.5 percent on cotton and 5 percent on other manufactures after 1813. Simultaneously, it maintained low duties on the export of Indian raw materials such as cotton and silk, whose production it monopolized by coercing skilled tradesmen into exclusive arrangements. Meanwhile, England imposed on Indian manufactures import duties that ranged between 30 and 80 percent (declining to between 10 to 30 percent after 1830). This inequitable arrangement quickly reduced India from manufacturing powerhouse to commodity provider. Trade figures revealed the transformation. To take the emblematic example: In 1800 India exported some five hundred bales of cotton to England and twenty-six hundred bales of cotton manufactures. By 1829 she exported some four thousand bales of cotton and a little more than four hundred bales of cotton manufactures.[95] The impact on traditional craft industries was brutal. By the early 1840s, English-educated Indians were bitterly complaining that Britain's policies were compelling the "once wealthy inhabitants" of the Konkan and Deccan to resort to "cultivation and tillage" in order to escape "indigence."[96]

The inequitable tariff system just described was unsettled by the Mutiny of 1857, which strained British India's finances. To raise revenue, in 1859 import duties on luxury items were increased to 20 percent and those on other items, including yarn and cotton products, were increased to 10 percent. But, under intense pressure from British manufacturers, especially Lancashire mill owners, the Government of India soon backpedaled. In 1861, the duty on yarn was reduced to 5 percent, and in 1862 to 3.5 percent, while duty on cotton products was reduced to 5 percent. Then, in 1864, the general duty on imports was reduced to 7.5 percent, and in 1867 a number of British products were entirely exempt from duty.[97] The effect, borne out by trade figures, was to accelerate Indian deindustrialization. To once more take the cotton trade as emblematic: in 1813 India had exported £2 million worth of yarn and cotton products to England. By 1858 she was importing upward of £11 million and by 1872 this number had risen to an all-time high of £19 million.

This outcome still did not satisfy Lancashire, which from 1871 onward began demanding that import duties on cotton goods be eliminated entirely. Ostensibly the justification was that free trade demanded so much: with her labor and fields, India ought to cultivate raw produce, whereas, with her capital and machinery, Lancashire ought to manufacture cotton products, whose lower price would benefit Indian consumers. The prevailing import duties, Lancashire's spokesmen claimed, were a protectionist measure that benefited inefficient Indian manufacturers at the cost of their poor and needy brethren. A growing number of Indian commentators saw it differently, however. In their view, what Lancashire really wanted was to nip in the bud India's infant industries, in particular Bombay's newly established mills, which were gradually becoming competitive, their exports of cotton products to England having recently almost doubled from £1.2 million in 1869 to £2 million in 1876. With Lord George Hamilton, the under secretary of state, promising to eliminate duties "so soon as the finances of India will permit," Indian observers sensed danger.[98] This was the context in which Bholanath Chandra published his highly influential essay "A Voice for the Commerce and Manufactures of India," which appeared in *Mookerjee's Magazine* in five parts between 1873 and 1876.

Chandra's starting point was the claim, developed in Kissen Mohan Malik's publication *A Brief History of Bengal Commerce* (1872), that the steady growth in the volume of India's trade, especially in terms of agricultural exports, implied that she was experiencing unparalleled "prosperity."[99] "I admit the expansion of trade," Chandra replied, "but I take leave to doubt that [its] net results have been at all favourable to our nation." The cause of concern was that Indians only provided agricultural labor, while manufacturing and commerce were in foreign hands. This was, he reminded his audience, a strange turn of events:

> No untruth is more strenuously sought to be impressed upon our minds than that we form an agricultural nation.... From time immemorial India has never been a consumer of foreign goods and manufactures ... It is she who

manufactured for other nations, while none manufactured for her. But by a mischievous inversion of that order of things, she is now a dependent upon foreign looms and forges for her supply.

To Chandra, the "development of indigenous industry [was] an important problem for the Indian statesman."[100] This was because the "pursuit of Commerce and Industry is politically necessary to ensure the wealth and material resources without which there can be no true greatness of a people."[101] Present trends boded ill for India in this regard because continually exporting cheap raw materials and then importing expensive manufactures would burden her with a permanent trade deficit, especially since other countries were "evolving the powers of their own native soils." There was also the serious problem that the markets for raw materials were prone to booms and busts. "They pay not now steadily, but spasmodically," Chandra noted, "under the influence either of a physical cause, or political contingency."[102] Hence, Indians should, he counseled, "sedulously strive for the subversion of the policy, which . . . has steeped the country . . . in an industrial slavery." In particular, they should demand "a policy that should abolish all duty upon the Exports to enable behind-hand India to compete with more intelligent nations, and that should levy an increased rate of duties upon the Imports to rescue her arts and industries from ruin, and give to the country, which has been robbed of its liberty, a true and substantial glory in exchange."[103]

Chandra knew of course that England would oppose such a policy. Even so it was at least her duty to "nurse" and "infuse new vigor" into Indian industry by providing technical education, supporting local banks and insurance houses, developing a native merchant navy, rationalizing taxation, and many other related prerequisites.[104] But, Chandra coolly observed: "To strip naked the disguised truth, the English want to reduce us all to the condition of agriculturists. It would be impolitic for them to rear up great or rich men among us. They are afraid of the consequences of intelligence and wealth in our nation. . . . Hence the fashion to cry us down into an agricultural people."[105] These obstacles did not faze Chandra since his ultimate aim was not to persuade the British but to rouse Indians—to transform his "weak and unmanly" countrymen into "strong and progressive" beings who would "help themselves."[106] In particular, they ought to combat English policy by importing patriotism into the marketplace—that is, by pursuing what would come to be called *swadeshi*. As he put it, India's opinion leaders

> should preach for the founding of independent Native Banks, Native Companies and Corporations, Native Mills and Factories, and Native Chambers of Commerce in the Presidencies. They should denounce the insensate practice of preferring foreign goods to home-made manufactures. They should inculcate the discipline of self-denial, and the cultivation of patriotic sentiments.[107]

By 1876 Chandra's tone had become more strident. The immediate irritant was the Tariff Bill of 1875, which had made a further concession to Lancashire by imposing a 5 percent duty on the import of American and Egyptian raw cotton, making it harder for Indian mills to compete in the production of finer cloth products. Chandra reminded his audience that it was "the height of absurdity to expect sympathy and encouragement" from Britain. "Self-help" was the only way: "Without using any physical force, without incurring any disloyalty, and without praying for any legislative succour, it lies quite in our power to regain our lost position . . . by resolving to non-consume the goods of England. . . . Moral opposition is unmatched in its omnipotence and efficacy. It defies all laws and restraints pressing down our industry."[108]

Chandra also responded to Malik, who had in the interim fired back in the pages of the *Mookerjee's Magazine*. In "The Commerce and Manufactures of India—Another View," Malik decried Chandra's essay as an uncouth "show of patriotism." It had, he insisted, conveniently overlooked the fact that "it was no intrigue or unfair play . . . that ruined our trade in cotton goods"; rather, Britain's "power-looms" had taken advantage of American cotton to provide higher-quality products at lower cost. As a result of Britain's skillful exploitation of technology and economies of scale, India's manufacturers had "died a natural death," which had hurt "a few thousand weavers," but had benefited "millions of the poor," who could now "cover their whole frame with the products of Manchester."[109] Chandra readily conceded that India had fallen behind technologically due to her conservatism and apathy. But Indians were now attempting to undo these mistakes—mill owners, for example, were quickly acquiring technology by importing capital goods. What remained out of reach, however, was a level playing field. "Real free-trade," Chandra reminded Malik, "implies the abolition of all tariffs and custom-houses." But this was not how Britain wanted to play the game. As Chandra saw it: "The secret of the success of the British adventurers lies not so much in the over-coming power of higher skill and greater capital, as in the operation of a scale of unequal duties—a small duty for England and heavy duties for India—cleverly adjusted so as to elevate one party and depress the other."[110]

Over the next two decades the number of commentators endorsing Chandra's critique grew. None was more widely read than Kashinath Trimbak Telang and Mahadev Govind Ranade, both accomplished scholars and pioneering judges of the Bombay High Court, who urged Calcutta to protect India's "infant industries."[111] These pleas had little effect, however. In 1879, in the midst of famine, import duties on cotton were reduced; then in 1882, import duties on British products were eliminated altogether. Only looming bankruptcy could shake Lancashire's hold over British India, albeit briefly. Given the expenditure incurred on the Great Game, in 1894 British India found herself confronting a £2 million deficit. As a consequence, a 5 percent duty on imports, including cotton, was reintroduced. At the same time, Britain imposed a "countervailing excise duty" of 5 percent on Indian mills, whose investment in the production of finer fabrics was causing Lancashire great anxiety.[112]

As it became painfully obvious that the Government of India would not protect India's "nascent industries," a new generation of politicians began urging consumers to exercise *their* power by boycotting British products and confining themselves "to indigenous (*Swadeshi*) articles of clothing as far as possible." This development worried the older generation, who had long endorsed free trade and objected only to inequitable tariffs. P. Ananda Charlu, a founder and former president of the Congress, neatly summarized their concern in "A Few Thoughts on the Poverty of India," a lecture delivered at the Chaitanya Library in Calcutta in 1897. Though he looked with "unqualified approval, upon the patriotic *Swadeshi* movements," said Charlu, because they "betoken humanitarian feelings of the noblest type," it was essential to recognize that the withering away of India's "customary industries" owed greatly to "a change in the tastes of the people." Given the "inevitable competition between handiwork and machine-power," such movements were "a slender reed to rely upon" when it came to the "industrial salvation of this country." The more durable course was to foster enterprise because "permanent and perennial sources of our industrial development, . . . to be progressive, must be natural, not heroic merely; for it is not everybody who will take away his eyes from the self and submit to large and continual orders on his generosity and purse."[113] India, with her "limitless store-house of raw materials," could surely be put on a "career of prosperity," he declared, if she found a way to combine "the purse and the brain." The "want of combination" between these "two potent agents" had a "deeper cause," however. It owed to "the want of mutual trust and want of adequate and dignified conception of labour." Thus, the need of the hour, he counseled, was to "reform ourselves." In particular, India's "penny-wise and pound-foolish" capitalists ought to follow Japan's example where investments in "up-to-date" technology permitted her industries to benefit from, rather than be disturbed by, free trade.

Charlu's appeal went largely unheeded. After the turn of the century, "Radicals" set on confronting Britain would steadily supplant "Moderates" in the Congress. As a result, calls for *swadeshi* would migrate from the page to the street, symbolized by the burning of foreign products. Only in 1919 would Britain, obliged to reward India for its contributions in World War I and worried about the growing influence of socialist ideals, finally allow her some freedom to set her own tariffs. But this would prove to be too little too late—by this point, the notion that international trade was predatory would be firmly entrenched in the public mind.

RACISM

Another front on which Britain disappointed English-educated Indian elites concerned discrimination against Indians in South Africa. Britain's willingness to condone such behavior convinced Indian elites that in spite of her stated intention to modernize India, Britain viewed even English-educated Indians as permanently inferior to her white subjects. This realization laid the foundation for their subsequent involvement in antiracism movements across the colonial world.

The abolition of slavery throughout the British Empire in 1833 unsettled a number of her colonies whose economies were based on the cultivation and extraction of raw materials, hitherto accomplished cheaply by employing slaves. With the newly emancipated fleeing agricultural plantations, these colonies soon confronted acute labor shortages. Since Britain's industries relied heavily on cheap imported raw materials such as sugar, cocoa, rubber, and coffee, desperate colonial authorities turned toward India, whose famished and "meek" millions were perceived as ideal replacements for slaves.[114] The outcome was the establishment of the indenture system, which from 1834 onward shipped over a million Indians overseas. The vast majority went to Mauritius and the Caribbean, which received nearly half a million laborers each over the century. Other destinations included South Africa, where the British colony of Natal alone received a little over 150,000 laborers between 1860 and 1911; Fiji, which received some sixty thousand laborers between 1879 and 1916; and Malaya and the Straits Settlements, which received upward of forty thousand laborers prior to the twentieth century.

The indenture system revolved around a worker voluntarily contracting to be employed overseas for up to five years in return for a fixed wage and basic amenities such as housing and medical care and eventually passage home. This system had severe defects. Laborers were often unaware of or misled about their future working conditions. Transported to the colonies in the most rudimentary conditions, many perished on the way. Upon landing they confronted harsh and unsanitary working and living conditions that led to high mortality rates. On top of this, contracts were commonly abused, and laborers had little recourse as local laws and local officials favored plantation owners. Finally, if returnees survived the voyage home, suspicions that they had violated rules about caste and diet could lead to accusations of impurity and even ostracism.

These defects were the subject of numerous British-led inquiries whose reports led to modest reforms, such as the creation in the colonies of the post of a protector of emigrants, as well as to sanctions, including the prohibition of migration to colonies that failed to meet basic labor standards. These changes were on the margin, however: hardship and abuse were more or less intrinsic to the indenture system, which sought to approximate the slave economy by relentlessly squeezing labor. Nevertheless, laborers still contracted in sizable numbers, and a large proportion declined free passage home upon the expiration of their contracts, preferring to settle in the colonies, where they were typically granted ten acres of land upon the completion of a second contract.

Few analyzed this phenomenon more carefully than Mahadev Govind Ranade, whose essay "Indian Foreign Emigration" (1893) offered a limited defense of the indenture system. Ranade's starting point was the background conditions under which the indenture system had come into existence, namely, the fact that India had a "surplus poor population . . . fitted to work as agriculturalist labourers." Though Ranade believed that the "permanent salvation" of these hard-pressed classes depended upon "the growth of Indian manufactures and commerce," he recognized that it would take much time both to cultivate the "change of habits" required to bring about a "change of occupations" and to stimulate local industry, which was "borne down . . . by the stress of foreign competition." As a result, "the overflow of the surplus population from the congested parts of the country to lands where labour is dear and highly remunerative," he concluded, could "alone afford the sorely needed present relief" to India's impoverished and underemployed masses.

Ranade recognized that "few people [were] aware of the comparative magnitude of this relief . . . afforded to our surplus population." His survey therefore drew attention to some striking facts. The number of emigrants "had been steadily increasing" and "nearly one half" of these 1,200,000 emigrants had settled in the colonies as "free labourers" upon the end of their contracts. Moreover, in spite of the difficult conditions, indentured laborers or so-called "coolies" were thriving, earning "two to three times" what they would make in India, their "general prosperity" being "fully attested to by the large remittances they make . . . and the savings they bring with them." The benefits of foreign emigration were not only material but also moral. From Ranade's perspective, the "most hopeful" feature of these outward flows was that upper castes and women were participating in increasing numbers as well. Only such "transplantation," he averred, could uproot the outdated "tastes, habits, temperaments, and prejudices" that social reformers like himself had struggled to alter through less drastic means. In his words: "if the old thraldom of prejudice and easy self-satisfaction and patient resignation is ever to be loosened, and new aspirations and hopes created in their place, a change of home surroundings is a standing necessity and a preparatory discipline."[115] Ranade's optimistic assessment was soon overtaken by events. His focus had been on the indenture system. But in the background, another stream of migrants—"free passengers"—was growing rapidly. These migrants included traders, accountants, teachers, lawyers, doctors, and clerks attracted by commercial opportunities in South Africa, and Natal in particular. Traders selling provisions to Indians and

Africans were the predominant element and included in their midst formerly indentured laborers who launched various informal enterprises upon
the end of their contracts. As a consequence of these trends, by 1893 approximately twenty-five thousand of the forty thousand Indians in the British
colony of Natal were "free passengers."

This development antagonized European settlers in South Africa on two
fronts. The first was racial: Europeans disliked the swelling numbers of "Asiatics" in their midst. The second was commercial: European enterprises
found it difficult to compete with their leaner Indian counterparts. The outcome was growing hostility toward Indians, which soon found its way into
legislation aimed at hobbling them and restricting further immigration. The
Boer republics of Transvaal and the Orange Free State led the way: in 1885
Transvaal passed a law denying "Asiatics" the franchise and requiring them
to live and trade in assigned areas only, and in 1891 the Orange Free State
prohibited "coloured" persons from farming or trading in its territories.
Natal proceeded a little more slowly. In 1888, it passed a law requiring Indians to carry passes, and in 1891 it ceased giving indentured laborers land
grants upon the completion of a second contract. When this failed to deter
"free passenger" immigration, in 1894 Natal disenfranchised Indians who met
the wealth criterion for voting rights. Subsequently, in 1895, it imposed an
annual £3 tax (nearly half of what a laborer earned in a year) on laborers who
did not reindenture or return to India upon the expiration of their contract.

These developments famously spurred Mohandas Karamchand Gandhi,
then in South Africa to manage the legal affairs of an Indian Muslim merchant, to launch the Natal Indian Congress in 1894. Under Gandhi's direction, the Congress contested Natal's laws on the ground that, being British
subjects, Indians were owed equal treatment under the law. Gandhi's efforts
to rouse public opinion against Natal were soon felt in India. A key turning point came in December 1895, when, under the sponsorship of G.
Parameswaran Pillai, editor of *The Madras Standard*, the Eleventh Indian
National Congress resolved:

> That the Congress deems it necessary to record its most solemn protest
> against the disabilities sought to be imposed on Indian settlers in South
> Africa, and it earnestly hopes that the British Government and the Govern-
> ment of India will come forward to guard the interests of these settlers in

the same spirit in which they have always interfered, whenever the interests of their British-born subjects have been at stake.

In his speech proposing the resolution, Pillai rallied his audience by appealing to their "fellow-feeling." The pitiable "condition of our brethren" in "distant lands" obliged the Congress to extend "our hand of fellowship to our suffering countrymen in South Africa," he urged. Pillai believed that the Congress had a role to play because the South African "crusade" against Indians stemmed from economic rather than racial considerations: "The real reason of all this agitation is strong competition in trade. Indians, owing to their simple habits and economic living, are able to carry on a very successful trade much to the prejudice of the white population." Since the cause of the conflict was economic rather than racial, the requisite solution was to apply diplomatic pressure. In his view, "Indians owe[d] all their sufferings to the fact" that British officials had "failed to treat Englishmen and Indians on a footing of equality." The Congress could thus help by pressuring the British Government to prevent South Africa from treating Indians "in a way unsuited to . . . their position as subjects of Her Britannic Majesty."[116]

The Congress resolution and the numerous editorials denouncing South Africa that followed in its wake had little effect. In 1896, Britain allowed Natal to proceed with disenfranchising Indians, who now outnumbered Europeans. This development prompted Gandhi to visit India, hoping to pressure the Government of India to object to the treatment of British Indians. A highlight was his speech in Madras in October 1896, "Grievances of Indian Settlers in South Africa." In it, Gandhi shocked his audience by detailing the treatment being inflicted on Indians in South Africa: Europeans deemed them "uncivilized," pushed them off footpaths, declined to serve them or to let them travel freely, and frequently employed violence against them. After complaining that "every Indian without distinction is contemptuously called a coolie," Gandhi sought to use these very laborers—predominantly lower- and middle-caste Hindus—to his own ends. Knowing how deeply Natal relied on indentured labor, he appealed to Indians to "help us to get emigration suspended." This was a tactic that British authorities had previously used to compel her colonies to institute labor standards; Gandhi now hoped to use it to advance the interests of Indian "gentlemen." He presented the tactic, however, as being in the interest of

indentured laborers. By compelling laborers to pay the annual £3 tax if they
did not reindenture or return home upon the expiration of their contracts,
the Natal authorities were, he correctly surmised, seeking to prevent the
indentured from rising "higher than the status of labourers." This was, he
insisted, a kind of "degradation." Gandhi acknowledged that this claim was
vulnerable to the observation that if circumstances in Natal were so intolerable, then why did the majority of indentured laborers not flee home? His
response was that these laborers were ignorant or timid:

> The fact that the indentured Indians as a rule do not avail themselves of the
> return passage . . . may prove that . . . [they] either do not mind the disabili-
> ties or remain in the Colony in spite of such disabilities. If the former be the
> case, it is the duty of those who know better to make the Indians realise their
> situation and to enable them to see that submission to them means degra-
> dation. If the latter be the case it is one more instance of the patience and
> the forbearing spirit of the Indian Nation.

There was, Gandhi admitted, another possibility. It was quite rational for
laborers to indenture themselves because, as Ranade had observed, the conditions they faced in India were even worse than in Natal. Gandhi mused:

> Who are these people who, instead of returning to India, settle in the Col-
> ony? They are the Indians drawn from the poorest classes and from the most
> thickly populated districts possibly living in a state of semi-starvation in
> India. . . . Is it any wonder, if these people after the expiry of their indenture,
> instead of "running to face semi-starvation," . . . settled in a country where
> the climate is magnificent and where they may earn a decent living? A starv-
> ing man generally would stand any amount of rough treatment to get a
> crumb of bread.

Gandhi did not reflect on whether it was appropriate to advance the interests of the Indian mercantile class in South Africa, such as the Memons that
employed him, by prohibiting Indian laborers from exiting their famine-
prone land. Instead, he ended his speech in Madras with the warning that
"if nothing further were to be done here and in England on our behalf, it is
merely a question of time when the respectable Indian in South Africa will
be absolutely extinct."[117]

Natal responded to Gandhi's tactics by blocking his return there. With Gandhi marooned on a ship off the coast of Durban, in December 1896 the Congress once again recorded "its most solemn protest against the disabilities imposed on Indian settlers in South Africa and the invidious and humiliating distinctions made between them and European settlers."[118] Undeterred, the South African colonies took further steps in 1897 to deter "free passenger" immigration. Transvaal, for instance, prohibited colored persons from walking on sidewalks and outlawed interracial marriages, while Natal enacted licensing requirements that made it harder for Indian traders to operate and then introduced immigration tests that effectively ended "free passenger" migration. Thus, in December 1898, the time was ripe for the Congress to once again take up the South African question. As before, Pillai took the lead. He stressed the gravity of the situation. Whereas previously wealthy Indians had been protesting discriminatory laws, now they were "struggling for their very existence," he lamented. Detailing the new indignities heaped on Indians, he appealed to the Congress to help. "Now is the time when we ought to go to their rescue," he urged, because "it is necessary that while we are struggling for our rights in this country, we should not forget those countrymen of ours who have emigrated to other lands."

Though Pillai still clung to the idea that "trade jealousy" lay "at the bottom of this unfortunate affair," others in the Congress started to openly point the finger at racism. For instance, V. Ramesam, the future chief justice of Madras, angrily declared that the disabilities imposed on Indians owed to "the prejudice of the white colonists to their Asiatic brethren of a less fair skin than themselves." Nor was the problem unique to South Africa, he added, since New South Wales in Australia had recently announced a law "compelling an Indian to pay a penalty of £1,000 if he enters the province." This view solidified following Britain's victory in the Boer War, which brought Transvaal and the Orange State under her control in 1902. When Britain expanded rather than eliminated the Boers' discriminatory laws, Indian elites fought more concertedly. In England, Mancherjee Bhownagree, the first Indian to be elected to Parliament on a Conservative ticket, raised embarrassing questions about conditions in South Africa. In Natal, Gandhi employed passive resistance, which led to modest concessions in 1913. In India, the battle was led by Ranade's disciple, Gopal Krishna Gokhale, who, somewhat ironically, helped shutter the indenture system by 1916.

These developments did little, however, to stem growing racial hostility toward Indians "in search of fresh fields and pastures new."[119] From 1901 onward practically every other British dominion, including Australia, Canada, and Kenya, and soon the United States as well, began closing their doors to Indian immigrants on explicitly racial grounds. Formerly indentured laborers, meanwhile, were sidelined when they settled in foreign lands, especially in Fiji and the Caribbean. As a consequence, Indian elites became ever more occupied with the fate of their countrymen abroad, making them increasingly vocal critics of racism, and apartheid in particular.

THE OPIUM TRADE

We have already examined a number of developments that led Indians to question Britain's commitment to liberal ideals. Let us now examine one further cause of disillusionment, namely British India's role in forcing opium upon China. Because the opium trade was lucrative, indeed essential to British India's finances, Indian criticism was initially muted. However, as the century went on, Indian elites became increasingly aware of the suffering that the trade was causing in China. The more liberal among them subsequently denounced the opium trade and called upon British India to withdraw from it.

Prior to the eighteenth century, opium was used in China principally for medicinal purposes and hence imported in small quantities. Starting in the early eighteenth century, it began to be smoked alongside tobacco. As addiction led to increased demand, Portuguese and Dutch traders stepped in to supply opium sourced from West and Central India.[120] Alerted to opium's baneful effects, the Chinese authorities issued in 1729 an edict prohibiting its use as an intoxicant. However, the venality of local officials meant that this order went largely unenforced.[121] As a consequence, imports, often under the guise of medicine, grew from a few hundred chests to well over four thousand chests per annum by the close of the century (each chest being 130 to 160 pounds).[122]

Over this period the East India Company had been consolidating its position in India. By 1757 it controlled much of the Gangetic plain with its rich soil and plentiful labor. Having noticed that the Native States of Malwa were supplying opium to the Portuguese in Daman and Diu, who then shipped it via Macau to China, the Company discerned a means of balancing its trade deficit with China.[123] To this end, in 1773 the Company assumed control over poppy cultivation and opium production in Bengal, giving it a sizable profit on the sale to exporters.[124] Still, Chinese hostility toward foreign traders meant that exports were initially limited. Prior to 1767 the number of chests shipped from British India "rarely exceeded two hundred" per annum. By 1781 this number had climbed to more than two thousand. In 1794 English traders anchored armed ships near Canton, which thereafter served as "fixed depots" to which Chinese smugglers could take recourse. As a consequence, by 1796 the export of Bengal opium had reached nearly four thousand chests per annum, prompting the Chinese authorities to issue an edict banning its import entirely. The Company had other plans, however. From 1797 onward it steadily expanded poppy cultivation and rationalized production in its opium factories. The increased supply, and the continued ability of smugglers to circumvent or bribe Chinese officials, kept Indian exports at four thousand chests per annum for the next two decades.[125]

In 1818 the Company succeeded in pacifying Central India, returning stability to a region previously wracked by internecine warfare. In short order, opium production escalated as the Native States of the Malwa region also sought to profit from the demand whipped up by the illicit trade with China. By 1831, with the free market having reduced prices and thereby increased demand, India was exporting nearly twenty thousand chests of opium, with a third coming from Bengal and two-thirds from Malwa.[126] In 1839 the Chinese finally responded to the upsurge by dispatching an upright administrator, the celebrated Lin Zexu, to crack down on the opium trade. Lin's confiscation and destruction of opium stocks held by English traders prompted Britain to launch the First Opium War. China's defeat in 1842 effectively marked the end of her efforts to stem the import of opium, and smuggling was hereafter conducted with near impunity.[127] As a result, by the middle of the century, China was consuming approximately fifty thousand chests (or more than three million kilos) of opium, drawn almost entirely from India.[128]

This turn of events did not go unnoticed in Western India, where opium revenues were starting to swell coffers. One memorable critique came in Bhaskar Pandurang Tarkhadkar's trailblazing "Letters of a Hindoo," which appeared in the Bombay Gazette in 1841. A product of Elphinstone College, Tarkhadkar contrasted Britain's alleged "integrity and good sense" with its "barbarities" in China. Her actions in China revealed, he bitterly observed, that her depredations in India were no accident: "self-interest is all in all to you, and to secure it you would do anything."[129] Subsequent events underscored the point. Following its defeat in the Second Opium War, China was forced in 1858 to accept Britain's demand to legalize the opium trade. As a consequence, by the early 1870s exports from India had increased to a staggering ninety thousand chests per annum, earning British India some six million sterling in revenue.

It was only in the final quarter of the nineteenth century that sustained efforts began to be made to counter the opium trade. As reports from Christian missionaries of the destruction wrought by such large-scale consumption of opium made their way back to Britain, anti-opium societies were formed. The most important of these was the Society for the Suppression of the Opium Trade, established in 1874 with the support of the wealthy Quaker industrialist Edward Pease and managed by Reverend Frederick Turner, whose critical essays on the subject had a wide readership. His views reached India through, among others, the erudite historian Shoshee Chandra Dutt, who in 1878 published an extensive review of Turner's *British Opium Policy and Its Results*. Drawing on Turner, Dutt challenged Anglo-Indians who claimed that "opium is the only national stimulant of China," by pointing out that the "national stimulants of the country for the last four thousand years have been tea, tobacco, wine, and spirits." Besides, the medical opinions "adverse to the use of opium" were "exceedingly well-grounded," he observed, which explained why the drug was banned in England.[130] Dutt conceded that it would not be easy for British India to exit the opium trade, because her finances depended heavily on opium revenues, which typically made up a fifth of government receipts. It was this very concern that earlier in the decade had thwarted attempts by radicals in Parliament to move motions condemning British India's opium revenues. Still, Dutt was willing to bite the bullet: "One thing is certain, namely, that no fiscal consideration can justify the British Government in continuing to inflict on China the grievous evil that the diffusion of opium in that country has given rise to. No Government ought to make private vice a source of public revenue."[131]

Over the following decade, additional tracts criticizing the opium trade made their way to India. One such tract that powerfully synthesized evidence of British venality was *The Indo-British Opium Trade* by Theodore

Christlieb, a prominent German evangelical. Its visceral impact can be gauged from a review essay published in 1881 by Rabindranath Tagore, then a mere twenty year old. Printed in the family-run Bengali periodical *Bharati*, the essay, "Chine Maraner Byabasa" ("The Death Traffic"), railed against Britain's "despicable meanness" in using "its strength to sell death." Tagore also drew attention to the "evils" done to India by the opium trade. Skirting Indian complicity—his grandfather, the magnate Dwarkanath Tagore, being among those who had profited from the opium trade—he underlined the danger of having a substantial portion of India's revenue derive from an "uncertain" trade, which was likely to decline as the Chinese sought to simultaneously expand production and curtail consumption of the opium.[132]

Though the critiques channeled via Dutt and Tagore were widely read, they were slow to have effect. To understand why, we need look no further than the speech delivered by Srish Chandra Basu, a prominent *zamindar* (landlord) and magistrate, at a meeting of the British Indian Association in 1882. The Society for the Suppression of the Opium Trade, Basu complained, comprised "fanatical agitators" whose "crusade" against the "imputed immorality" of the opium trade was "ignorant." This trade, he noted, provided India between seven and nine million sterling per annum, which enabled "beneficial reforms" in the form of increased public investment. Since no one wanted to see such expenditure cease, the revenue shortfall caused by exiting the opium trade could only be met by introducing direct taxation, which would further impoverish Indians. Given the unpleasant choices, it made no sense, Basu concluded, to surrender "such a fertile source of income ... for the sake of a mere sentiment." This was all the more so because exiting the trade would not lead to the "moral regeneration" of the Chinese, who would simply procure opium from elsewhere.[133]

Criticism of the kind voiced by Basu led the Society for the Suppression of the Opium Trade to propose in 1891 that England ought to help India cover the deficit that would be brought about by the elimination of opium revenues. To this suggestion English politicians had a common response: it was, in James Fitzjames Stephens's inglorious words, "one of the most foolish dreams" to think that English taxpayers would pay out of their pockets to rescue "the Chinese from the consequences of their own self-indulgence."[134] Such unyielding sentiment explained why the Congress refrained from making any "pronouncement on the great Opium question."

Without some "temporary assistance" from Britain in lieu of foregone revenue, William Wedderburn, a former Congress president, wrote in *The Times of India* in 1892, the country faced the prospect of "the stoppage of the present scanty expenditure upon those objects which are specially dear to the people."[135] The Congress's embarrassing silence was underlined by the English parliamentarian Alfred Webb, who was asked to preside over the 1894 Congress. Webb, a prominent radical, discomfited his hosts by observing that while the opium trade had long engaged "the attention of many of the more thoughtful and conscientious of your friends," he found "little reference" to it in the Congress's proceedings. Webb had no trouble guessing why—the subject, he admitted, had "difficulties surrounding it."[136]

In the end, matters went the way Tagore had foreseen. When growing competition from China's domestic opium producers caused Indian exports to dry up, Britain eventually acceded to China's long-standing plea to curtail the trade. In 1907 came the Ten Years Agreement, which committed China and British India to reducing poppy cultivation. One of those to welcome the agreement was Gokhale, who declared in the Imperial Legislative Council,

> I confess I have always felt a sense of deep humiliation at the thought of this revenue, derived as it is practically from the degradation and moral ruin of the people of China. And I rejoice that there are indications of a time coming when this stain will no longer rest on us. . . . [For] whatever may be the measure of England's responsibility in forcing the drug on China, the financial gain from the traffic has been derived by India alone, and we must, therefore, be prepared to give up this unholy gain without any compensation from anybody.[137]

LEARNING FROM THE WEST

Let us close this overview by discussing the overarching theme in nineteenth-century reflections on international politics. The central question that Indians asked themselves over the course of the century was this: Why had India been brought so low? Why was it, as Swami Vivekananda famously asked at the end of the century, that forty million Englishmen were able to rule over three hundred million Indians? The great and lasting schism in the debate over this question was about whether India would find her rightful place in the international order by learning from the West *or* by reviving her glorious ancient civilization, a dispute that would go on to dominate pre-1947 discussions over the role that India ought to play on the world stage.

At the start of the century, as we have seen, it was believed that India had fallen behind because she had failed to cultivate modern knowledge. However, following the spread of modern education, many newly educated elites placed the blame on the unwillingness of their countrymen to act in the common good, which they in turn attributed variously to a lack of morality, discipline, and patriotism. One important example in this vein was Nagendra Nath Ghosh's essay "Indian Views of England" (1877), which sought to highlight "what there is in English ideas and English life which we can study with profit to ourselves." Behind "the civilization we all admire," wrote Ghosh, a staunch modernizer who had spent a half-decade in London before being called to the Inner Temple in 1876, were two moral impulses deriving from Christianity. The first was rationalism or the willingness to tolerate dissent, which prevented "rigidity." The second was an emphasis on duty, understood as upholding "a certain ideal perfection of self," namely, that individuals ought to endure hardships "manfully." These moral impulses, he observed, were supplemented by three societal attributes: individuals' "business-like character," which fostered diligence; the orderly character of "home life" that favored productivity; and above all, a well-developed sense of "public morality," which issued in the general expectation of "strict good faith" and thereby fostered social "solidarity." These features were far from present in the Indian context, Ghosh lamented. Rationalism was suspect because it prompted unwelcome questions about the logic underpinning Hinduism's norms, especially caste. Hinduism also promoted an antisocial conception of duty, calling for self-abnegation rather than perseverance. From a societal perspective too, India could not be further from the West: individuals were sentimental rather than resolute; family life was infested with ceremony and pettiness; and public morality was so deficient that social cohesion was "quite unknown." These patterns, Ghosh argued, had to change, or else moral advancement and material prosperity would remain out of India's reach. Hence, he blasted those who appeased "popular vanity" by claiming that India was blessed with "precious" customs:

He ... who would keep out of our view the sterling excellences of European nations and the manifold agencies to which those excellences are due, who would, with sweet seductive stories of what we once were, make us forget what we now are ... such a man as this would deserve to be called not a Patriot, not a lover of his Motherland, but the most insinuating of her Enemies, the basest of her Betrayers. We have been deluded too long, and grievously have we paid for our delusion. It is high time for us now to wake from our dreams.[138]

The most influential of the reflections on India's subjugation placed the blame not on her morals or her manners but on defects in her communal life. This claim received its profoundest treatment in Bankim Chandra Chatterjee's oeuvre. Of particular importance is his "The Shame of Bharat" (1879), which investigated why "has India been enslaved for such a long time." Bankim's reply traced India's subjugation to two features of her communal life. One was that Indians had long been "devoid of any wish to be free," which made them unwilling to resist their colonizers. "They never feel in their hearts," Bankim observed, "that being ruled over by their own people is good and leads to happiness, and that foreign rule oppresses and belittles them." He attributed this sentiment to Hindu philosophy, which cultivated "an indifference to worldly happiness, which in turn leads to a tendency to be inactive." The other cause "of their long servitude" was their "lack of unity, their lack of a sense of nationalism, their lack of a wish to work for the good of their country." He ascribed this unfortunate tendency to caste as well as geography and invasions, which divided Indians on the basis of "habitation, language, race and religion." The upshot was that Indians did not need to convert to Christianity or become Englishmen. If they wished to redeem themselves, they needed to appreciate, and cultivate among their compatriots the desire to be free and to cooperate in the common good. As Bankim put it, "The English are a great benefactor of India. They are teaching us many new things. ... Of all the gems we are getting from the mental treasure-trove of the English, we have mentioned only two of them ... love of freedom and nationalism."[139] Since Hinduism had hitherto impeded the cultivation of these desirable virtues, Bankim advised Hindus to reevaluate their scriptures and traditions on the basis of utility. This reworking of Hinduism reached its high point in his *Dharmatattva*

(1888), which features a dialogue between a Master and a Disciple on the question of what constitutes happiness. The Master's answer is that happiness depends on cultivating an individual's faculties, including those required to excel in war. But how could this contribute to happiness, the Disciple asks, when war might lead to death and destruction? The Master explains:

> Defence of one's own country is an action directed to God as much as self-preservation and preservation of the near and dear ones. All *dharma* and progress will disappear from the world if everything is destroyed or degraded due to mutual aggression or comes under the domination of the most sinful and greedy nations. Hence for the well-being of all creatures, everyone should defend his own country.

Patriotism was *not* an excuse for the narrow-minded nationalism on display in Europe, the Master cautioned, because *dharma* enjoins that "one should not seek any benefit by doing harm to others." Thus, if India cultivated a suitable kind and degree of patriotism, it would, the Master promised, "occupy in future the highest position in the world."[140]

Bankim's counsel was underscored by Indians who, having dared to cross the seas, had begun reporting on lands where Europeans had subjugated indigenous populations (a genre of writing that would grow exponentially as anticolonial nationalism would sweep the globe in the early part of the twentieth century). One of the most striking examples was the prominent social reformer Ramabai Sarasvati's *The Condition of the People of the United States*. Written during her visit to the United States to attend Anandibai Joshi's graduation in 1886, Ramabai's remarkable travelogue introduced Indians to American norms and practices. Though she admired the United States, Ramabai did not fail to educate her compatriots about the corresponding fate of their Native American "brethren." The two peoples, she pointed out in the passages excerpted here as "The Ruin of the Native Americans," had a "very immediate connection." Both had been "bestowed" to Europeans by the Pope's "feigned generosity," the one to Spain and the other to Portugal. Though she had recently converted to Christianity, she did not disguise her disgust at the transaction. "Africa, America, India and their neighboring islands—what were they to the Pope, the land of his fathers?," she asked sarcastically. More importantly still, both societies had succumbed to "Whites" for the same reasons. One was their "ignorance," which had rendered them defenseless before modern weapons. The other was seeking "outsider's help" in settling "feuds," which had let the "White people" turn them into "puppets." As Ramabai reminded her compatriots,

> Due to the contentious disputes amongst our countrymen, foreigners could gain ingress and we lost our Independence, this much is evident to every person that reads the history of Hindustan. Our Native American brethren met the same fate. While they were fighting among themselves, the White people gained ground. . . . Thus it becomes apparent that both the weak Indians who helped the Whites destroy enemies of their own race, and similarly ignoble persons in our own country, ultimately hurt their own people, of their own make and blood, with their actions.[141]

Though Bankim and Ramabai both stressed how important patriotism was for survival, the unabashed and brutal imperialism that Italy, Germany, and Belgium were starting to display in Africa naturally led their compatriots to question whether this sentiment, which encouraged noble self-sacrifice, would be sufficient to withstand modern Europe. For a taste of the awe evoked by the scale and power of modern Europe, we need look no further than *My Jubilee Visit to London*, which recounted the 1st Madras Lancers' Subadar Muhammad Beg's outing on the occasion of Queen Victoria's Diamond Jubilee in 1897.

Originally written in Hindustani, Beg's account drew attention to the physical contrast between Englishmen and Indians. Like nearly every Indian who visited England during this time, Beg was struck by the "active energetic habits" of the English, which contrasted sharply with the "indolence" of the average Indian. The "end of life in the West is active work," he observed, while the "end of life in the East seems to be an easy-chair." The outcome in the former case, the Subadar's practiced eye discerned, was a physically capable citizenry—a "nation of soldiers." To this collective virtue was joined the "tested perfection" of the English state. Whether recollecting military parades, naval reviews, or shooting matches, Beg could only marvel at the "strength, organisation, and discipline" he was witnessing. The broader impression, he informed his countrymen, was this: "It struck me how closely superior strength is associated with an idea of permanency.

Whatever is weak is a reminder of the transient nature of our existence, whereas whatever is strong is just the reverse. The impression British strength makes on one's mind, both on land and on sea, evokes the expression, 'What wonderful people these, who can conquer them?'"[142] Though travel reports such as Beg's brought home how far the colonized world was falling behind in terms of military might, even worldly-wise Indians continued to struggle to recommend following Europe's example. Baman Das Basu's essay "What Can England Teach Us?" (1897) is a revealing example of their unease. Basu, who had trained in medicine in England, published this essay under the pseudonym "Indo-Anglian" when serving in the Indian Medical Service, a career that included grueling stints in Sudan and Afghanistan. Not relishing "being in harness in company with military imperialists," he would subsequently take premature retirement and go on to become a prolific commentator with many popular essays to his credit.[143]

Like Bankim, Basu saw there was much his compatriots needed to learn from England in order to "be able to maintain their position in this world." Having lived in England, he drew attention to facets of English life, such as the "worship" of "heroes," which inspired "the general mass," and communal solidarity, which contrasted sharply with the tendency of Indians to "cut each other's throats." But, most important of all, he stressed, his compatriots needed to cultivate "worldliness." They had to understand that "to do a good turn to his own nation, a Western patriot does not hesitate to cut the throats of another people," and thus act accordingly, else they would be "liable to be exterminated." Even so, Basu could not help but wince at the full implication of his own view. He counseled imbibing the "national selfishness" of the English "*minus* the robbing instinct."[144] Thus, for instance, while it was foolish to think that Britain would encourage Indian manufacturing, he urged patriots to defend their country through *swadeshi*.

The following generation, exemplified by Aurobindo Ghosh's rousing essay "Morality of Boycott" (1907), would be less shy than Basu. Taking rising Japan as their inspiration, they would declare "the sword of the warrior as necessary to the fulfilment of justice and righteousness as the holiness of the saint."[145] But this more muscular posture, which would produce bursts of violence and scattered conspiracies such as the Ghadar movement (and, much later, the Indian National Army under Rash Behari

Bose), would be fiercely repressed by the British, leaving the field to unworldly ideals of the kind discussed in the following chapter.

TEACHING THE WEST

Having examined the view that, to take her rightful place in the international order, India needed to learn from the West, let us survey the rival point of view. This was the idea that India ought to challenge rather than imitate the West because, by teaching mankind to curtail material desire and accept difference, her philosophy alone could heal a world disfigured by greed and hatred.

By the latter half of the nineteenth century, most of Asia was under the sway of European powers. The recent course of history notwithstanding, a sizable section of the Indian elite, especially those associated with Hindu revivalism, counseled their compatriots not to emulate the West on the grounds that their own civilization had ultimately greater worth. One prominent spokesperson was Raj Narain Bose, the leader of the principal sect of the Brahmo Samaj. In his widely reported lecture "The Superiority of Hinduism to Other Existing Religions" (1882), Bose responded to Christian missionaries, who had long assailed Hinduism as a false religion, by offering two reasons why Hinduism was superior to the Abrahamic faiths. The first was that Hinduism was "more liberal than other religions" because "Christians and Mahomedans assert that, unless one be a Christian or a Mahomedan, he is to suffer the pains of eternal hell," whereas Hindus believed that "if a man follows the religion in which he believes, to the best of his power, he will be saved." Since it was inevitable that "different men think differently of God," Bose reasoned, Hinduism's "tolerant spirit" was truer to the "law of nature," and therefore preferable to Christians' and Muslims' "extremely unreasonable and uncharitable" opinions. The second was that Hinduism exhibited a more "comprehensive" morality that addressed the totality of human existence. It ignored "neither the soul, nor the mind, nor the body, nor society," Bose observed. This made it especially suited to resisting the moral corruption engendered by modernity. "The present civilization is a hollow one," Bose declared, where "glitter" and "external refinement" papered over "rottenness" and the "grossest vices."[146] As a result, Indians could "never become great by means of imitation." It was only by "re-attaining its ancient religious and moral civilization" that India could become "the best and the foremost of all nations on the earth."[147]

The former of the two points that Bose had pressed so firmly—the value of pluralism—was subsequently pressed home by Keshub Chandra Sen, the leader of a rival sect of the Brahmo Samaj. One of the few Indians whose name was known throughout the country and abroad as well, Sen had long championed the cause of "universal brotherhood." In "Asia's Message to Europe," delivered at Calcutta's Town Hall in 1883, he underlined what Europe could learn from Asia. "Europe's aggressive civilization," he complained, had inflicted "a cruel slaughter" on Asia's customs, institutions, and industries. Let there be, he urged his audience, "no more war, but henceforth peace and amity, brotherhood and friendliness." But how could Europeans be persuaded to display brotherliness when the English, the French, and the Germans were all seeking hegemony? The impulse for brotherhood could be fostered, Sen argued, by appreciating the pluralism widely prevalent in Asia, whose civilizations had long sought out what was common in humankind. "What Asia has done intuitively," he declared, Europe would have to do "reflectively." Europe ought to emulate Asia's "unity in variety," he contended, because human history showed that there "is a natural and an irresistible tendency in man's progressive nature towards social fellowship." Individuals and groups appreciated communal life because it enriched their lives culturally and materially. But communal life could only be maintained when collectives were "not destructive, but constructive," i.e., when they allowed individuals and groups to not only expand but also maintain existing sympathies and identities. Hence, if Europeans wanted to be on the side of civilization rather than barbarism, Sen concluded, they ought to follow Asia's example by encouraging "international fellowship." "Let us all march then into broader fields and larger intercourses," he proclaimed, "till we form a blessed and world-wide community of God's children, for that is indeed the destiny of our race."[148]

The latter of Raj Narain Bose's claims—that Hinduism stressed the moral over the material—owed much to generations of Orientalist study of classical Indian literature. This tradition received its grandest statement in Friedrich Max Müller's lecture "India: What Can It Teach Us?" (1883), which contrasted Europe and India by saying that whereas the "best talent" of the former had been devoted to "the study of the development of the outward or material world," the latter held "a place second to no other" in the study of the "inward and intellectual world." As a consequence, it was to India, he urged, that Europe should turn to "draw that corrective which is most wanted in order to make our inner life more perfect, more comprehensive, more universal, in fact more truly human."[149] This claim found numerous subscribers in the decade that followed. Among them was Annie Besant, who would go on to lead the Theosophical Society, found Central Hindu College, and eventually preside over the Congress. Consider, for instance, her lecture "India, Her Past and Her Future" (1893), which drew attention to Müller's praise for India's "unique civilisation." Its uniqueness, she noted, consisted in the fact that its political, social, and familial structures were all organized toward fostering "spiritual progress." Dismissing the "veneer of a western and materialistic civilisation" produced by the spread of English education, Besant declared that India's "mission" was not to accomplish "political greatness" but to become "the teacher of the world in spiritual truth."[150]

The idea that Indians ought to propagate their civilizational ethos found its greatest exponent in Vivekananda. The question before the world, Vivekananda told his audiences, was "what makes one nation survive and the others die?" Europe thought the answer was to acquire power "by hook or crook." But history showed acquisitive nations "rising and falling almost every century—starting up from nothingness, making vicious play for a few days, and then melting."[151] The moral was that, to endure, a nation ought instead to cultivate "mildness, gentleness, forbearance, toleration, sympathy, and brotherhood"—virtues that would allow it to accommodate the differences that are an inevitable part of social existence.[152] And since materialism tended to smother these virtues that fostered sociability, it became essential to practice renunciation. "Giving up the senses," he concluded, is what "makes a nation survive."[153] As Vivekananda recounted in 1897 before the Triplicane Literary Society in Madras:

> I was asked by a young lady in London, "What have you Hindus done? You have never even conquered a single nation." That is true from the point of view of the Englishman, the brave, the heroic, the Kshatriya—conquest is the greatest glory that one man can have over another. That is true from his point of view, but from ours it is quite the opposite. If I ask myself what has been the cause of India's greatness, I answer, "The cause is that we have never conquered." That is our glory.[154]

Vivekananda sensed that India's example needed to travel far. "The whole of the Western world is on a volcano," he cautioned, "which may burst tomorrow" (indeed World War I erupted a little over a decade later). Hence, he championed the idea that religion was India's "theme" in a much more ambitious sense. "The foundation of her being, the raison d'être of her very existence," he wrote in a draft titled "India's Message to the World," was "the spiritualisation of the human race."[155] This duty fell upon India because Hinduism was best suited to impart the "unworldliness" that nations needed to learn before there could be peace. Hinduism's characteristic "mildness," its lack of interest in propagating its ideals through "fire and sword," also made it the ideal instructor. "Up, India, and conquer the world with your spirituality,"[156] said Vivekananda, promising that the message of love and renunciation would be her "gift to the world."[157]

Having concluded that the "non-recognition of the rights of others" was the "cause of all evil, of all international conflicts, of all war and persecution," Vivekananda and his brother-monks devoted themselves to propagating this message, traveling across Europe and the United States to preach on behalf of "unselfishness." "International Ethics," a lecture delivered in 1898 in Boston by Kaliprasad Chandra, better known as Swami Abhedananda, is a prime example of this endeavor. In his lecture, Abhedananda urged his audience to see that peaceful coexistence ultimately depended not on goodwill or dogma but on the fundamental "recognition of oneness in spirit," on the realization that social and religious differences are merely superficial. In other words, incessant conflict could only be tamed

> not by bloodshed, but by understanding the principle of nature. By the principle of nature I mean the great plan, the grand truth which is manifested in every department of nature; and that truth is "Unity in Variety." If we can understand this law, this plan of nature and if we observe it in our everyday life then we shall be unselfish, then we shall be able to recognise the rights of others, then we shall be friendly to others, and help others as we help ourselves.[158]

THE PAST AND THE PRESENT

Our overview is now complete. The preceding discussion permits three broad conclusions. First, we have seen that, contrary to conventional wisdom, Indians were thinking carefully about international relations well before 1947. While the bulk of the essays in this volume are drawn from English-speaking metropolitan India, the translations it contains indicate that similar discussions were occurring in regional languages as well. Second, we have also seen that leading figures in Indian public life strongly disagreed with one another on questions relating to international politics. This is borne out, for example, by debate over preparations for the Great Game (in chapter 3) and the morality of the opium trade (in chapter 7). This fuller history thus challenges the idea that there is a characteristic Indian response to international politics, such as the oft-touted doctrine of non-violence. Third, it should now be clear that many controversial issues in India's foreign relations have longer histories than is commonly realized. For instance, anxieties about extraterritorial allegiances (in chapter 4) or about self-reliance (in chapter 5) have been around far longer than contemporary personalities and political parties.

These broad conclusions set the record straight. But why, it may be asked, should we care about them? What is their contemporary relevance? Do they only clear up misconceptions and thus help better *understand* the past or do they *explain* something about the present? The latter ambition may be controversial. Are we really to believe, hard-bitten observers and practitioners will scoff, that the past unveils the present—that "the child-hood shows the man, as morning shows the day?"[159]

Here it is necessary to clarify that this overview does not claim that nineteenth-century discussions on international politics *directly* explain contemporary Indian foreign policy decisions. Such influence is certainly possible. The great figures of that era are still read and cited as inspirations by decision-makers today. But it would require a very different kind of volume to flesh out such a claim. It is the business of political science to identify the pulls and pressures that lead to particular decisions at particular moments. That is not this volume's purpose. But ideas can have explanatory power in another sense: they explain how choices came to be framed, motivated, and legitimated. This is the business of intellectual history. The conjecture this volume offers is that when we stand back from explanations about why a particular decision was made, and ask why that decision was considered *a good idea*, the trail of answers is likely to lead to an idea originating in nineteenth-century India. This is the sense in which this volume has a strong claim to contemporary relevance.

Of course much more needs to be done to validate this conjecture. An anthology is the beginning, not the end, of an investigation. This is especially so in the present context. Given how little material from nineteenth-century India is publicly available, this volume has focused solely on bringing these items to wider notice. As a result, we have only been able to briefly note, toward the close of each subsection, the impact that the nineteenth-century debates had on subsequent ideas and events. A forthcoming sequel to this volume, focusing on the twentieth century, will make such connections still clearer.[160] It will show how deeply the critiques contained in this volume impacted following generations, and in fact continue to resonate in contemporary India (present-day pleas to replace imports with domestic manufacturing can, for instance, easily be traced back to the discussion on self-reliance in chapter 5).

This caveat notwithstanding, there is one important connection between the past and present that is worth underscoring here. This volume shows that in the nineteenth century there emerged a divide between those who thought that India needed to learn worldliness, and those who thought that it was the world that needed to learn from India. This debate, evidenced in chapters 8 and 9, bequeathed later generations a weighty question: Should India strive to be a great power?

This piece of intellectual history seems especially relevant today. There is already plenty of evidence to show that this question was not settled in the twentieth century. Voices urging India to shun great power politics may have been loud, but there were always contrary voices—in the Constituent Assembly, in Parliament, in the media, and in the corridors of power—counseling India to cultivate power and influence.[161] Shocks, embarrassments, and triumphs made the balance seesaw, but there was no decisive, collective answer. Nor, as we noted earlier, has this debate been settled in recent decades. Though voices arguing that India should be a great power may now appear ascendant, there are plenty that still fiercely oppose the idea. This is not simply an instance of the dead hand of history—old grudges and hardened positions—weighing down on the present. There are genuine anxieties to contend with. Those on the Left believe that partaking in great power politics will endanger domestic priorities such as a focus on social welfare (mirroring the critique in chapter 3). Those on the Right, especially Hindu nationalists, have grave doubts about building the economic and social base required to achieve great power, because they worry that gross materialism will weaken India's culture and ethos (mirroring the critique in chapter 9).[162]

What this means is that a collective choice still remains to be made. For the past century, the security umbrella provided by the British Empire, and subsequently the Nehruvian policy of nonalignment, allowed Indians to more or less avoid the question of whether their country should enter, with all seriousness, into the rough and tumble of great power politics. We are still in the waiting room of history. This is why debates from the nineteenth century are recognizable rather than quaint: the great question India confronts today is the same question it confronted back then. The only difference is that now, with great power competition truly underway in Asia, India will soon be compelled to confront this momentous question squarely. A clearer sense of its past may help it develop its answer, or at least help others understand why such an answer is hard to come by.

NOTES

1. Robert D. Blackwill and Ashley J. Tellis, "The India Dividend: New Delhi Remains Washington's Best Hope in Asia," *Foreign Affairs* 98, no. 5 (2019).

2. For instance, see Alyssa Ayres, *Our Time Has Come: How India Is Making Its Place in the World* (New York: Oxford University Press, 2018); Teresita C. Schaffer and Howard B. Schaffer, *India at the Global High Table: The Quest for Regional Primacy and Strategic Autonomy* (Washington, DC: Brookings Institution Press, 2016); Shashi Tharoor, *Pax Indica: India and the World of the 21st Century* (New Delhi: Penguin, 2013); David M. Malone, *Does the Elephant Dance?: Contemporary Indian Foreign Policy* (New York: Oxford University Press, 2014); Sunil Khilnani, Rajiv Kumar, Pratap Bhanu Mehta, Prakash Menon, Nandan Nilekani, Srinath Raghavan, Shyam Saran, and Siddharth Varadarajan, *NonAlignment 2.0: A Foreign and Strategic Policy for India in the 21st Century* (New Delhi: Penguin, 2014).

3. S. Jaishankar, *The India Way: Strategies for an Uncertain World* (New Delhi: HarperCollins, 2020); Shyam Saran, *How India Sees the World: Kautilya to the 21st Century* (New Delhi: Juggernaut, 2017); Shivshankar Menon, *Choices: Inside the Making of India's Foreign Policy* (Washington, DC: Brookings Institution Press, 2016); Vijay Gokhale, *The Long Game: How the Chinese Negotiate with India* (New Delhi: Penguin, 2021); Shivshankar Menon, *India and Asian Geopolitics: The Past, The Present* (Washington, DC: Brookings Institution Press, 2021); Sanjaya Baru, *India and the World: Essays on Geoeconomics and Foreign Policy* (New Delhi: Academic Foundation, 2016); Arvind Gupta and Anil Wadhwa, eds., *India's Foreign Policy: Surviving in a Turbulent World* (New Delhi: Sage, 2020).

60

4. For instance, see Rajesh Basrur and Kate Sullivan de Estrada, *Rising India: Status and Power* (New York: Routledge, 2017); Waheguru Pal Singh Sidhu, Pratap Bhanu Mehta, and Bruce D. Jones, eds., *Shaping the Emerging World: India and the Multilateral Order* (Washington, DC: Brookings Institution Press, 2013); Baldev Raj Nayar and T. V. Paul, *India in the World Order: Searching for Major-Power Status* (New York: Cambridge University Press, 2003); Stephen P. Cohen, *India: Emerging Power* (Washington, DC: Brookings Institution Press, 2004); Sandy Gordon, *India's Rise as an Asian Power: Nation, Neighborhood, and Region* (Washington, DC: Georgetown University Press, 2014); Johannes Plagemann, Sandra Destradi, and Amrita Narlikar, eds., *India Rising: A Multilayered Analysis of Ideas, Interests, and Institutions* (Oxford: Oxford University Press, 2020).

5. C. Raja Mohan, *Modi's World: Expanding India's Sphere of Influence* (New Delhi: HarperCollins, 2015); Ian Hall, *Modi and the Reinvention of Indian Foreign Policy* (Bristol: Bristol University Press, 2019); Sinderpal Singh, ed., *Modi And The World: (Re)Constructing Indian Foreign Policy* (Singapore: World Scientific, 2017); Shakti Sinha, *Vajpayee: The Years That Changed India* (New Delhi: Penguin, 2021); Sanjaya Baru, *The Accidental Prime Minister: The Making and Unmaking of Manmohan Singh* (New Delhi: Penguin, 2015); Jaswant Singh, *In Service of Emergent India: A Call to Honour* (New Delhi: Rupa, 2006); L. K. Advani, *My Country, My Life* (New Delhi: Rupa, 2008); Vinay Sitapati, *Half-Lion: How PV Narasimha Rao Transformed India* (New Delhi: Penguin, 2017); Montek Singh Ahluwalia, *Backstage: The Story Behind India's High Growth Years* (New Delhi: Rupa, 2020); Jairam Ramesh, *Intertwined Lives: P. N. Haksar and Indira Gandhi* (New Delhi: Simon and Schuster, 2019); Jairam Ramesh, *A Chequered Brilliance: The Many Lives of V. K. Krishna Menon* (New Delhi: Penguin, 2019); Narayani Basu, *V. P. Menon: The Unsung Architect of Modern India* (New Delhi: Simon and Schuster, 2020); Hindol Sengupta, *The Man of Saved India: Sardar Patel and His Idea of India* (New Delhi: Penguin, 2018); Andrew B. Kennedy, *The International Ambitions of Mao and Nehru: National Efficacy Beliefs and the Making of Foreign Policy* (Cambridge: Cambridge University Press, 2012).

6. Notable recent works include Srinath Raghavan, *War and Peace in Modern India: A Strategic History of the Nehru Years* (Basingstoke, UK: Palgrave Macmillan, 2010); Zorawar Daulet Singh, *Power and Diplomacy: India's Foreign Policies During the Cold War* (New Delhi: Oxford University Press, 2019); Sumit Ganguly, *Engaging the World: Indian Foreign Policy Since 1947* (Oxford: Oxford University Press, 2016); David Malone, C. Raja Mohan, and Srinath Raghavan, eds., *The Oxford Handbook of Indian Foreign Policy* (New York: Oxford University Press, 2015); Manu Bhagavan, ed., *India and the Cold War* (Raleigh: UNC Press, 2019). County-specific studies include Rudra Chaudhuri, *Forged in Crisis: India and the United States Since 1947* (New York: Oxford University Press, 2014); Nicolas Blarel, *The Evolution of India's Israel Policy: Continuity, Change, and Compromise Since 1922* (New Delhi: Oxford University Press, 2015); Tanvi Madan, *Fateful Triangle: How China Shaped U.S.-India Relations During the Cold War* (Washington, DC: Brookings Institution Press, 2020); Harsh V. Pant, *The China Syndrome: Grappling with an Uneasy Relationship Hardcover* (New Delhi: HarperCollins, 2010); Kanti Bajpai, Selina Ho, and Manjari Chatterjee Miller, *Routledge Handbook of China-India Relations* (New York: Routledge, 2020); Harsh V. Pant, *China Ascendant: Its*

Rise and Implications (New Delhi: HarperCollins, 2019); Kanti Bajpai, Jing Huang, and Kishore Mahbubani, eds., *China-India Relations: Cooperation and Conflict* (New York: Routledge, 2016); Sandra Destradi, *Indian Foreign and Security Policy in South Asia: Regional Power Strategies* (London: Routledge, 2012); Rajesh Basrur and Sumitha Narayanan Kutty, eds., *India and Japan: Assessing the Strategic Partnership* (New Delhi: Springer, 2018); Rohan Mukherjee and Anthony Yazaki, eds., *Poised for Partnership: Deepening India-Japan Relations in the Asian Century* (New Delhi: Oxford University Press, 2016).

7. Brief discussions can be found in Bimal Prasad, *The Origins of Indian Foreign Policy: The Indian National Congress and World Affairs, 1885–1947* (Calcutta: Bookland, 1962); T. A. Keenleyside, "Diplomatic Apprenticeship: Pre-Independence Origins of Indian Diplomacy and Its Relevance for the Post-Independence Foreign Policy," *India Quarterly* 43, no. 2 (1987); J. N. Dixit, *The Makers of India's Foreign Policy: Raja Ram Mohun Roy to Yashwant Sinha* (New Delhi: HarperCollins, 2004); A. K. Damodaran, "Roots of Foreign Policy," *India International Centre Quarterly* 14, no. 3 (1987): 53–65; P. M. Joshi and M. A. Nayeem, eds., *Studies in the Foreign Relations of India, from the Earliest Times to 1947* (Hyderabad: State Archives, Govt. of Andhra Pradesh, 1975); Thomas Pantham and Kenneth L. Deutsch, eds., *Political Thought in Modern India* (New Delhi: Sage, 1986). Some recent scholarship that touches on this era includes Sneh Mahajan, *British Foreign Policy, 1874–1914: The Role of India* (London: Routledge, 2015); Mithi Mukherjee, "'A World of Illusion': The Legacy of Empire in India's Foreign Relations, 1947–62," *International History Review* 32, no. 2 (2010): 253–271; Vineet Thakur, "The Colonial Origins of Indian Foreign Policymaking," *Economic and Political Weekly* 49, no. 32 (2014): 58–64.

8. "India," *Encyclopedia Britannica*, February 18, 2021 (www.britannica.com/place /India).

9. There is a sizable literature on the role of ideas—and relatedly of norms, culture, and identity—in foreign policy. Important studies include Jeffrey W. Legro, *Rethinking the World: Great Power Strategies and International Order* (Ithaca: Cornell University Press, 2005); Manjari C. Miller, *Why Nations Rise: Narratives and the Path to Great Power* (New York: Oxford University Press, 2021); Neta C. Crawford, *Argument and Change in World Politics: Ethics, Decolonization, and Humanitarian Intervention* (New York: Cambridge University Press, 2002); Joseph S. Nye, *Do Morals Matter?: Presidents and Foreign Policy from FDR to Trump* (New York: Oxford University Press, 2019); Richard J. Samuels, *Securing Japan: Tokyo's Grand Strategy and the Future of East Asia* (Ithaca: Cornell University Press, 2007); Alastair Iain Johnston, *Cultural Realism: Strategic Culture and Grand Strategy in Chinese History* (Princeton: Princeton University Press, 1995); Anne L. Clunan, *The Social Construction of Russia's Resurgence: Aspirations, Identity, and Security Interests* (Baltimore: Johns Hopkins University Press, 2009); Jeffrey W. Meiser, *Power and Restraint: The Rise of the United States, 1898–1941* (Washington, DC: Georgetown University Press, 2015); Ronald R. Krebs, *Narrative and the Making of US National Security* (New York: Cambridge University Press, 2015); Walter Russell Mead, *Special Providence: American Foreign Policy and How It Changed the World* (New York: Routledge, 2013); Peter Trubowitz, *Defining the National Interest: Conflict and Change in American Foreign Policy* (Chicago:

University of Chicago Press, 1998); Amitav Acharya, *Whose Ideas Matter?: Agency and Power in Asian Regionalism* (Ithaca: Cornell University Press, 2011); Peter J. Katzenstein, *The Culture of National Security: Norms and Identity in World Politics* (New York: Columbia University Press, 1996); Judith Goldstein and Robert O. Keohane, *Ideas and Foreign Policy: Beliefs, Institutions, and Political Change* (Ithaca: Cornell University Press, 1993).

10. Legro, *Rethinking the World*, 1. A small but growing body of literature focuses on the role of ideology, identity, and culture in Indian foreign policy. Important works include Manjari Chatterjee Miller, *Post-Imperial Ideology and Foreign Policy in India and China* (Palo Alto: Stanford University Press, 2013); Jacques E. C. Hymans, *The Psychology of Nuclear Proliferation: Identity, Emotions, and Foreign Policy* (Cambridge: Cambridge University Press, 2006); Priya Chacko, *Indian Foreign Policy: The Politics of Postcolonial Identity from 1947 to 2004* (London: Routledge, 2013); Kate Sullivan, "India's Ambivalent Projection of Self as a Global Power: Between Compliance and Resistance," in *Competing Visions of India in World Politics: India's Rise Beyond the West*, ed. Kate Sullivan (London: Palgrave Macmillan, 2015), 15–33; Deep K. Datta-Ray, *The Making of Indian Diplomacy: A Critique of Eurocentrism* (New York: Oxford University Press, 2015); Harsh V. Pant, ed., *India's Foreign Policy: Theory and Praxis* (New Delhi: Cambridge University Press, 2019), part 1; Kadira Pethiyagoda, *Indian Foreign Policy and Cultural Values* (London: Palgrave Macmillan, 2020); Vineet Thakur, *Postscripts on Independence: Foreign Policy Ideas, Identity, and Institutions in India and South Africa* (New Delhi: Oxford University Press, 2018); Nalini Kant Jha, "Traditional Foundations of Nehru's Foreign Policy in Contemporary Context," *India Quarterly* 62, no. 1 (2006); K. J. Holsti, "National Role Conceptions in the Study of Foreign Policy," *International Studies Quarterly* 14, no. 3 (1970): 233–309.

11. Vipin Narang and Paul Staniland, "Institutions and Worldviews in Indian Foreign Security Policy," *India Review* 11, no. 2 (2012): 77.

12. George K. Tanham, *Indian Strategic Thought: An Interpretive Essay* (Santa Monica: RAND, 1992), v; "Can India Become a Great Power?," *Economist*, April 5, 2013. See also K. Subrahmanyam, *Shedding Shibboleths: India's Evolving Strategic Outlook* (New Delhi: Wordsmiths, 2005), 7; Jaswant Singh, *Defending India* (Delhi: Macmillan, 1999), 16–17, 40–41; K. Sundarji, *The Blind Men of Hindoostan: Indo-Pak Nuclear War* (New Delhi: UBS, 1993); S. N. Prasad, "Introduction," in *Historical Perspectives of Warfare in India: Some Moral and Materiel Determinants*, ed. S. N. Prasad (New Delhi: Centre for Studies in Civilizations, 2002), 36–42. For an overview of the subsequent debate, see Kanti Bajpai, Amitabh Mattoo, and George K. Tanham, eds., *Securing India: Strategic Thought and Practice in an Emerging Power* (Delhi: Manohar, 1996); Bernhard Beitelmair-Berini, "Theorizing Indian Strategic Culture(s): Taking Stock of a Controversial Debate," in *Theorizing Indian Foreign Policy*, ed. Misha Hansel, Raphaëlle Khan, and Mélissa Levaillant (Abingdon: Routledge, 2017), 91–111; C. Christine Fair, "India," in *Comparative Grand Strategy: A Framework and Cases*, ed. Thierry Balzaq, Peter Dombrowski, and Simon Reich (New York: Oxford University Press, 2019), 171–91; Harsh V. Pant, "Indian Strategic Culture: The Debate and Its Consequences," in *Handbook of India's International Relations*, ed. David Scott (London: Routledge, 2011),

14–22; Sui Xinmin, "India's Strategic Culture and Model of International Behavior," *China International Studies* 45 (2014): 139–62.

13. Kanti Bajpai, "Indian Strategic Culture," in *South Asia in 2020: Future Strategic Balances and Alliances*, ed. Michael R. Chambers (Carlisle, PA: Strategic Studies Institute, 2002), 245–304; Kanti Bajpai, "Indian Conceptions of Order and Justice," in *Order and Justice in International Relations*, ed. Rosemary Foot, John Lewis Gaddis, and Andrew Hurrell (Oxford: Oxford University Press, 2004); Rajesh M. Basrur, *Minimum Deterrence and India's National Security* (Singapore: NUS Press, 2009); Narang and Staniland, "Institutions and Worldviews in Indian Foreign Security Policy," 76–94; Itty Abraham, "India's 'Strategic Enclave': Civilian Scientists and Military Technologies," *Armed Forces and Society* 18, no. 2 (1992); Ian Hall, "The Persistence of Nehruvianism in India's Strategic Culture," in *Strategic Asia, 2016–17: Comparing Strategic Cultures in the Asia Pacific*, ed. Ashley Tellis and Michael Wills (Washington DC: National Bureau of Asian Research, 2016). The precursors to this literature included T. A. Keenleyside, "Prelude to Power: The Meaning of Non-Alignment Before Indian Independence," *Pacific Affairs* 53, no. 3 (1980); A. P. Rana, "The Nature of India's Foreign Policy: An Examination of the Relation of Indian Non-Alignment to the Concept of the Balance of Power in the Nuclear Age," *India Quarterly* 22, no. 2 (1966); Paul F. Power, *Gandhi on World Affairs* (Washington, DC: Public Affairs, 1960); Charles Heimsath and Surjit Mansingh, *A Diplomatic History of Modern India* (Bombay: Allied, 1971).

14. C. Raja Mohan, *Crossing the Rubicon: The Shaping of India's New Foreign Policy* (New Delhi: Penguin, 2005); Sumit Ganguly, "India After Nonalignment," *Foreign Affairs*, September 19, 2016. For a succinct overview of prior goals, see M. S. Rajan, "The Goals of India's Foreign Policy," *International Studies* 35, no. 1 (1998); Vijaya Lakshmi Pandit, "India's Foreign Policy," *Foreign Affairs* 34, no. 3 (1956): 432–40.

15. Important works in this vein include Shivshankar Menon, "Strategic Culture and IR Studies in India," 3rd International Studies Convention, Jawaharlal Nehru University, New Delhi, December 11, 2013; Shivshankar Menon, "Kautilya Today," Workshop on Kautilya, Institute for Defense Studies and Analyses, October 18, 2012; Subrata Mitra and Michael Liebig, *Kautilya's Arthashastra: The Classical Roots of Modern Indian Politics* (Baden-Baden: Nomos, 2016); P. K. Gautam, Saurabh Mishra, and Arvind Gupta, eds., *Indigenous Historical Knowledge: Kautilya and His Vocabulary*, vol. 1, (New Delhi: PentagonPress, 2015); W. P. S. Sidhu, "Of Oral Traditions and Ethnocentric Judgements," in Bajpai, Mattoo, and Tanham, *Securing India*, 175–79; Rodney W. Jones, "India's Strategic Culture and the Origins of Omniscient Paternalism," in *Strategic Culture and Weapons of Mass Destruction*, ed. Jeannie L. Johnson, Kerry M. Kartchner, and Jeffrey A. Larsen (New York: Palgrave Macmillan, 2009), 117–36; Aparna Pande, *From Chanakya to Modi: Evolution of India's Foreign Policy* (New Delhi: HarperCollins, 2017); Jayashree Vivekanandan, *Interrogating International Relations* (New Delhi: Routledge, 2011); Bharat Karnad, *Nuclear Weapons and Indian Security: The Realist Foundations of Strategy* (New Delhi: Macmillan, 2005), 3–29; Swarna Rajagopalan, "'Grand Strategic Thought' in the Ramayana and Mahabharata," in *India's Grand Strategy: History, Theory, Cases*, ed. Kanti Bajpai, Saira Basit, and V. Krishnappa (New Delhi: Routledge, 2014), 31–62; Shrikant Paranjpe, *India's Strategic Culture: The Making*

of National Security Policy (New Delhi: Routledge, 2013); Raj Shukla, "Contours of India's Grand Strategy," in *The New Arthashastra: A Security Strategy for India*, ed. Gurmeet Kanwal (New Delhi: HarperCollins, 2016), 323–40; Ali Ahmed, "Does India Think Strategically?: Searching Military Doctrines for Answers," in *Does India Think Strategically?: Institutions, Strategic Culture, and Security Policies*, ed. Jacob Happymon (New Delhi: Manohar, 2015), 149–72; Raja Menon and Rajiv Kumar, *The Long View from Delhi: To Define the Indian Grand Strategy for Foreign Policy* (New Delhi: Academic Foundation, 2010).

16. Ashley J. Tellis, C. Raja Mohan, and Bibek Debroy, eds., *Grasping Greatness: Making India a Leading Power* (New Delhi: Penguin Random House, 2021); Manjari Chatterjee Miller, "India's Feeble Foreign Policy: A Would-Be Great Power Resists Its Own Rise," *Foreign Affairs* 92, no. 3 (2013); Aparna Pande, *Making India Great: The Promise of a Reluctant Global Power* (New York: HarperCollins, 2021); Bharat Karnad, *Why India Is Not a Great Power (Yet)* (Oxford: Oxford University Press, 2015); Anit Mukherjee, *The Absent Dialogue: Politicians, Bureaucrats, and the Military in India* (New York: Oxford University Press, 2019); Sumit Ganguly, "Modi's Foreign Policy Revolution?," *Foreign Affairs*, March 8, 2018; Manjari Chatterjee Miller and Kate Sullivan de Estrada, "Pragmatism in Indian Foreign Policy: How Ideas Constrain Modi," *International Affairs* 93, no. 1 (2017): 27–49; Bharat Karnad, *Staggering Forward: Narendra Modi and India's Global Ambition* (New Delhi: Penguin, 2018).

17. Pratap Bhanu Mehta, "Still Under Nehru's Shadow?: The Absence of Foreign Policy Frameworks in India," *India Review* 8, no. 3 (2009); Tanham, *Indian Strategic Thought*, v–vii.

18. Stephen Hay, ed., *Sources of Indian Tradition: Modern India and Pakistan* (New York: Columbia University Press, 1958), part 6; Rachel McDermott, Leonard Gordon, Ainslie T. Embree, Frances Pritchett, and Dennis Dalton, eds., *Sources of Indian Traditions: Modern India, Pakistan and Bangladesh* (New York: Columbia University Press, 2014), chaps. 2–5. Valuable collections that shed light on *twentieth*-century debates include Kanti Bajpai and Siddharth Mallavarapu, eds., *India, the West, and International Order* (New Delhi: Orient Blackswan, 2019); A. Appadorai, ed., *Documents on Political Thought in Modern India*, vol. 2 (Bombay: Oxford University Press, 1976), chap. 10; D. Mackenzie Brown, *The White Umbrella: Indian Political Thought from Manu to Gandhi* (Berkeley: University of California Press, 1964).

19. Brahma Chaudhuri, "India," in *Periodicals of Queen Victoria's Empire: An Exploration*, ed. J. Don Vann and Rosemary T. Van Arsdel (Toronto: University of Toronto Press, 1996), 175–200; R. P. Kumar, *Research Periodicals of Colonial India, 1780–1947* (New Delhi: Academic, 1985).

20. A comprehensive database titled *Ideas of India*, covering more than one hundred nineteenth-century periodicals, can be freely searched via www.ideasofindia.org. Other recently inaugurated databases, which require subscriptions, are *South Asia Archive* (www.southasiaarchive.com); *Granth Sanjeevani* (www.granthsanjeevani .com); *South Asian Newspapers* (www.readex.com); British Newspaper Archive (www.britishnewspaperarchive.co.uk); *Indian Newspaper Reports* (www.ampltd.co .uk); and South Asia Open Archives (www.saoa.crl.edu).

21. For a tantalizing example, see V. Ramakrishna, "Women's Journals in Andhra During the Nineteenth Century," *Social Scientist* 19, nos. 5/6 (1991): 80–87.

22. There were notable examples of travel writing, including Sunity Devee, *The Autobiography of an Indian Princess* (London: John Murray, 1921); Meera Kosambi, ed. and trans., *Pandita Ramabai's American Encounter* (Bloomington: Indiana University Press, 2003), chaps. 1–3; Mary Bhore, *Some Impressions of England* (Poona: Bhau Govind Sapkar, 1900); Harihar Das, *Life and Letters of Toru Dutt* (Oxford: Oxford University Press, 1921), chaps. 2–3; Parvatibai Chitnavis, *Amacha Jagacha Pravasa* [Our Travels Around the World] (Mumbai: Manoranjan, 1915). A valuable recent overview is Jayati Gupta, *Travel Culture, Travel Writing and Bengali Women, 1870–1940* (New York: Routledge, 2021).

23. Thomas B. Macaulay, "Minute on Education," in *Selections from Educational Records*, pt. 1, *1781–1839*, ed. Henry Sharp (Calcutta: Bengal Government Press, 1920), 107–17. Anglo-Indians questioned the overemphasis on Macaulay's Minute. William Wilson Hunter, for example, wrote: "Before Macaulay set foot in India native opinion had declared so strongly for English teaching, in place of the old traditional learning, that Macaulay's eloquent Minute merely played the part of the shout at which the walls of Jericho fell." Wilson, *State Education for the People* (London: George Routledge, 1890), 3.

24. T. Madava Row, "An Essay on Native Education," in *The Fifth Annual Report from the Governors of the Madras University, 1845–46* (Madras: Christian Knowledge Society's Press, 1847), 34–47.

25. Row, 34–47.

26. Benoy Kumar Sarkar, "Hindu Theory of International Relations," *American Political Science Review* 13, no. 3 (1919): 407–8.

27. Annie Besant, "India's Mission Among Nations," in *The Birth of New India* (Madras: Theosophical, 1917), 85–86.

28. Isaiah Berlin, "The Bent Twig: A Note on Nationalism," *Foreign Affairs* 51, no. 1 (1972): 30.

29. Romesh Chunder Dutt, *Three Years in Europe* (Calcutta: S. K. Lahiri, 1896), 99.

30. For instance, see Pankaj Mishra, "Narendra Modi and the New Face of India," *Guardian*, May 16, 2014; Pratap Bhanu Mehta, "India in a Corner," *Indian Express*, February 15, 2018; Chris Ogden, *Hindu Nationalism and the Evolution of Contemporary Indian Security: Portents of Power* (New York: Oxford University Press, 2014), 68.

31. Bankim Chandra Chatterjee, *Essentials of Dharma*, trans. Manomohan Ghosh (Calcutta: Sribhumi, 1977), 54.

32. Bal Gangadhar Shastri Jambhekar, "Knowledge Is Power," *Bombay Durpun*, August 24, 1832.

33. *Opening of the Madras University on the 14th April 1841* (Madras: Pharaoh, 1852), 49–51.

34. *The Fifth Annual Report from the Governors of the Madras University, 1845–46* (Madras: Pharaoh, 1852), 7–8.

35. *Fifth Annual Report from the Governors of the Madras University, 1845–46* (Madras: Christian Knowledge Society's Press, 1847), 34–47.

36. Ram Gopal Ghosh, "The Influence of the University System of Education on Native Society," *Bengal Magazine* 7 (September 1879), 78.

37. Nagendra Nath Ghose, "English Education in India from a Native Point of View," *Calcutta Review* 76, no. 156 (1884): 330–31.

38. Chunder Nath Bose, *High Education in India: An Essay Read at the Bethune Society on 25th April 1878* (Calcutta: Jogesh Chunder Banerjee, 1878).

39. Bishan Narayan Dar, "Some Characteristics of Indian English-Educated Youths," *Indian Magazine* 16, no. 191 (1886): 573, 580, 577, 582, 585–86, 577.

40. For example, see G. F. I. Graham, *Life and Work of Syed Ahmed Khan* (London: William Blackwood, 1885), 124–25; Omar Khalidi, ed., *An Indian Passage to Europe: The Travels of Fath Nawaz Jang* (Oxford: Oxford University Press, 2006), 3.

41. [Bholanath Chandra], "Vindication of the Hindoos as a Travelling Nation," *Calcutta Review* 46, no. 92 (1867): 391, 394, 427, 432.

42. F. H. Brown, "Indian Students in Great Britain," *Edinburgh Review* 217, no. 443 (1913): 139; Harihar Das, "The Early Indian Visitors to England," *Calcutta Review* 13 (October 1924): 101–9.

43. [Chandra], "Vindication of the Hindoos as a Travelling Nation," 432, 434.

44. A Brahmin Liberal, "Crossing the Sea for Hindus," *Journal of the National Indian Association*, no. 157 (1884): 20.

45. Caroline Healey Dall, *The Life of Dr. Anandabai Joshee, a Kinswoman of the Pundita Ramabai* (Boston: Roberts Brothers, 1888), 70–81; [Anandabai Joshi], *Speech by a Hindu Lady* (Bombay: Native Opinion, 1883), British Library, 1415.a.62.(8.).

46. *Full Report of the Proceedings of the Sobha Bazaar Meeting in Connection with the Sea-Voyage Movement* (Calcutta: Indian Daily News, 1892), i, iii–iv, 1.

47. R. Ananta Krishna Sastri, "Sea Voyages Among the Hindus," *Madras Review* 2, no. 7 (1896): 453.

48. S. E. Gopalacharlu, "Sea Voyages by Hindus (I): May Hindus Cross the Ocean?," *Imperial and Asiatic Quarterly Review* 4, no. 7 (1892): 51–52.

49. Swami Vivekananda, "Letter to Alasinga, August 20, 1893," in *The Complete Works of Swami Vivekananda*, vol. 5 (Almora: Advaita Ashrama, 1960), 12.

50. *The Hindu Sea Voyage Movement in Bengal* (Calcutta: J. N. Banerjee, 1894), ii.

51. Bankim Chandra Chatterji, "Letter Regarding the Movement," in *The Hindu Sea Voyage Movement in Bengal*, 16, 19, 17.

52. For example, see T. N. Mukharji, *A Visit to Europe* (Calcutta: W. Newman, 1889), xi, 27; Behramji M. Malabari, *The Indian Eye on English Life* (London: Archibald Constable, 1893), 10–11.

53. On this see Devesh Kapur, *Diaspora, Development, and Democracy: The Domestic Impact of International Migration from India* (Princeton: Princeton University Press, 2010), 52; Michael Fisher, *Counterflows to Colonialism: Indian Travelers and Visitors in Britain* (New Delhi: Permanent Black, 2004); Rozina Visram, *Ayahs, Lascars, and Princes: Indians in Britain, 1700–1947* (London: Pluto, 1986).

54. "Indians in England," *Indian Magazine* 17, no. 194 (1887): 57–62; "Indian Gentlemen in the West," *Indian Magazine and Review* 25, no. 278 (1894): 75–84.

55. *The Hindu Sea Voyage Movement in Bengal*, v.

56. "The Russians in the East," *Calcutta Review* 43, no. 85 (1866): 93, 78, 82, 78, 96, 96, 75.

57. India, "England and Russia," *Oriental Miscellany* 1, no. 9 (1879): 366, 364, 365, 366, 369–70.

58. *Indian Leaflets No. 10: Why Do Indians Prefer British to Russian Rule?* (Calcutta: British Indian Association, 1885), 1, 3.

59. Dinshah Ardeshir Taleyarkhan, *Selections from My Recent Notes on the Indian Empire* (Bombay: Times of India Steam, 1886), 48, 48–53, 50, 51, 52, 53.

60. "The New Army Expenditure," *Voice of India* 3, no. 9 (1885): 468–75.

61. G. V. Joshi, "The Native Indian Army," *Quarterly Journal of the Poona Sarvajanik Sabha* 8, no. 3 (1886): 19, 21–22, 27, 30, 15, 36, 41–42.

62. A. M. Zaidi, ed., *INC: The Glorious Tradition*, vol. 1 (New Delhi: Document Press, 1987), 28, 32–33, 38, 47–48, 67–68, 79–80, 90, 108–9, 133.

63. Dadabhai Naoroji, "Expenses of the Abyssinian War," in *Essays, Speeches, Addresses and Writings of the Hon'ble Dadabhai Naoroji*, ed. Chunilal Lallubhai Parekh (Bombay: Caxton, 1887), 53.

64. Dadabhai Naoroji, "The Moral Poverty of India, and Native Thoughts on the Present British Indian Policy," in Parekh, *Essays, Speeches, Addresses and Writings of the Hon'ble Dadabhai Naoroji*, 471, 477.

65. K. T. Telang and Mancherjee Merwanjee Bhownugree, "Memorial from Bombay Branch to the Right Hon. W. E. Gladstone Relative to the Afghan War," *Journal of the East India Association* 13 (May 1881): 146, 150.

66. Edward B. Eastwick and Rampal Singh, "Memorial to Secretary of State for India Against India Contributing to the Expenses of the Egyptian Expedition," *Journal of the East India Association* 15 (February 1883): 88.

67. *Indian Leaflets. No. 11: The Appalling Costliness of the Indian Army* (Calcutta: British Indian Association, 1885), 5. See also *Indian Leaflets No. 9: 21 Per Cent. Growth of Indian Military Expenditure in 20 Years* (Calcutta: British Indian Association, 1885).

68. *The Indian National Congress* (Madras: G. A. Natesan, 1910), 2, 19, 24.

69. Dinshaw E. Wacha, "Indian Military Expenditure," in *Report of the Seventh Indian National Congress, Held at Nagpur* (1891), 24, 23, 26, 24–25.

70. *The Indian National Congress*, 39, 81, 87.

71. In the nineteenth century, the term referred to British residents of India, not to their mixed-race descendants, the latter being termed *Indo-Britons.*

72. James Long, "The Position of Turkey in Relation to British Interests in India," *Journal of the East India Association* 9 (December 1875): 185, 185, 182, 185, 184.

73. James Long, "The Eastern Question in Its Anglo-Indian Aspect," *Journal of the East India Association* 10 (May 1877): 234, 235, 234, 236, 234, 246. See also Cheragh Ali, *The Proposed Political, Legal, and Social Reforms of the Ottoman Empire and Other Mohammadan States* (Bombay: Education Society's Press, 1883).

74. Aziz Ahmad, "Sayyid Aḥmad Khān, Jamāl al-dīn al-Afghānī and Muslim India," *Studia Islamica*, no. 13 (1960): 67.

75. Wilfred Scawen Blunt, *India Under Ripon: A Private Diary* (London: T. Fisher Unwin, 1909), 105.

76. Sheikh Jamaluddin Afghani, "Les Anglais en Égypte," in "Notes Sur le Séjour de Djamal al-Din al-Afghani en France," ed. Homa Pakdaman, *Orient*, no. 35 (1965): 211. Translated here by Sravya Darbhamulla.

77. Sheikh Jamaluddin Afghani, "Lettre Sur l'Hindoustan," *L'Intransigeant*, April 24, 1883. Translated here by Sravya Darbhamulla.

78. Elie Kedourie, "Further Light on Afghani," *Middle Eastern Studies* 1, no. 2 (1965): 193.

68

INTRODUCTION

79. Blunt, *India Under Ripon*, 63; "Sir Salar Jung on the Eastern Question," *Voice of India* 5 (1887): 590.
80. Salar Jung, "Europe Revisited II," *Nineteenth Century* 22, no. 128 (1887): 502–3, 504.
81. Ghulam-us-Saqlain, "The Mussalmans of India and the Armenian Question," *Nineteenth Century* 37, no. 220 (1895): 929, 931, 935, 936–37, 935, 930. See also Rafiuddin Ahmad, "England in Relation to Mahomedan States," *National Review* 21, no. 122 (1893): 187; A. H. Keane, *Asia* (London: E. Stanford, 1882), 305.
82. Malcolm MacColl, "The Musulmans of India and the Sultan," *Contemporary Review* 71 (February 1897): 287, 288, 286–87, 287.
83. Shrabani Basu, *Victoria and Abdul: The True Story of the Queen's Closest Confidant* (New York: Vintage, 2011), 188–90; Jamil Sherif, Anas Altikriti, and Ismail Patel, "Muslim Electoral Participation in British General Elections," in *Muslims and Political Participation in Britain*, ed. Timothy Peace (Abingdon: Routledge, 2015), 32–33.
84. Julia Baird, *Victoria: The Queen: An Intimate Biography of the Woman Who Ruled an Empire* (New York: Random House, 2016), 456.
85. MacColl, "The Musulmans of India and the Sultan," 293.
86. Azmi Özcan, *Pan-Islamism: Indian Muslims, the Ottomans and Britain, 1877–1924* (Leiden: Brill, 1997), 102.
87. Syed Ahmed Khan, "The Caliphate," *Aligarh Institute Gazette*, September 11, 1897, 26–32.
88. Khan, 26–32.
89. Syed Ahmed Khan, "The Law of Jehad," *Pioneer*, September 28, 1897.
90. Syed Tanvir Wasti, "Sir Syed Ahmad Khan and the Turks," *Middle Eastern Studies* 46, no. 4 (2010): 535. See also M. N. Qureshi, *Pan-Islam in British Indian Politics* (Leiden: Brill, 1999), 33.
91. Rafiuddin Ahmad, "A Moslem's View of the Pan-Islamic Revival," *Nineteenth Century* 42, no. 248 (1897): 519–20, 520, 519, 522, 525, 526, 524, 525.
92. Ahmad, "Sayyid Aḥmad Khān, Jamāl al-dīn al-Afghānī and Muslim India," 73–76.
93. On this period, see Syed Tanvir Wasti, "The Political Aspirations of Indian Muslims and the Ottoman Nexus," *Middle Eastern Studies* 42, no. 5 (2006); Mushirul Hasan, "Pan-Islamism Versus Indian Nationalism: A Reappraisal," in *They Too Fought for Freedom: The Role of Minorities*, ed. Asghar Ali Engineer (New Delhi: Hope India, 2005).
94. Nicolas Blarel, *The Evolution of India's Israel Policy: Continuity, Change, and Compromise Since 1922* (New Delhi: Oxford University Press, 2015), chap. 1.
95. Romesh Chunder Dutt, *The Economic History of India Under Early British Rule* (London: Kegal Paul, Trench, Trübner, 1902), 293–95.
96. Philanthropy, "Letter to The Editor," *Bombay Gazette*, July 7, 1841, 22–23. An important study here is J. V. Naik, "Forerunners of Dadabhai Naoroji's Drain Theory," *Economic and Political Weekly* 36, nos. 46/47 (November 24, 2001), 4428–32.
97. Romesh Chunder Dutt, *India in the Victorian Age: An Economic History of the People* (London: Kegan Paul, Trench, Trübner, 1904), 401–2.
98. Dutt, 348; Peter Harnetty, *Imperialism and Free Trade: Lancashire and India in the Mid-Nineteenth Century* (Vancouver: University of British Columbia Press, 1972), 33.

99. Kissen Mohun Mullick, *Brief History of Bengal Commerce* (Calcutta: Hindoo Patriot Press, 1871–72).
100. [Bholanath Chandra], "A Voice for the Commerce and Manufactures of India (I)," *Mookerjee's Magazine* 2 (March 1873): 82, 90, 121.
101. [Bholanath Chandra], "A Voice for the Commerce and Manufactures of India (II)," *Mookerjee's Magazine* 2 (June 1873): 233–34.
102. [Bholanath Chandra], "A Voice for the Commerce and Manufactures of India (IV)," *Mookerjee's Magazine* 3 (August 1874): 368–69.
103. [Chandra], "A Voice for the Commerce and Manufactures of India (I)," 110, 98.
104. [Chandra], "A Voice for the Commerce and Manufactures of India (IV)," 378–79.
105. [Bholanath Chandra], "A Voice for the Commerce and Manufactures of India (III)," *Mookerjee's Magazine* 2 (December 1873): 621.
106. [Chandra], "A Voice for the Commerce and Manufactures of India (IV)," 373, 376.
107. [Chandra], "A Voice for the Commerce and Manufactures of India (I)," 110.
108. [Chandra], "A Voice for the Commerce and Manufactures of India (V)," 12–13.
109. Kissen Mohun Mullick, "The Commerce and Manufactures of India—Another View," *Mookerjee's Magazine* 2, no. 8 (May 1873): 202–11, 202–3.
110. [Chandra], "A Voice for the Commerce and Manufactures of India (V)," 7–9, 38, 41.
111. Mahadev Govind Ranade, "Indian Political Economy," *Quarterly Journal of the Poona Sarvajanik Sabha* 15, no. 2 (1892); Kashninath Trimbak Telang, "Free Trade and Protection from an Indian Point of View," in *Selected Writings and Speeches* (Bombay: K. R. Mitra, 1888).
112. Dutt, *India in the Victorian Age*, 538.
113. P. Ananda Charlu, *A Few Thoughts on the Poverty of India: A Paper Read at the Anniversary Meeting of the Chaitanya Library* (Calcutta: Juno Printing Works, 1897), 6–17.
114. P. C. Emmer, "The Meek Hindu: The Recruitment of Indian Labourers for Service Overseas, 1870–1916," in *Colonialism and Migration: Indentured Labour Before and After Slavery*, ed. P. C. Emmer (Dordrecht: Martinus Nijhoff, 1986), 187.
115. Mahadev Govind Ranade, "Indian Foreign Emigration," in *Essays on Indian Economics: A Collection of Essays and Speeches* (Madras: G. A. Natesan, 1906), 130–31, 133, 165–66, 166, 134.
116. *Report of the Eleventh Indian National Congress, Held at Poona* (Poona: Arya Bhushan Press, 1896), 104, 105, 106.
117. Mohandas K. Gandhi, "Grievances of Indian Settlers in South Africa," in *Speeches and Writings of M. K. Gandhi* (Madras: G. A. Natesan, 1922), 18, 5, 4, 11, 12, 14, 15–16, 22.
118. *Resolutions Passed at the Twelfth Indian National Congress Held at Calcutta* (Calcutta: Bharati Press, 1897), 2–3.
119. *Report of the Fourteenth Indian National Congress, Held at Madras* (Madras: G. A. Natesan, 1898), 88, 90, 91, 92, 94, 90.
120. Shoshee Chunder Dutt, "British Opium Policy and Its Results," in *India, Past and Present* (London: Chatto and Windus, 1880), 376–77; James B. Lyall, "Note on the History of Opium in India and of the Trade in It with China," in *Final Report of the Royal Commission on Opium*, vol. 7 (London: Her Majesty's Stationery Office, 1895), 7, 17.

121. Lyall, "Note on the History of Opium in India," 17; Joseph Edkins, "Historical Note on Opium and the Poppy in China," in *First Report of the Royal Commission on Opium*, vol. 1 (London: Eyre and Spottiswoode, 1894), 156.

122. Amar Farooqui, *Smuggling as Subversion: Colonialism, Indian Merchants, and the Politics of Opium, 1790–1843* (Lanham, MD: Lexington, 2005), 15–16, 29–30.

123. Lyall, "Note on the History of Opium in India," 6, 18; Dutt, "British Opium Policy and Its Results," 344; Farooqui, *Smuggling as Subversion*, 15; *Final Report of the Royal Commission on Opium*, vol. 6, pt. 1 (London: Her Majesty's Stationery Office, 1895), 48–53.

124. R. M. Dane, "Historical Memorandum," in *Final Report of the Royal Commission on Opium*, 7:34–45.

125. Dutt, "British Opium Policy and Its Results," 345; E. H. Walsh, "The Historical Aspects of the Opium Question," *Calcutta Review* 102, no. 204 (1896): 262.

126. Dutt, "British Opium Policy and Its Results," 347.

127. H. N. Lay, *Note on the Opium Question, and Brief Survey of Our Relations with China* (London: M. S. Rickerby, Walbrook, E. C., 1893), 5–9; Dutt, "British Opium Policy and Its Results," 352–53; Frederick Storrs Turner, "Opium and England's Duty," *Nineteenth Century* 11, no. 60 (1882): 248–49.

128. Frederick Storrs Turner, *British Opium Policy and Its Results to India and China* (London: Samson Low, Marston, Searle and Rivington, 1876), 308.

129. A Hindoo [Bhaskar Pandurang Tarkhadkar], "Letter No. V," *Bombay Gazette*, September 16, 1841, 262. On this, see J. V. Naik, "Contemporary Indian Nationalist Reaction to the Opium War," *Proceedings of the Indian History Congress* 60 (1999): 501–6.

130. Dutt, "British Opium Policy and Its Results," 386, 386–87, 384.

131. Dutt, 397.

132. Rabindranath Tagore, "The Death Traffic," *Sino-Indian Journal* 1, no. 1 (July 1947): 110, 114–15.

133. Srish Chandra Bosu, "Opium Question," in *Public Speeches of Babu Srish Chandra Bosu Sarvadhicari* (Calcutta: Nababibhkar Press, 1897), 14, 15, 16. See also Dadabhai Naoroji, "India and the Opium Question," in Parekh, *Essays, Speeches, Addresses and Writings of the Hon'ble Dadabhai Naoroji*, 364.

134. James Fitzjames Stephen, "The Opium Resolution," *Nineteenth Century* 29, no. 172 (1891): 852, 854.

135. William Wedderburn, "India and the Opium Question," in *Speeches by Sir William Wedderburn*, ed. Raj Jogeshur Mitter (Calcutta: S. C. Basu, 1899), 201, 203, 201. See also *Final Report of the Royal Commission on Opium*, 3:129, 151.

136. Alfred Webb, "Inaugural Address Tenth Indian National Congress 26th December 1894," in *Inaugural Addresses by Presidents of the Indian National Congress*, ed. Dinker Vishnu Gokhale (Bombay: Ripon, 1895), 224.

137. Gopal Krishna Gokhale, "Budget Speech, 1907," in *Speeches of Gopal Krishna Gokhale* (Madras: G. A. Natesan, 1906), 162–63.

138. Nagendra Nath Ghose, *Indian Views of England* (Calcutta: Thacker, Spink, 1877), 2, 3, 7, 13, 22, 25, 33–34, 38, 38, 39, 5, 40.

139. Bankim Chandra Chatterjee, "Bharat Kalanka," in *Bankim Rachnabali*, vol. 2, ed. Jogesh Chandra Bagal (Calcutta: Mahendra Nath, 1954). Translated here by Arunava Sinha.

140. Bankim Chandra Chatterjee, *Essentials of Dharma*, trans. Manomohan Ghosh (Calcutta: Sribhumi, 1977), 24, 159,147.

141. Pandita Ramabai [Ramabai Sarasvati], *Yunaited Stetsci Lokasthi ani Pravasavrtta* [The Condition of the Peoples of the United States] (Mumbai: Nirnaysagar, 1889), 13–41. Translated here by Sravya Darbhamulla.

142. Subedar Muhammad Beg, *My Jubilee Visit to London* (Bombay: Thacker, 1899), 52–56. Subedar was the rank equivalent to captain.

143. Ramananda Chatterjee, "Baman Das Basu," *Modern Review* 48, no. 6 (1930): 667–75.

144. Indo-Anglian [Baman Das Basu], "What Can England Teach Us," *Modern Review* 3, no. 2 (1908): 158–60.

145. Aurobindo Ghosh, *Bande Mataram: Political Writings and Speeches, 1890–1908*, in *The Complete Works of Sri Aurobindo* (Pondicherry: Sri Aurobindo Ashram, 2002), 127.

146. Raj Narain Bose, "Superiority of Hinduism to Other Existing Religions: As Viewed from the Stand-Point of Theism (IV)," *Theosophist* 4, no. 1 (1882): 13, 14.

147. Raj Narain Bose, "Superiority of Hinduism to Other Existing Religions: As Viewed from the Stand-Point of Theism (V)," *Theosophist* 4, no. 2 (1882): 35.

148. Keshub Chunder Sen, "Asia's Message to Europe," in *Keshub Chunder Sen's Lectures in India* (London: Cassell, 1904), 51, 62, 63, 77, 78–79, 117, 80.

149. Friedrich Max Müller, *India: What Can It Teach Us?* (London: Longmans, Green, 1883), 14, 6.

150. Annie Besant, "India, Her Past and Her Future," in *The Birth of New India* (Madras: Theosophical, 1917), 40, 44, 59, 60.

151. Swami Vivekananda, "Reply to the Address of Welcome at Madras," *From Colombo to Almora* (Madras: Vyjayanti, 1897), 121–22.

152. Swami Vivekananda, "First Public Lecture in the East," in *From Colombo to Almora*, 18.

153. Vivekananda, "Reply to the Address of Welcome at Madras," 121.

154. Swami Vivekananda, "The Work Before Us," in *From Colombo to Almora*, 190.

155. Swami Vivekananda, "India's Message to the World," in *Complete Works of Swami Vivekananda*, vol. 4 (Calcutta: Advaita Ashrama, 1955), 315.

156. Vivekananda, "The Work Before Us," 194.

157. Swami Vivekananda, "Ceylon," in *From Colombo to Almora*, 11.

158. Swami Abhedananda, "International Ethics," *Prabuddha Bharata* 4, no. 30 (1899): 10.

159. John Milton, *Paradise Regained* (Chiswick: C. Whittingham, 1823), 47.

160. For instance, see Rahul Sagar, "Before Midnight: Views on International Relations, 1857–1947," in *Oxford Handbook on Indian Foreign Policy*, ed. David Malone, C. Raja Mohan, and Srinath Raghavan (Oxford: Oxford University Press, 2015); Rahul Sagar, "Leading Ideas," in *Grasping Greatness: Making India a Leading Power*, ed. Ashley J. Tellis, C. Raja Mohan, and Bibek Debroy (New York: Columbia University Press, 2022).

161. For instance, see Rahul Sagar and Ankit Panda, "Pledges and Pious Wishes: The Constituent Assembly Debates and the Myth of a 'Nehruvian Consensus,'" *India Review* 14, no. 2 (2015); Rohan Mukherjee and Rahul Sagar, "Pragmatism in Indian

Strategic Thought," *India Review* 17, no. 1 (2018); Rahul Sagar, "The Hindu Nationalist View of International Politics," in *India's Grand Strategy: History, Theory, Cases*, ed. Kanti Bajpai (New Delhi: Routledge, 2014).

162. Rahul Sagar, "Hindu Nationalism and the Cold War," in *India and the Cold War*, ed. Manu Bhagavan (Chapel Hill: University of North Carolina Press, 2019).

PART I

Regaining Greatness

Chapter One

ENGLISH EDUCATION

KNOWLEDGE IS POWER, 1832
Bal Gangadhar Shastri Jambhekar

"Knowledge," says Lord Bacon, "is power." The truth of this maxim, which is so particularly apparent in these times, has not equally influenced the conduct of different nations, nor produced in an equal degree, a taste for learning among them. It is undeniable that the first light of knowledge dawned from East on the West; and it is proved on authority equally unquestionable, that the natives of Asia possessed the first rudiments of it thousands of years ago. It therefore excites our surprise to observe the difference between the perfection to which the arts and sciences have attained in Europe, and the very little improvement which has been effected in them in Asia during such a long period.

Whatever may be the cause of this disproportionate intellectual advancement in these two quarters of the world, we feel assured, that one of them is that the advantages of knowledge have not been appreciated in this country in their proper light. In illustration of this view, we need only remark, that had the Asiatic philosophers bestowed the same attention on useful arts and sciences, as they have done on more abstruse and subtle branches of knowledge, such as metaphysics and logic, much more good might have been expected from their labours. But it appears, that they regarded all knowledge as useful only in religion, or as a means of gaining victory in argument, and in no way connected with the common purposes of life. Hence the very little progress of the Hindoos and Mohammedans in mechanics, geography, history, etc.

But everyone must admit, that change of time and circumstances occasions a necessity for relinquishing the established modes and adopting new ones. The circumstances and order of things have, within the last twenty years, undergone a material change in this country—a change which has swept off many of the ancient institutions, and which makes it daily more and more imperative upon the natives of it, to bestow their attention on the useful arts and sciences; their practical application to the common purposes of life; and in short, to gain every acquisition, which has rendered European nations superior to Asiatics, and from the want of which their country has so much suffered. The ancient learning of the country, whatever may have been the advantages of it in former days, must gradually lose its value in connection with the necessities and wants of human life. Lord Brougham observes, that, "the practical uses of any science or branch of knowledge, are undoubtedly of the highest importance; and there is hardly any man, who may not gain some positive advantage in his worldly wealth and comforts by increasing his stock of information."[1]

It is this kind of knowledge, which some of the charitable Institutions in this city, have it in view to impart to the natives in general. . . . While on this point, we cannot withhold a place from the following very sensible remarks in *The Reformer* of Calcutta on this subject:

The time is now arrived, when every nation must either rise in the scale of civilization or sink in the depths of contempt and misery. Prosperity in this age appears to be a term synonymous with civilization and the cultivation of the arts and sciences. Indeed, in every age they have been so more or less, but in the present their dependence on one another is too palpable to be overlooked by the most superficial observers. Let us only consider the preeminence to which England has arrived by the diffusion of knowledge among her inhabitants. Her astonishing machineries which have multiplied her means of acquiring wealth to an inconceivable degree, owe their origin to the cultivation of the arts and sciences. Is it not owing to the power which knowledge has given to the people of so small and so distant a country as England, that they have been enabled to conquer and keep possession of these vast territories far more congenial to the prosperity of the human race than the sterile soil of England? Why is it thought the most extravagant dream to suppose that India should ever conquer England? Is it not because the latter enjoys the blessings of knowledge in a far greater degree than the former? Is it not to the power of knowledge that we must trace back the vast superiority of England over this country, ay, not only over this, but over a great many others? And yet our opulent friends are for the most part so short-sighted and of such narrow views that they prefer a thousand foolish enjoyments of the senses to the lasting benefits of knowledge; they prefer to waste their estates and accumulated wealth on the most foolish diversions rather than spend a rupee in the cause of education. All general remarks have exceptions and we are ready to admit that there are many among the Natives who contribute towards these laudable objects as far as their circumstances will permit. We complain not of these few, but of the mass of our country-men whose eyes yet appear to be shut against the benefits of education.[2]

AN ESSAY ON NATIVE EDUCATION, 1846
T. Madhava Rao

When we look into the records of human affairs, when we explore the repositories of experience, and dive into the profundities of past centuries, what an interminable series of unforeseen vicissitudes passes before our view! Those mighty empires which were once objects of admiration; those proud sanctuaries of the arts and sciences, which were models for imitation; those renowned seats of wealth and civilization, from which alone the tide of improvement flowed to fertilize barbarian soils; all these have now sunk into the obscurities of insignificance, either by retracing their steps, or by remaining in the same invariable condition, throughout the wild waste of centuries. It is to be confessed that unfortunate India now ranks among such nations of antiquity. Guarded on two sides by the sea, and defended by an impregnable chain of mountains on the third, possessed by a genial climate and commanding all the varied and abundant productions of a pro-lific soil, our original ancestors were secure from foreign invasion, and had ample leisure for the prosecution of knowledge of various descriptions. Accordingly, we can now indulge in the proud boast, that our ancient pro-genitors were the earliest cultivators of knowledge; we can flatter ourselves that ours is the hallowed land, in which, arts, sciences, and literature first sprung up. But although knowledge was prosecuted in the early ages with ardour and perseverance—although India moved on for a time with accelerating celerity in the path of civilization, yet not long after, a complete stagnancy, or rather a kind of retrogradation took place, which has brought our country so low in the scale of nations. . . .

Indisputable experience shows that no nation can make any advancement whatever, while war rages around, and devastations exterminate the blessings of peace. . . . But fortunately for our countrymen, India has been rescued, perhaps by an immediate interposition of Providence, from the galling yoke of unrelenting tyranny, under which she groaned for several centuries. A milder form of government has succeeded, and peace, justice and freedom have taken the place of anarchy, tyranny, and bondage. Even now the influence which past miseries exercised on the Hindoos, has not ceased to act. . . . A mistaken and almost preposterous notion of the infallibility of ancestral wisdom, precludes every generous attempt to exercise the powers of the intellect, or to extend the limits of human knowledge. A grievous destitution of general intelligence, a lamentable ignorance of their own position in the scale of nations, and a disgraceful deficiency of all independent feelings, have continued to render the condition of the Hindoos as deplorable as is possible. . . .

Here then a great question of immense importance is offered to our serious consideration; a question that affects the destiny of whole millions and involves the dearest interests of the native community—one which is well worth the consideration of the stranger as well as the native, the philanthropist as well as the patriot. This is, what will raise India from her prostate condition? It may be briefly answered that it is a general dissemination of knowledge and education alone throughout all classes, that will bring about a complete regeneration of the Hindoo community. . . .

Now, the great question which presents itself to our view, is respecting the nature of the education that is to be communicated to the Hindoo, and the manner in which it is to be imparted. This subject has been often discussed with great vehemence but decided with little certainty. Differing opinions have been entertained, and various persons have proposed various systems of education. However, all have agreed in the judgement, that directing the minds of our youth to the study of our own literature is of little use, and that the time and labour spent in the pursuit are little better than an unprofitable waste. This conclusion is justified by many considerations, some of the most important of which I shall here briefly mention.

First of all, the greatest portion of what may be called our literature and science is to be found couched in the Sanskrit tongue, and previous to any attempt to study them, a thorough knowledge of this language is indispensably requisite. The acquisition of this necessary instrument to tear the almost impervious veil, under which Sanskrit lore lies hidden, is a barrier which has discouraged all, and has been overcome by a few. . . . After all, even supposing that these difficulties have been conquered, what shall we gain? Our science consists of a set of innumerable and complicated rules, without demonstration; and the student has to encumber his memory with difficult formula, without any thing to guide the intellect in recollecting them. . . . Our metaphysics consist of subtle distinctions, useless niceties and contradicting doctrines. Our theology is all that deserves notice and praise.

A depreciation of our literature is not at all intended here. On the contrary it is to be highly valued and is to be regarded as a work of wonder, when we take into consideration, the early time of its formation. All that is meant is, that it is inferior compared with the improved literature of Europe. These various considerations, with the fact that Sanskrit is an old and obsolete language compel us to prefer some modern tongue for the education of Hindoo youths. Those that are masters of large fortunes, and have leisure at their command; those that find no necessity for entering the world in early life, may very advantageously devote their time in studying some modern European language, which is the key to the repositories of the literature and science of the western world. By so doing they can easily acquire a thorough knowledge of that acuteness and ingenuity, that refinement and civilization and those discoveries and inventions, which have made Europe the first continent in wealth and prosperity. Thus, they may avail themselves of the combined exertions and aggregate experience of ages and make use of them to raise our country to a level with its present sovereign. But of all the European tongues, the English recommends itself peculiarly to our consideration, from the fact that it is the language of our rulers and the language of the first nation on the face of the earth.

With regard to the nature of the English education that is to be imparted to a native, we have to remark that it is not to be of quite a different character to that which is fitted for a European youth. . . . It is not necessary that the Hindoo should be carried through the complicated mazes of classic lore; it is not requisite that he should study all the poets of the English language; but what is of far greater importance to himself and to his countrymen, is that he should direct his attention towards the sciences and arts of the Western continent. He should be taught to imitate the habits and manners, customs and opinions of nations more civilized than his own. The prejudices peculiar to his religion and country must be gradually undermined; the spell of superstitious veneration for ancient institutions must be broken—liberal and far sighted views must be implanted in him; independent feelings instilled in his mind; and he must be made to feel the supreme importance of a strict adherence to the rules of morality which should not be violated as well amidst the storms of adversity as in the sunshine of prosperity. Such in a few words, must be the nature of education of the higher classes of the Hindoos—an education that will, in time, bring about a complete moral and political regeneration of the Indian continent. . . .

Education does not consist, as a native generally supposes, in the mere acquisition of the capacity to read and write. It may be defined, in its most comprehensive sense, to be a judicious training of the intellectual faculties—a proper development of those powers which lie latent in man, so as to preserve the mind in a most wholesome condition, and to enable the person to conduct himself according to the rules of virtue and wisdom, in order that he may benefit himself and advantage his own species. Such being the important end of what is called a liberal education, it is distinctly seen that those schools, which are set up in different parts of India, by natives, for the instruction of youths in the vernacular languages, are of very little use. . . . To remove this defect, all kinds of translations from the English into the vernacular languages should be encouraged; so that in time all European knowledge may be rendered accessible to those, who are conversant only with the native languages. . . . While thus the progress of the English language and the improvement of the vernaculars are encouraged, the Sanskrit tongue is not to be allowed to perish in silence; but some encouragement must be given to it also, and a knowledge of it preserved in order that the vernaculars may receive improvements by the adoption of words and phrases from a language, whose nature enables us to form compounds, without any difficulty. English Seminaries must be established in the different Provinces for the education of the higher classes of the natives; vernacular schools must be instituted in different districts to instruct the lower orders. These are to be liberally endowed with funds; high inducements ought to be held out, and strenuous exertions made, to instill in the native, an inextinguishable thirst for knowledge and to kindle in his breast a flame of emulation to surpass European youths in every respect. When once these advantages will be attained, the Hindoos will not rest satisfied with a mere perusal of the English works of science and literature; they will not rest contented with treading a beaten path; but now and then some towering genius may rise, and exploring some unknown track, make discoveries which may not fall short of those of Watt, or Newton, or any other illustrious ornament that English annals can boast of. . . .

To contribute to a general diffusion of knowledge, to burst the clouds of superstition and prejudice, and to enlighten the dark dens of ignorance, and, in short, to bring about a complete emancipation of the native mind, must be the sole object of one and all. . . . Indeed, in such an attempt to effect a deliverance of the Hindoo mind, no exertions can be unprofitable, and no energies ill-directed. On the contrary, the highest object of glory, at which human ambition can aim, is to enlighten the minds of our countrymen, and to raise a fallen people high in the scale of nations. It is impossible for us to conceive what wondrous, but silent revolutions would be effected by the diffusion of a knowledge of the western sciences in India. . . . As general intelligence spreads equally among all classes, those unlimited resources, which bountiful nature has bestowed upon our country, with a lavish hand, will be fully developed. New channels will be opened for the employment of Indian capital; the wealth-teeming plough will be carried over the desolate bosom of uncultivated forests; extensive manufactures will be established throughout the country; and those varied productions of our soil, which are now carried to remote corners of the globe to be converted into articles of utility, will afford an unlimited supply of materials to the Indian manufacturer. The wants and enjoyments of our countrymen will be indefinitely augmented; and they will freely wield at their command the varied pleasures of a civilized life. No longer will the impervious clouds of ignorance shut out the genial rays of knowledge; no more will superstition and prejudice barricade the path of civilization; on the contrary, science and literature will begin to flourish again in their natal seat; foreign arts and foreign improvements will be introduced, and European wonders will be seen to rise on an Asiatic soil. Future generations will witness the gigantic locomotive engine rumbling along with miraculous celerity over the vast plains of the Indian continent; the steamer will be seen plying in the copious streams which irrigate our country; that labour which is now thrown away from an ignorance of the principles of science, will be far more profitably employed; enterprising works will be undertaken, and the people will show that they have spirit to conceive, and perseverance to execute, whatever is requisite for the benefit of their country.

As knowledge spreads itself among the Hindoos, they will gradually rise to eminence, and soon will the astonished nations of Europe behold a rival gloriously rising in the east, capable of coping with them for superiority. No longer will England with all the perfections of age, and America with all the exuberance of youth, boast of matchless pre-eminence. A whole body of a hundred and forty million will be cemented into one community by the influence of similar habits and the same government; intestine discord, such as raged a few centuries ago, will be exterminated. The whole nation will be formed into an irresistible phalanx, which scarce any power on earth can dissolve. The government will entirely be guided in its conduct by the sense of the people, who will weigh every one of its measures. Every act will have to pass the ordeal of public discussion; and, as is the case in England at present, every artificer, and every mechanic in India, will be seen examining and analyzing the schemes of politics, pursued by the statesmen at the head of the administration. Some sceptic folly may deem these results the idle reveries of a deranged imagination. The only sure specific to produce a different conviction, is to consult the pages of history and observe what revolutions took place to change the condition of ancient countries, in the same circumstances as in India.

Here then we may conclude with a repetition of the important observation, that a general spread of education alone will rouse India from that indolence which has lulled her for ages, in a kind of lethargic slumber, and will launch her in the progressive stream of improvement to compete for superiority with those nations which are fast advancing their course; that a diffusion of western knowledge alone will dispel the dark shades of ignorance that have fallen upon our country, and will raise her to that meridian splendor of intellectual eminence and national prosperity, which the most civilized nation on the earth is capable of attaining.

HIGH EDUCATION IN INDIA, 1878
Chandranath Basu

In the long course of human history, great empires have risen, flourished and disappeared. . . . England's empire in India is one of the greatest facts in history—a fact, at once serious, wonderful, and unique. But will posterity, will future ages remember this fact? I, for one, think it quite certain that it will be remembered. But I am equally certain that it will not be remembered for the sake of the many material symbols of power, intelligence, and enterprise which meet the eye in all parts of this magnificent empire. The Hugli bridge or the Sutlej bridge—however great and marvelous as works of engineering skill—will not perpetuate the memory of this empire. A cyclone or a storm-wave may tear or sweep away both in a moment. The great railroads which intersect the country in all directions will not perpetuate the memory of this empire. A month's disuse will cover them with jungle and hide them from mortal eyes. . . .

I say, therefore, that England's claim to the grateful remembrance of distant ages will rest, and rest exclusively, on the performance of the grand work of intellectual renovation and regeneration in which she is engaged in India. Our roads, railways, bridges, and canals are doing much good; but they will do no good when the power which has constructed and the power which is working or maintaining them will be withdrawn. They are all conditional blessings. But regenerated India, capable of supplying her material wants out of her own resources, will be unto herself an unconditional blessing, and a permanent guarantee of progress and material welfare. India thinking for herself, India acting for herself, India working for herself—this, I say, will be the one historic memento of England's empire in Asia; and this, I also say, must be preceded by India revolutionized in thought and temper.

The most important revolution can only be effected by a sound liberal education. . . . I know that this high English education has produced a schism in Hindu society, a schism in the Hindu family, a schism in the Hindu heart. I know that high English education has seriously disturbed the economic organisation of the country and added infinite material misery to infinite mental misery. I know this high English education has destroyed the Hindu's root ideas of social and political life, converted order into anarchy, and replaced impassive equanimity with universal and unseemly restlessness. I know all this and very much more; and yet I think that high English education is a thing not to be hated or condemned.

I would ask all those, who feel surprised and startled to find so much misery and disorder flowing from high education in this country, to consider the character and magnitude of the revolution through which Hindu society is now passing. It seems to me that this revolution is far more radical in its character and far more comprehensive in its purpose than even the greatest political revolution seen in history. It has always seemed to me that the French Revolution itself was not produced by causes more numerous or more organic than those to which we owe this vast social revolution in India. The French Revolution was the result of political and clerical despotism; and its chief causes were political injustice and religious absolutism. The force, which impelled the Revolutionist to deeds of unparalleled violence and atrocity, was a force which had no deeper spring than the sense of political misery and clerical imposture. But the case is far different and much more serious here in India. Our English education tells us that we live under tyrannies more numerous and more radically mischievous than those which produced the great political revolution of 1789. It tells us that, here in India, we have a social tyranny, a domestic tyranny, a tyranny of caste, a tyranny of custom, a religious tyranny, a clerical tyranny, a tyranny of thought over thought, a tyranny of sentiment over sentiment. And it not only tells of all these tyrannies but makes us feel them with terrific intensity. Judge then whether the educated Hindu has not greater reason to be a revolutionist than the Frenchman of the eighteenth century who had only two small tyrannies to remove. Judge then whether the educated Hindu, who looks so restless and impatient and indiscreet in language, thought, and action, is not a model of forbearance compared with the revolutionist whose hatred of two tyrannies sent hundreds and thousands to the guillotine. Judge this, I say, and wonder that the educated Hindu is not more indiscreet, impatient and uneasy than you actually find him. He has, forsooth, lost all faith in the very constitution of his home and his society—in the relation of class to class, of family to family, of individual to individual, of father to son, of husband to wife; and yet you find in him so little discontent, so little indiscretion, so little impatience! . . .

India in the past was profoundly metaphysical and spiritual, and therefore essentially subjective and introspective. She studied the mind in many of its aspects and remained one grand piece of philosophical thought from beginning to end. She cared not for the world and the things of the world; and so she rose not above the condition of a simple tiller of the soil. No one then claimed of her a share of her earthly possessions and she found that she was sufficient unto herself. And so she went on thinking and feeling until she forgot everything but thought and feeling. And then when the Mussalman came, she felt and regretted that she had dreamed away the longest epoch in human history. But what had once been possible and possible for so long a time, will not be possible now and hereafter. For India is not now what she had been when there was nothing in the world but India. . . .

In plain prose, England has introduced India into the great comity of nations, has drawn India into the scheme of material life, of which she herself is perhaps the most perfect representative. India is now, in fact, a country of Europe, not of Asia, without that intellectual culture, however, which has made Europe what it is. To be able to maintain this new position, to be able to fulfil this new destiny, India must receive that high scientific education which has resulted in modern Europe. Speculative thought, of which she is perhaps the grandest earthly expression, availed her not in the past, and will be simply incompatible with the necessities of her new material solution. For hard bodily work and deep mental abstraction exclude each other. Nor is this all. If India has an intellect—and we have seen that she has one of a very elevated type—and if the cultivation of the intellect be an important condition of national life, the Hindu intellect must be supplied with food and nourishment. But is this food and nourishment, or at least the best portion of it, to come from within as in ancient India or from without as in modern Europe?

I think the question admits of but one solution. In the first place, history reveals the important fact that, at least for a considerable period after the formation of a society or community of men, the function of their intellect is chiefly determined by their material condition. This fact has, it seems to me, a grave meaning for Hindus of the present day. Being so utterly unlike their ancestors of the Mussalman period in regard to their material situation, these Hindus may be viewed in the light of a newly formed people. And as a newly formed people, they must accept the law of intellectual culture which no newly formed people has been able to ignore or override. But we have already seen that, in her new material situation, India must accept science as a duty and a necessity.

In the second place, India's new position among the nations of the earth is a clear index to the intellectual work she must now perform. For all essential purposes India and the rest of the world had been, till a very recent period, complete strangers to each other. For all essential purposes India had been able to ignore the rest of the world. Other nations, no doubt, came to her; but she seldom went to other nations. The case is very different now. England has introduced India to the nations of Europe—has made her, in fact, a member of great family of nations. Now, in order to be one of many, one must know the many in thought and feeling. People who do not know each other cannot live together. And if India is to live as one of many nations—if she is not to disappear from the sight of other nations—if she is not to remain forever a crystallized relic of a remote antiquity, she must know what other nations are. Europe, to whom she has been introduced, is reading her closely and trying to cultivate her acquaintance. And it is absolutely necessary that she, to whom Europe has been introduced, should study Europe and make her acquaintance. If she fails to do this, she will be faithless and untrue to her new national or rather international position— faithless and untrue to herself and her dearest interests. She cannot neglect Europe without losing her new international position. And if she loses her new international position, she will be absolutely without a position in the world. For it is not difficult to understand that her new material situation, over which, as the necessary result of her new political situation, she has no control whatever, will absolutely prevent her from reverting to that isolated and inactive position which she was able to occupy in ancient times. She must, therefore, study Europe.

But Europe is essentially scientific. Science, strictly so called, engages a large part of her attention, and what is not strictly science is studied by her on the strictly scientific method. Her history, her psychology, her jurisprudence, her political economy, her political philosophy have all accepted the scientific method of inquiry, and she has given a conclusive proof that she and science are synonymous terms by subjecting religion itself to a severe scientific analysis. Indeed, it is impossible to know Europe without knowing science and the principles of scientific thought. . . . I think, therefore, the study of science ought to occupy the largest and most important place in Indian intellectual education. For it is only by the study of science that the Hindu can be expected to overcome that subjective bias of his mind which has cost him so dear and deprived him of a distinguished place among the nations of the earth. And what is much more important than this, it is only for the study of science that the Hindu can be expected to enter into the thought, as he has already entered into the industrial economy, of the modern man. For this thought and this economy are necessary correlatives and cannot be divorced from each other. . . .

If we would live a material life, we must love matter and acquire confidence in its powers. So long as we do not obey this law, so long our efforts to be practical must be fruitless, or, at the best, will produce very inadequate results. So long as the character of the national intellect is not changed, so long as the intellectual atmosphere of the country does not become an atmosphere of practical thought, so long as the national mind does not realise the meaning and the spirit of the material world as intensely as our ancestors realized the meaning and the spirit of the spiritual mind—so long, it seems to me, the nation will be both morally and intellectually incapable of adopting an industrial scheme of life. Until this necessary consummation, industry, if introduced at all, may be accepted by some few born workmen among us; but it will not be accepted by the nation. The nation, to be able to do this, must have a new intellectual faith and a new intellectual temper. I need hardly say that science alone will give us that faith and that temper. . . .

SOME CHARACTERISTICS OF INDIAN
ENGLISH-EDUCATED YOUTHS, 1886
Bishan Narayan Dar

That the fate of every society depends upon its rising generation, is a commonly accepted truth, and deserves the special attention of those of us who are watching closely and with interest the progress of events in India. Those who approve of the changes that are taking place in India, and those who do not: those who think that European influence is destined to become the regenerating force of our society, and those who think that it is a hindrance to our real progress, are alike agreed on this point—that whatever of good or evil happens to India in future, will be due, in a large measure, to the actions of those young men who have been and are being brought up in English schools and colleges. . . .

It is an historical fact, that in countries where political feelings are not very strong, new reforms are generally introduced and condemned (as the case may be) in the name of religion. The reformer says that he wants to make certain changes, in accordance with some higher truths hidden beneath the absurdities of his religion. His opponents persecute him, on the ground that the reforms he proposes are contrary to the tenets of that religion. . . . Young men too, on account of their new ideas and practices, are called infidels by our people. Can we say that the charge of infidelity brought against them is totally unfounded? I do not think we can. If I understand rightly the sentiments of the young generation, the cardinal difference which exists between it and the elder generation is this: that while religion is the enthusiasm of the latter, social liberty is the enthusiasm of the former. . . .

Young men, it is said, are irreligious, and have no respect for the past; their atheism is the fruit of English education and the root of social evils and immoralities. I think those who advance this charge are unjust alike to the rising generation and to English education. . . . Mark the strange irony of fate—that English literature and English civilisation, which have revived a new interest in our literature and religion, and unearthed for us tangible relics of a civilisation the very idea of which had passed into the region of myths and fables, are accused of having made us atheists and disrespectful to the past! . . .

But in all that is said against the religious tendencies of young men, there is this truth: that the disintegration of religious beliefs and the rise of a new political spirit—both the products of English influence—have turned (as far as they have at all succeeded) the current of popular enthusiasm from religion to purely social movements. The two things which have always excited the enthusiasm of mankind are religion and patriotism; and no nation has been able to achieve any great thing which was not pervaded by intense religious or patriotic feelings. In India, religious enthusiasm has nearly vanished away, and a purely patriotic zeal has not yet taken its place. And herein lies the interest, perhaps the danger, of the present crisis. In all social changes, it is good to recognise the truth, that ideas change sooner and more easily than feelings. The fear of ghosts remains long after men have ceased to believe in their existence. Now, applying this truth to the present revolution in India, we find that while English education has given a new turn to our habits of thought, and changed our ideas upon almost all subjects regarding man and nature, it has not been equally successful in changing our feelings. It has destroyed our belief in old customs and traditions; it has done everything to weaken the theological, and strengthen the secular, spirit of our society; it has taught us to believe in the indefinite progress of humanity and to subordinate individual to national interests: and these teachings, through the medium of popular education, are passing, by a gradual process of infiltration, down to the lowest strata of our society. And what is the consequence of this change? Religious ideas have changed, religious enthusiasm has cooled down; but no patriotic spirit has yet diffused itself through the society. We all *know* that it is good to be patriotic; but we do not *feel* the warmth of patriotism. Thus, the very first essential of social progress—enthusiasm of some kind—is wanting in us at the present moment.

. . . By these remarks I do not mean that English civilisation is altogether responsible for the disappearance of every kind of enthusiasm among the people. What it did was to change certain of our religious conceptions, and to offer us new and secular ideals; and, if we had possessed any national feelings, the enthusiasm lost in religion would probably have been gained in social progress. But as we do not possess any consciousness of nationality, our enthusiasm, having lost hold of our religious feelings, and being unable to find in us any other congenial and generally diffused feeling around which to entwine itself, has nearly died away. That it is destined to revive again, I do not entertain any doubt. . . . Our feelings will take a long time to change; but they will change, if everything goes on well. And the more our feelings begin to harmonize with our ideas—even those ideas which we possess at present—the stronger and intenser will grow in us that national and patriotic sentiment which is the chief guarantee of social progress.

In social matters, a great change is passing over our public opinion, under the silent pressure of Western civilisation. It is a noteworthy fact, that though our customs and superstitions held their own against Mohammedan influence for more than six hundred years, yet under the mild light of British rule, which is only about a hundred years old, they are gradually vanishing away. . . . I think the chief cause why our customs, ideas and habits are changing so much more rapidly now than they did during the Mohammedan rule, lies in the spread of Physical Science, the rudiments of which we are now taught from our very infancy. . . . The study of elementary physical geography has revolutionized the Indian mind more deeply than the study of all Persian authors put together.

Our old men, who yet feel the touch of the vanished hand of Mohammedan kings, cannot understand the elasticity of the younger generation. They seldom felt the pressure of Mohammedan civilisation upon their habits and beliefs, and, consequently, cannot realise the position of young men whose minds are exposed to different and more powerful influences. And this, I think, is the secret of the charge of unsteadiness, recklessness, and want of respect towards their elders, so often hurled against them. It is said that these young men are very fickle, because they change their opinions from day to day; that they are very reckless and revolutionary, because they have no regard for their society, and are blown hither and thither by the impulse of the moment, like flies by every wind that blows; that they have no respect for the beliefs and customs of their elders, because, blind-folded by the false glamour of English education, they do not see the good which is embalmed in the sacred heirloom of the past.

While admitting a certain amount of truth in these accusations, I must protest that they owe their origin to the complete misunderstanding of some very important circumstances. We must bear in mind that the old and the young live, as it were, in two different strata of civilisation. Our indigenous civilisation is separated from modern civilisation by a gulf of centuries. When people talk of this disparity, as if it were an evil for which young men were responsible, do they ever consider what the disparity means? Is not the sudden and unexpected meeting of the Indian and the European civi-lizations a sufficient cause to account for this change? Where else in the history of the world can we find two streams of such conflicting ideas min-gling together? . . . Thus, if a fault it is to reflect in their manners and convictions the sort of education they receive and the civilization under whose influence their minds are nurtured, it is a fault, not of young men, but of that inexorable destiny which has placed us under the British rule.

What I consider to be some of the chief characteristics of Indian youths, are not fickleness, recklessness, and a disregard of the feelings of their elders, but love of liberty and a disregard of authority, a restless desire for change, and belief in the indefinite progress of humanity. All these characteristics I look upon as the product of English education. Where education is not, these characteristics are not; and the more the former is spreading, the more the latter are getting common. Perhaps this may make some people think that I am looking only at that side of the picture which tells of sweet-ness and light, but not at the other side, which has some very objectionable bias upon it. The following pages will, I hope, dispel this impression. Though I hold certain good things to be the characteristics of Indian youths, yet I must say at the outset that those characteristics are yet *in making*; that though it is the tendency of English education to form them, yet it sometimes inflicts a great deal of harm before it can achieve its object.

One of the chief ideas which have been transported into India from Europe, and revolutionized the whole current of Indian thought, is the idea of Progress, in the modern sense of the word. I think, if there is one thing more than another which distinguishes the young from the old generation in our country, it is its belief in the indefinite progress of humanity. . . . I think if Europe had given us only this one idea of Progress, it would have been quite enough to transform the whole future history of India. The idea that we can be better than what we are, that in the march of civilisation we also can distinguish ourselves by trying to keep pace with the fastest runners, is a noble and elevating idea; and a product of English education as it is, it is sure to expand with its expansion, and become one of the most powerful levers of our mental, moral, and social advancement.

But we must bear in mind, that immense as is the good it has done, and is likely to do, to our young men in future, it leads them sometimes to a very grave error, against which they should always guard themselves. Many an Indian youth throws himself into the position of an Englishman and begins to think of the past and the future of *his* country as an Englishman would do of his. This, I consider, is a grave error. An Englishman thinks of his ancestors as barbarians, rude, illiterate, and the like. He looks upon all that he sees around him—printing-press, railways, telegraph, gas, and electricity—as things of yesterday, the achievements of a civilisation far superior to that under which his ancestors lived. In every respect he is far superior to his forefathers and has no particular reason to be proud of being a descendant of one of the followers of Hengist and Horsa, or William the Conqueror. In fact, he considers the progress of European society to be hampered to a great extent by the customs and traditions of feudalism surviving up to this day. But can an Indian contemplate the course of Indian history with the same feeling? No. That there once existed a mighty civilisation in India, nobody can deny; and though in a great many respects it is not suited to the present age, yet it developed to their full extent certain qualities and faculties of the human mind, without which there can be no *completeness* in our progress, and which it will be ill for us to lose. . . . By this remark I do not want to encourage the mischievous faith in the infallibility of Aryan wisdom; but what I contend is this, that in our thirst for progress, we must not forget that no real progress in India can at present take place without giving a due place to the teachings of our great religious teachers, moralists, and lawgivers, in our systems of thought.

A strong and restless yearning for change, which is allied to the idea of the gradual amelioration of the human race, is another most marked characteristic of Indian youths. In this nineteenth century, when change is the law of progress, when to cease changing is to cease improving, Indian society shows a strong aversion to change. Perhaps this attitude might not have been very injurious when the whole current of affairs was in its favour. Two hundred years ago, perhaps, it did not matter much whether we changed in certain respects or not. The spirit of conservatism reigned everywhere: political institutions resting upon the divine right of kings, religious institutions resting upon the divine right of priests, were safe from the ravages of change. But now change is a necessity. It augurs ill for us, that while everything is moving around us we are standing still. Those who have received English education are beginning to feel this necessity; and a new adventurous spirit is growing up among them, which jars with the spirit of their society. Some are afraid of this tendency, but I am not. I do not think it has grown too strong, and requires to be checked. I think the danger is the other way. . . . They have to deal with a perverse and stiff-necked generation, which is the chief support of the empire of routine; owing to their connection with Europe, they have to keep pace with affairs in Europe; they have to do what it has fallen to the lot of few people to do—they have, without any previous preparation, to compete with one of the most active and most enlightened nations of the world, in every department of human activity; and that they may be able to perform this arduous task successfully, it is necessary that their thirst for change and their capacity of assimilating to themselves the various tendencies of the age be further encouraged and intensified. . . .

Love of liberty, and a disregard of authority is another noteworthy feature of Indian youths, which it will be worthwhile to dwell upon at some length. The old generation of Indians is pervaded by an instinctive regard for the established order. It hates innovation, and its constant endeavor is to be guided by custom and tradition. The spirit of doubt and inquiry, the desire to test old beliefs by the rules of modern science, individuality of character, liberty of thought and action, are the things which it hates from the bottom of its heart, and which English education is slowly but surely instilling into the mind of the rising generation. . . . I wish the fears entertained as to the reactionary tendencies of young men were true; but, unfortunately, they are not. Young men are not revolutionary; neither will they be so for some time to come. And if we reflect coolly and calmly upon this matter, we shall soon find the reason why it is extremely hard for them to be revolutionary men in this revolutionary age. They live in an atmosphere of conservatism. Their early education and their home and social influences have a conservative tendency. . . . But, besides these, there is another modifying force, which is often lost sight of. I mean the inherited drill of ages, which has created in their minds a most deep-rooted conservatism. . . . The work of ages cannot be undone in a day. Our present instincts and tendencies are the resultant of forces that have been co-operating for ages; and no sudden change in our outward surroundings, such as the introduction of a European element into India, can change them. Centuries must pass away before new instincts and habits can be formed. These are the forces which act upon the rising generation, and it must be an extraordinary generation indeed, if with the help of a little English education, it can overcome them in so short a time. . . .

I think if there is any phase of our present revolution which is really lamentable, it is that of the general hypocrisy of our educated youths. It is a melancholy truth, that revolutionary periods are also the periods of hypocrisy. . . . Periods of change and convulsions are the very times when it is necessary that new convictions, which have not got the sanction of established opinion, should be openly expressed and boldly followed by those who hold them; but as these are the very times when moral courage involves a great deal of self-sacrifice, men lose their straightforwardness of character, and sacrifice their principles to their immediate interests, in the name of expediency. This, I consider, is the saddest and dismalest phase of the present crisis in India. The masses of the Indian people stick to many absurd customs, but they are sincere in their belief; but that young men, holding quite different principles, should still, for the sake of general convenience, give any encouragement to those customs, is all insincerity and hypocrisy. Who can deny the fact that the whole, mental and moral fabric of an Indian youth, who has been trained in an English institution, is a protest against the tendencies of his society? But in spite of all this, his one desire is to pacify his society by sacrificing his principles; to reconcile the irreconcilables by practicing "pious frauds." "I do not believe in *Prashchit*, but I perform it in order to please my sect," says an Indian youth. "I do not believe in caste; but I do not want to hurt the feelings of my people by proclaiming my belief openly," says another. "I am against forced widowhood; but I can't marry my widowed sister or daughter, as it would make my friends, and especially my female relations, very angry," says a third. Now, what is all this, if it is not hypocrisy? . . .

But it is one of the most hopeful signs of the time, that with the progress of English education, there is gradually growing up a new spirit of liberty and individuality among a certain portion of young men, destined, in course of time, to overcome all hostile forces, and diffuse itself through the whole Indian community. Hard and painful is its struggle at present against the time-honored prejudices of the country. . . . I have no patience with those who say that the spirit of liberty which these young men have imbibed is of a very objectionable nature, that they rebel against public opinion simply for the sake of rebellion, that their individuality means freedom from all social restraints. . . . Those young men who are imbued with a true love of liberty, who feel the dignity of human nature, and whose idea of self-respect it is to possess the individuality of character, and not to be the facsimile of some other person, are the real regenerators of India—the true upholders of the honour, the character, and the prestige of the Indian race.

Besides these, there is another characteristic of Indian youths, to which I want to draw attention for a moment. It is my opinion that young men, as a rule, lack that martial spirit of self-sacrifice, and readiness to endure pain for others without flinching, which their forefathers possessed; and the decline of these noble qualities is going on *pari passu* with the spread of European civilisation in India. Indian youths may be superior to their elders in those qualities which pass under the name of amiable and humane; but in heroic virtues, in courage—even in mere physical courage—in the willingness to court pain for pain's sake, they are decidedly inferior to them. The remark so often made, that young men are pleasure-loving and lack self-denial, is based upon truth. They are luxurious, pleasure-loving, wanting in the qualities of self-abnegation and courage; and this may, in a large measure, be attributed to the influence of modern civilisation. We shall first see what were the circumstances which favoured the growth of heroism and courage in ancient times, and then those other circumstances which are of recent date, and under which they are fast withering away.

Everyone knows that there used to be constant feuds in ancient times in India. . . . Despotism was the chief form of government in those days, and it was the interest of despots to keep their army in good order. All these things tended to keep up a martial spirit among the people. Being constantly in danger of losing their life or property, or both, they were always prepared to meet these dangers. Military drill was common, and a life of perpetual warfare made men reckless as regards encountering pain and peril. This state of things is no doubt fraught with many evils; but it has one redeeming feature too, and it is this: that by making men live in a state of perpetual strife, and exposing them continually to dangers which they must face, either for their safety or that of others, it creates in them a sort of heroic spirit which nerves them, without flinching and without hesitation, to grapple with pain.

Our early method of education was also calculated to nurture this spirit. In ancient times, student-life was a life of hardship and even of beggary. Of the many wise things which we find in Manu's *Dharma Shastra*, the wisest, perhaps, is his method of the early education of Aryan youths. These young men had to leave their home and the pleasures of home in order to lead a life of toil and trouble in some *pathshala* (school). . . . Their early training, by making them familiar with the experiences of pain and privation, disciplined them for the fiercest battles of life. I have no doubt that a great deal of heroism and self-denial of the ancient Hindus was the result of this peculiar method of education.

Another element which contributed largely to the growth of heroic qualities in the Indians was their joint-family system. I am no advocate of this system, which has, most certainly, done a great deal of mischief to India. But no one will deny that it is favourable to the growth of some very good and admirable qualities of human nature; and specially in a society wanting in the spirit and fervour of nationality, it is one of the main things which nurture them and preserve them from decay. . . . Take, for instance, the treatment of the poor and the sick. . . . To live together under one roof and to help each other, was taught to the members of every family as a religious and moral duty; and the consequence was, as there were rare cases of men who, in times of extreme difficulty or illness, had not some of their own relations to look after them, public help on such occasions was seldom wanted. . . . And the performance of this duty was a moral culture to them, inasmuch as, on every occasion of any physical, mental, or pecuniary trouble, it called into play all those feelings of love, pity, generosity, and self-denial, without which human society cannot exist for a day, and in the increase of which lies the true test of civilisation. . . . Domestic attachment and many other heroic qualities are even now very common in those sections of Indian society which have not yet been very much influenced by European ideas; but wherever the latter are spreading, the former are dwindling away. . . .

Now, these were three elements which kept up in our predecessors a spirit of heroism, self-sacrifice, and a courageous disregard of pain and peril; and it is these elements, or some others similar to them, which are wanting in India at the present moment. True, that in place of anarchy and confusion we have law and order; true, that in place of perpetual feuds we have permanent peace. But a little reflection shows that law, order, and peace, *minus* those activities which we find in Europe, are the very things which have contributed to the decline of a martial spirit in our young men. The police and the judge now do everything for us; the idea of danger never troubles our minds, and the consequence is that we lose all presence of mind when dangers do suddenly come. . . .

Then again, looking at the early training of Indian youths, I cannot help thinking that no system of education was ever calculated to make them so pleasure-loving, and so afraid of the very sight of pain, as the present one. . . . I am fully sensible of the softening, humanizing influence which this mode of training exercises upon young minds, by refining their tastes, by making them feel the comforts and pleasures of modern civilisation, and by creating in them new susceptibilities. Still, one cannot ignore the fact, that along with refined tastes and fine susceptibilities, there has come over our young men a sort of Epicureanism, a moral effeminacy, which, while spurring them on to everything which contributes, or is likely to contribute, to their own pleasure, makes them shrink from undertaking any work which involves a moral hardship and the sacrifice of personal advantages. This I consider to be the natural fruit of their education; and so long as this education is what it is, nothing better can be expected from them. . . .

Believe me, gentlemen, that no man ever became a great character who did not learn the virtue of self-mortification at an early age; and no nation ever became a great nation which did not contain a large number of men ready to make every sacrifice of personal comfort and pleasure for the sake of others—ready to court pain and danger, and face them boldly when they come. It was men of this stamp who made India what it was in the past; and it will be men of the same stamp again who will raise it to the level of the most civilised nations of the earth. The earnest endeavours of our reformers ought to be, to preserve from wreck the noble qualities of heroism and self-sacrifice, in the midst of a flood of new tastes and ideas, seething and surging like the waves of an angry sea; and to see that in our unbounded, and sometimes one-sided, admiration of modern civilisation, we do not lose the noblest attributes of humanity.

NOTES

"Knowledge Is Power" originally appeared as Bal Gangadhar Shastri Jambhekar, "Knowledge Is Power," *Bombay Durpun*, August 24, 1832. "An Essay on Native Education" originally appeared as T. Madava Row, "An Essay on Native Education," in *The Fifth Annual Report from the Governors of the Madras University, 1845–46* (Madras: Christian Knowledge Society's Press, 1847), 34–47. "High Education in India" originally appeared as Chunder Nath Bose, *High Education in India: An Essay Read at the Bethune Society on 25th April 1878* (Calcutta: Jogesh Chunder Banerjee, 1878). "Some Characteristics of Indian English-Educated Youths" originally appeared as Bishan Narayan Dar, "Some Characteristics of Indian English-Educated Youths," *Indian Magazine* 16, no. 191 (November 1886): 570–86.

1. Henry Brougham, *A Discourse of the Objects, Advantages, and Pleasures of Science* (London: Baldwin and Cradock, 1829), 6.
2. The author of the cited passage was Prasanna Kumar Tagore, the editor of *The Reformer*, the first Indian-owned English-language newspaper.

Chapter Two

CROSSING THE SEAS

VINDICATION OF THE HINDOOS AS A
TRAVELLING NATION, 1867
[Bholanath Chandra]

... That the Hindoos have never been a travelling people, is the common opinion of foreigners as well as of themselves. It is inculcated in one of their traditions current from a remote age, and is confirmed by a reference to their institutions, usages, and habits of life.... [A Hindoo] is never induced to go abroad either by a liberal curiosity, or the pursuit of gain. His climate, his food, and his religion—all encourage inaction. His rules of caste check all propensity to locomotion from the scenes of his birth and nursery. He has his favorite proverb, that "it is more happy to be seated than to walk, and more happy to sleep than to be awake." He is hemmed in by prejudices which he dares not break through; he has his religious abhorrence of setting his feet on board ship; his horror of the *kaala-pani* or the sea.

... Certainly, there is no denying the truth of the antipathy of the present Hindustanis or Bengalis to any kind of peregrination whatsoever, excepting pilgrimages. That which may be assumed to have been a partial weakness in their ancestors, has in them settled down into a hereditary national repugnance. But facts can be enumerated to show that the ancient Hindoos were not so wholly opposed to all foreign travelling, as is the common supposition; that they were not fond of enacting the dramas of their lives only within the limits of their own country; that enterprise formed an ingredient in the composition of their character; that they sought political acquaintance with foreign people; that they maintained commercial relations with distant nations; and that they visited different countries to contemplate the wide diversities of men and manners. . . .

The *Rig-Veda* shows the ancient Hindoos to have been a naval people. Menu bears testimony to their sea-voyages as well as to their land journeys. The other Hindoo writers, and even the Puranic authors who mystify all accounts, confirm the same fact. The Greek writers speak of Hindoo navies, of Hindoo mariners, of Hindoo pilots, of Hindoo merchants, and even of Hindoo intermarriage with a Greek princess. There were Indian religious missions, and Indian political and commercial embassies, to China on the East, and Rome on the West. There was the ancient Hindoo colony at Java, just like the modern English colonies at the Cape, or in Australia. The Chinese pilgrim, Fa Xian, speaks of his having returned home in a Hindoo vessel, guided by a Hindoo crew. The Arab writers speak of Hindoo physicians and Hindoo astronomers, teaching their sciences at Baghdad. All these are positive facts, tending to the positive determination of the question of ancient Hindoo travelling. Under the impenetrable obscurity which hangs over the deeds of the ancient Hindoos, these are the few isolated facts that have yet transpired and been gathered from the materials at present accessible to us. It is because these casual and detached facts are generally overlooked in a hasty study of Indian history, that people are often precipitated into the opinion which we have sought to contradict and refute. To include in that opinion both the ancient and modern Hindoos, is also a great mistake. That the former were by far a more travelling people than a mere superficial knowledge of them might lead us to suspect, has been made obvious by the facts seriately and chronologically cited in the foregoing pages. . . .

True, that the effects of foreign travelling often appear in what Lord [Francis] Bacon calls "the pricking in some flowers of that a traveler hath learned abroad into the customs of his own country."[1] If no such effect is visible in the institutions and manners of the Hindoos, it ought to be attributed more to their conceit than to that exemption from restlessness and curiosity which is supposed to have made them abstain from all foreign intercourse. The Hindoos grew up alone and unaided in the civilization which placed them in the foremost rank among mankind and made them the teachers of the other nations of antiquity. Finding themselves superior to all the tribes living around them, they saw little to admire in the institutions of their neighbours, and nothing to imitate or borrow from them. Their national pride made them choose to live as it were in a "close borough," disdaining all communication with the outside. When the Greeks rose to a similar civilization, they too looked down with scorn upon all foreigners, and regarded them as barbarians. Notwithstanding, the Hindoos were not blind to recognize merit where it existed. This is seen in the Hindoo writers of the fifth century speaking with respect of the astronomy of the *Yavans* or Greeks. One of them even wrote a treatise called the *Romaka Siddhanto*, or Roman astronomy. The policy prohibiting innovations from abroad, was acted upon only in the instance of religious or political matters. It was only when they were afraid of their interests being hurt, that the Brahmins took precautions against the permeation of any foreign light to India. Such a policy may have been cherished from a remote age, but its strict observance, did not become necessary until the decadence of the Hindoos into a dismembered, superstitious, idolatrous, and effeminate nation. It is always a policy of the weak against the strong, to avoid disastrous collisions—the contact of the earthen-pot with a brass-pot. There is a very common tradition preventing a Hindoo from crossing the Indus. Few can fail to trace it to the repeated invasions from beyond the Indus . . . which were sources of dread to the degenerate Hindoo. The prohibition is plainly a political admonition to warn Hindoo ambition from extending its influence beyond the Indus, lest any provocation should call forth the vengeance of an enemy in the weakened state of the Hindoos. The interdict would have been ineffectual without the accompaniment of religious terrors; and, for the first time, it sowed the seed of that aversion to foreign travelling in the Hindoo mind, which, in the lapse of ages, has grown into a chronic and hereditary repugnance. . . .

Much has been said to vindicate the Hindoos of former times, and it remains now to speak a few words about the present natives. The ancient Hindoo was he who belonged to the pre-Puranic period, when his intelligence and wealth were considerable, his notions of God pure and lofty, and his spirit liberal and enterprising; when he had his own government, laws, and institutions, and his own national politics and economics; when he had his own armies to protect his dominion upon land, and his own navies to protect his interests upon the sea. The position he occupied and the state of things in which he lived, made him a different creature altogether from the being who now bears his name and claims to be his descendant. The modern Hindoo properly dates from and after the Puranic period. Born and bred in subjection, ignorance, and superstition, he has grown an alien to his race in all respects, excepting those of lineage and hereditaments. He is disgraced by idolatry and hemmed in by prejudices. He has no political existence. The Moslem first deprived him of his dominion on land, and the Arabs, the Portuguese, the Dutch, and the English successively drove him from the sea. The trade and manufactures of his country have passed into foreign hands. He has been reduced to a mere hewer of wood and tiller of the soil. Centuries of Brahminical tyranny, of national disunion, and of foreign subjection and misrule, have demoralized and depraved his character. He has long forgotten the glorious deeds of his nation, and now looks upon their adventures as those of a romance. He is void of all geographical knowledge, and his notions of the sea are as wild as the wildest dream. He has no incentive to action and spends his life in one long inertia. He has no hopes beyond those centered in self, and no adventures beyond those occurring within his threshold. He rusts in idleness and stagnates in ignorance and poverty.

In spite of all his drawbacks, however, the modern Hindoo is not without his travels. He is known to make pilgrimages to the most distant shrines—to Vrindavan on the Jamuna, to Pushkar in Rajputana, to Dwarka in Gujarat, to Suchindram near Cape Comorin, to Jagannath at Puri, to Badrinath upon the Himalayas, and to Hinglaj on the coast of Makran. There are religious mendicants who travel to Baku, the sacred fire on the Caspian; who go to Astrachan, and sometimes even to Moscow. Individuals of a Hindoo tribe from Shikarpur, a city near the Indus, settle as bankers and merchants in the towns of Persia, Turkestan, and the southern dominions of Russia. . . .

The celebrated Rajah Rammohan Roy, the only instance of a glorious character to which Bengal can point in the whole compass of its modern history, was the first native to set the example of breaking through the ice of prejudice and embark for England. . . . The next instance is that of Dwarkanath Tagore, who, taking his passage in a mail steamer, travelled through Italy and France, on his way to England. He returned from his first voyage, and then went back to spend his last days amongst the *élite* of England. On the second occasion, he took with him one of his sons and a nephew, and two native medical students who were to finish their education in England. The success of the medical students encouraged others to follow in a similar path. There was one Bengali who accompanied a Unitarian missionary gentleman to America. Indeed, a native of Bengal, like Gyanendra Mohan Tagore, teaching Hindoo jurisprudence in the London University, reminds us of Plutarch instructing the citizens of Rome in the philosophy of the Greeks. Indian snake-charmers finding their way to London, are also like the Indian astrologers who found their way to ancient Rome. There are Indian lascars who often attract a crowd in the streets of London by the music of their tom-tom and other novelties. The example of the Bengalis has begun to be followed by the natives of Bombay. Already have half-a-dozen agency houses been established in London by the Parsis. The Gujaratis, who have been a maritime people from the Vedic period, and who were seen by the early Portuguese navigators to trade as far down the Indian Ocean as the Mozambique, and the mouth of the Zambesi, have also established similar houses at Hong Kong and Shanghai. The Marwaris, too, are trading in the track of the Gujaratis. Many Bengalis are employed as writers at Akyab and Rangoon. The opening of the Civil Service to the competition of Her Majesty's Indian subjects has set a spur to the ambition of Hindoo youths, with whom a voyage to England is now a foregone conclusion. Already has the grandson of Dwarkanath Tagore come back a successful candidate from that competition. Two native gentlemen have also returned having finished their studies at the Inner Temple and have been admitted to the bar of the High Court; while a third is still prosecuting his studies with the same object in view.

It has been our aim in these pages to vindicate our nation from an unjust opprobrium, and, at the same time, to disabuse the native public mind of the prejudices and erroneous notions that have been a bar to their progress and prosperity. At present no enlightened Hindoo thinks of anything so much as to see his countrymen take a place amongst the nations of the world. Intelligence, enterprise, and wealth must alone pave the way to the attainment of that wished-for object. The qualification of intelligence is the fruit of that education to which the nation must first of all direct its undivided and persevering attention. The possession of wealth is dependent upon enterprise, and a nation to be enterprising must cultivate habits of travelling and enlarge the circle of its experience. The evidence which has been submitted to the reader seems hardly to leave a doubt as to our nation having been a travelling people from a pre-historic period. The benefit of forty years' education has set the natives to think, but not yet to act. It has enabled them to appreciate the use of the press and the platform, but has not as yet opened their eyes to the material benefits of foreign travelling and foreign trade. The necessity for a more enterprising spirit than has hitherto distinguished the natives of this country, is beginning to be felt. . . . True, that the bench, the bar, the Government offices, and the counting houses, are all open to the ambition of the natives, but they all form a field too small for the teeming millions of India. . . . If they find the fields around them too hot for competition, they should turn their attention to other quarters. If it is found difficult to make money by preferring to live at home, they should overcome their repugnance to a life of sojourn. If their operations be not attended with success in India, they should make up their minds to go to China, to Australia, to the Mauritius, to England, and to America, to try new fields and new resources. Education without enterprise is like sowing seeds upon a sluggish soil that never yields a speedy crop. A widely diffused enterprising spirit is always the antecedent to that widely diffused national prosperity, by means of which alone can our nation ever hope to occupy a conspicuous position in the eyes of mankind. Such was the state of India once, such ought to be the state of India again.

MY FUTURE VISIT TO AMERICA, 1883
Anandibai Joshi

. . . Our subject to-day is, "My future visit to America, and public inquiries regarding it." I am asked hundreds of questions about my going to America. I take this opportunity to answer some of them. . . .

Why do I go to America? I go to America because I wish to study medicine. I now address the ladies present here, who will be the better judges of the importance of female medical assistance in India. I never consider this subject without being surprised that none of those societies so laudably established in India for the promotion of sciences and female education have ever thought of sending one of their female members into the most civilized parts of the world to procure thorough medical knowledge, in order to open here a College for the instruction of women in medicine. There is probably no country that would not disclose all her wants and try to stand on her own feet. The want of female doctors in India is keenly felt in every quarter. Ladies both European and Native are naturally averse to expose themselves in cases of emergency to treatment by doctors of the other sex. There are some female doctors in India from Europe and America, who, being foreigners and different in manners, customs and language, have not been of such use to our women as they might. As it is very natural that Hindu ladies who love their country and people should not feel at home with the natives of other countries, we Indian women absolutely derive no benefit from these foreign ladies. They indeed have the appearance of supplying our need, but the appearance is delusive. In my humble opinion there is a growing need for Hindu lady doctors in India, and I volunteer to qualify myself for one.

Are there no means to study in India? No. I do not mean to say there are no means, but the difficulties are many and great. There is one College at Madras, and midwifery classes are opened in all the Presidencies; but the education imparted is defective and not sufficient, as the instructors who teach the classes are conservative, and to some extent jealous. I do not find fault with them. That is the characteristic of the male sex. We must put up with this inconvenience until we have a class of educated ladies to relieve these men.

I am neither a Christian nor a Brahmo. To continue to live as a Hindu and to go to school in any part of India is very difficult. A convert who wears an English dress is not so much stared at. Native Christian ladies are free from the opposition or public scandal which Hindu ladies like myself have to meet within and without the *zenana*.[2] If I go alone by train or in the street some people come near to stare and ask impertinent questions to annoy me. Example is better than precept. Some few years ago, when I was in Bombay, I used to go to school. When people saw me going with my books in my hands, they had the goodness to put their heads out of the window just to have a look at me. Some stopped their carriages for the purpose. Others walking in the streets stood laughing and crying out so that I could hear:—

"What is this? Who is this lady who is going to school with boots and stockings on?"

"Does not this show that the Kali Yuga has stamped its character on the minds of the people?"

Ladies and gentlemen, you can easily imagine what effect questions like these would have on your minds if you had been in my place!

Once it so happened that I was obliged to stay in school for some time, and go twice a day for my meals to the house of a relation. Passers-by, whenever they saw me going, gathered round me. Some of them made fun, and were convulsed with laughter. Others, sitting respectably in their verandahs, made ridiculous remarks, and did not feel ashamed to throw pebbles at me. The shopkeepers and venders spit at the sight of me, and made gestures too indecent to describe. I leave it to you to imagine what was my condition at such a time, and how I could gladly have burst through the crowd to make my home nearer!

Yet the boldness of my Bengali brethren cannot be exceeded, and it is still more serious to contemplate than the instances I have given from Bombay. Surely it deserves pity! If I go to take a walk on the Strand, Englishmen are not so bold as to look at me. Even the soldiers are never troublesome; but the Babus lay bare their levity by making fun of everything. "Who are you?" "What caste do you belong to?" "Whence do you come," "Where do you go?" are, in my opinion, questions that should not be asked by strangers. There are some educated native Christians here in Serampore who are suspicious; they are still wondering whether I am married or a widow; a woman of bad character or ex-communicated! Dear audience, does it become my native and Christian brethren to be so uncharitable? Certainly not. I place these unpleasant things before you, that those whom they concern most may rectify them, and those who have never thought of the difficulties may see that I am not going to America through any whim or caprice.

Why do I go alone? It was at first the intention of my husband and myself to go together, but we were forced to abandon this thought. We have not sufficient funds; but that is not the only reason. There are others still more important and convincing. My husband has his aged parents and younger brothers and sisters to support. You will see that his departure would throw those dependent upon him into the arena of life, penniless and alone. How cruel and inhuman it would be for him to take care of one soul and reduce so many to starvation! Therefore I go alone.

Shall I not be excommunicated when I return to India? Do you think I should be filled with consternation at this threat? I do not fear it in the least. Why should I be cast out, when I have determined to live there exactly as I do here? I propose to myself to make no change in my customs and manners, food or dress. I will go as a Hindu, and come back here to live here as a Hindu. I will not increase my wants, but be as plain and simple as my fore-fathers, and as I am now. If my countrymen wish to excommunicate me, why do they not do it now? They are at liberty to do so. I have come to Bengal and to a place where there is not a single Maharashtrian. Nobody here knows whether I behave according to my customs and manners, or not. Let us therefore cease to consider what may never happen, and what, when it may happen, will defy human speculation.

What will I do if misfortune befall me? Some persons fall into the error of exaggerated declamation, by producing in their talk examples of national calamities and scenes of extensive misery which are found in books rather than in the world, and which, as they are horrid, are ordained to be rare. A man or a women who wishes to act does not look at that dark side which others easily foresee. On necessary and inevitable evils which crush him or her to dust, all dispute is vain. When they happen they must be endured, but it is evident they are oftener dreaded than experienced. Whether per-petual happiness can be obtained in any way, this world will never give us an opportunity to decide. But this we may say, we do not always find visi-ble happiness in proportion to visible means. It is not a thing which may be divided among a certain number of men. It depends upon feeling. If death be only miserable, why should some rejoice at it, while others lament? On the other hand, death and misery come alike to good and bad, virtuous and vicious, rich and poor, travelers and housekeepers; all are con-founded in the misery of famine and not greatly distinguished in the fury of faction. No man is able to prevent any catastrophe. Misery and death are always near, and should be expected. When the result of any hazardous work is good, we praise the enterprise which undertook it; when it is evil, we blame the imprudence. The world is always ready to call enterprise imprudence when fortune changes.

Some say that those who stay at home are happy, but where does their happiness lie? Happiness is not a readymade thing to be enjoyed because one desires it. Some minds are so fond of variety that pleasure if perma-nent would be insupportable, and they solicit happiness by courting dis-tress. To go to foreign countries is not bad, but in some respects better than to stay in one place. [The knowledge of history as well as other places is not to be neglected. The present state of things is the consequence of the former, and it is natural to enquire what were the sources of the good that we enjoy or the evils we suffer. To neglect the study of sciences is not prudent; it is

not just if we are entrusted with the care of others. Ignorance when voluntary is criminal, and one may perfectly be charged with evils who refused
to learn how he might prevent it. When the eyes and imagination are struck
with any uncommon work, the next transition of an active mind is to the
means by which it was performed. Here begins the true use of seeing other
countries. We enlarge our comprehension by new ideas and perhaps recover
some arts lost by us, or learn what is imperfectly known in our country. So
I hope my going to America will not be disadvantageous.]

[I have seriously considered our manners and future prospects and find
that we have mistaken our interests.] Everyone must do what he thinks
right. Every man has owed much to others. His effort ought to be to repay
what he has received. [This world is like a vast sea, mankind like a vessel
sailing on its tempestuous bosom. Our prudence is its sails; the sciences
serve us for oars; good or bad fortunes are the favorable or contrary winds
and *judgement* is the rudder; without this last the vessel is tossed by every
billow and will find ship-wreck in every breeze.] Let us follow the advice of
Goldsmith who says: "Learn to pursue virtue of a man who is blind, who
never takes a step without first examining the ground with his staff."[3] I take
my Almighty Father for my staff, who will examine the path before He leads
me further. I can find no better staff than He.

And last you ask me, why I should do what is not done by any of my sex?
[To this I cannot but say that we are bound by the rights of society to the
labours of individuals. Everyone has his duty and he must perform it in
the best way he can; otherwise his fear and backwardness are supposed to
be a desertion of duty. It is very difficult to decide the duties of individuals.
It is enough that the good of the whole is the same with the good of an
individual. If anything seems best for mankind, it must evidently be best
for an individual and that duty is to try one's best, according to his sentiments to do good to the society.] According to Manu, the desertion of duty
is an unpardonable sin. So I am surprised to hear that I should not do
this, because it has not been done by others. [I cannot help asking them in
return "who should stand the first if all will say so?"] Our ancestors whose
names have become immortal had no such notions in their heads. I ask my
Christian friends, "Do you think you would have been saved from your
sins, if Jesus Christ, according to your notions, had not sacrificed his life
for you all?" Did he shrink at the extreme penalty that he bore while doing
good? No, I am sure you will never admit that he shrank! Neither did our

ancient kings Shibi and Mayurdhwaj. To desist from duty because we fear failure or suffering is not just. We must try. Never mind whether we are victors or victims. Manu has divided people into three classes. [Those who do not begin for fear of failure, are reckoned among the meanest; those who begin but give it up through obstacles belong to the middle class; and those who begin but [do] not give it up till they attain success, through repeated difficulties, are the best. Let us not therefore be guilty of the very crime we absolutely hate. The more the difficulties, the greater must be the attempt. Let it be our boast never to desist from anything begun. Sufferance should be our badge.]

MAY HINDUS CROSS THE OCEAN?, 1892
S. E. Gopalacharlu

There exists among Brahmins a very generally received opinion that if one of their community crosses the sea and remains for a time in a foreign country, he is liable by that act to be expelled from his caste. . . . After a careful study of the various authorities, it seems to the present writer that this opinion has no real foundation, and that the crossing of the ocean is not forbidden to Brahmins by their scriptures. But before citing the various passages that go to prove the correctness of this view, a few preliminary remarks ought to be made.

Some may consider that it is unnecessary to discuss this subject at all, on the ground that there is no sufficient reason to induce any of the "twice-born" to cross the sea. In our opinion, however, there are many benefits to be gained by foreign travel, and this without sea-travel is almost impossible.

Until the invasion of the Mohammedans, the inhabitants of India generally knew but little about those of other lands; but in later times, especially since the establishment of British rule in this country, a great interest has been awakened in foreign countries, and the habits, manners, and customs of their inhabitants. This new interest naturally aroused a desire on the part of my fellow-countrymen to see for themselves the things and people of whom they had heard, and accordingly a number of gentlemen from Bengal, the Maratha county and the North-West Provinces have been to England, and the number of those who go is increasing year by year. The people of the north set the example, and it was found that they returned from England after having received a good education, and obtained as a result good positions in life in this country, the Southern Indians wished to follow their example, and some of them did so. But these on their return were visited by all the pains and penalties of transgressors against our strict caste rules. They were refused admittance into the community, and otherwise were made to suffer much pain and misery. Not only Brahmins, but also non-Brahmins, were excommunicated on account of their travelling by sea, and the consequence has been that many who would otherwise have gone abroad have been deterred from so doing by the social consequences incurred by others.

When we, Indians, look at the condition of our own country, we find much to regret. Our ancient prosperity seems to have deserted us. The arts and sciences that were known to our fathers have been forgotten. Native education has reached the lowest ebb, and we have actually to thank foreigners for the education received by our children. Our manufactures have fallen into decay, and we find that generally speaking, with the exception of those engaged in agriculture, our people are compelled to rely on subordinate positions under foreigners as a means of gaining their livelihood. Our country is poverty-stricken, and our population is increasing. Except the public services and the two professions of law and medicine, there is no career open to our young men; the professions are over-crowded, and there are more applicants for public service than can possibly enter it. . . .

If those who wish to do so are able, without unnecessary let and hindrance, to go to foreign countries, many of these evils will gradually cease. When our people see for themselves how commerce is carried on abroad, they will be able to employ the same methods here, and increased prosperity will be the result. Our artisans and workmen require to know about the improved tools and processes of manufacture used by the foreigners, and unless some of our people go abroad it is not likely that this knowledge will be gained for the country. It is humiliating to think of how many of the articles in daily use in this country by almost all classes are imported from abroad instead of being manufactured here. We do not use a single pin that has not been made in Europe, and even our paper—except the most common qualities—has to be made for us by foreigners. Our cultivators are ignorant of the best and most economical methods of agriculture, and so our land is not as productive as it ought to be. On every account it is necessary that some of our more intellectual men should visit England and other European countries in order to find out what means may be taken for the improvement of the condition of this country. We should remember the example of the Russian Emperor Peter the Great, who went to England and worked in a shipyard, and then went back to teach his own people how to work.

Until recently we have been comparatively indifferent to the condition of our own country. Now a spirit of inquiry and reform seems to be stirring, and the air is full of plans of reform and improvement. But if the existing prejudice against sea-travel is to continue, and those who are willing to go to England are to be deterred by the prospect of misery and persecution on their return, as is now the case, it will be found that the various schemes are likely to fail, on account of the ignorance of the country at large of foreign methods.

Our forefathers obtained thorough skill in various arts to the number of sixty-four. They were in a position to teach and instruct the mass of the people. Useful knowledge, says Manu, must be obtained, even if from inferior classes. All sorts of arts and sciences may be received from all men. Spiritual knowledge may be obtained even from the lowest class of men. . . . Many of us think that various high offices ought to be held by Hindus, but as things are at present, it is not likely that such offices can be properly held except by those who have received a systematic modern training in Europe. Even among the Europeans foreign travel is considered a necessary part of education.

. . . Is it not worse than folly to continue to harbor a prejudice that will cause the best of our children who may happen to go abroad, to be treated on their return with contempt and cruelty, to be no longer admitted to dwell in our streets, to break the most sacred ties of relationship, and treat them, in fact, as little better than brute beasts? Is there not something inhuman in the prohibition of such sea-travelled Brahmins to even see their wives, whom they so tenderly love? . . . Such bigotry is indeed difficult to understand. Our Aryan forefathers protected our *Dharmas*, our literature, our religion, our philosophy, from century to century without any danger even from the invading foreigners. But now there is danger to our religion on many sides. Our children are growing up educated in new ways, and many of them forsake the faith of their fathers—not to exchange it for some other form of worship, but to become mere materialists and atheists. Nothing is so likely to prejudice the more intelligent among them against our religion as the keeping up of this foolish and cruel system of persecution against those who travel by sea for the sake of improving themselves and their countrymen. It is the existence of abuses such as this that will cause our religion to decay, and unless we prune them away we shall be like men who inherited good houses from their fathers but let these houses sink into ruin for want of a little timely repair.

In the *Vedas* certain duties are described which were afterwards changed by the code of Manu and other sages. The duties laid down by Manu have been modified by Parashara and other modern *Rishis*. In the introduction to the *Parasaramadhaviya*, Madhavacharya gives his decision that, according to the circumstances of the country, the law should be changed from time to time. Therefore, if we arrange our duties according to the condition of the circumstance of the country, of the people, and of the time, without altering any main principles, without contradicting the authority of the *Vedas*, or Manu and other sages, we shall be acting in accordance with our own immemorial custom. The time has now come when it is absolutely necessary for us to make an exhaustive review of our *Shastras* on this important point, and it is useless to delay so doing. . . .

THE HINDU SEA VOYAGE MOVEMENT IN BENGAL, 1894
Standing Committee on the Hindu Sea-Voyage Question

. . . Hindoo young men, in appreciable numbers, proceed to England to receive education in the universities, to qualify for the Bar, to compete for the Indian Civil Service, for the Medical Service, and in various other ways to equip themselves for the practical work of life. The number is on the increase, of gentlemen, who, if all restrictions were removed, would like to proceed to Europe for purposes of travel, and all the pleasures and profits it brings. There is a growing desire also in some quarters to make excursions to the West for commercial purposes. It cannot be a matter of indifference to the Hindoo community if the gentlemen who come back from Europe after perfecting their education and enlarging their experience are to be received back into society or excluded from it. It cannot be a matter of indifference also whether adventurous gentlemen should have free scope given to them in the matter of travel, or they should have their ambition curbed by social restrictions. The welfare of a country is the welfare of its individuals, and no subject can be of greater national importance than the discussion of the limits which custom may have prescribed to the liberty of movement of the men who compose the nation.

On economic grounds alone the question of sea-voyages is of great practical importance. People may feel themselves driven by sheer necessity to try their fortune in remote countries, to seek new careers, learn the arts of foreign nations, and come back home with added qualification and augmented resources. If these poor, adventurous souls should be denied the opportunities they sought, it is not they alone that would be sufferers, but the country as well. Social restrictions, however, are likely to prove an effectual barrier to most of them, and the legitimacy of those restrictions therefore deserves serious consideration. The possibility of natives of India marching out in quest of occupation to distant lands may now appear to be too remote, and as a dream. But there are reasons to believe that if the restrictions were repealed or relaxed, opportunities of adventure would often be utilized.

Hindoo society is governed by rules which have their basis in the Hindoo religion. That religion is enshrined in the *shastras*, of which the recognised, authoritative interpreters are the Pandits. The Pandits give their *vyavasthas* or ordinances founded upon the texts. These are accepted by the leaders of the different castes which make up society, and they thus come to regulate usage. On the subject of sea-voyage, therefore, the first thing necessary was to obtain the opinions of the Pandits. That step has already been taken. It was not of course to be expected that the opinion of every single Pandit in Bengal should be obtained, but many of the leading Pandits have been consulted. . . . The next step that was taken was to refer the subject to some of the leading members of Hindoo society, all of the higher castes, and their opinions have also been recorded. Attention may be specially called to the opinion of so distinguished an apostle of Hinduism as Bankim Chandra Chatterjee. Lastly, a large body of public opinion from various sources, which had been elicited by the discussion, has been set forth in its proper place. It includes the opinions as well of eminent Englishmen as of newspapers, Hindoo and English. These opinions have a value which must not be overlooked. Pandits interpret the *shastras*; social leaders judge practicability; but an intelligent public have also a right to be heard, for, unfettered by considerations of authority and custom, they are able to utter the voice of abstract reason. Mere reasonableness is not an excuse for an innovation, but it will hardly be denied that a practice which is manifestly contrary to reason cannot long remain unmodified, and that so long as it does exist it will work mischief. The opinions, therefore, of intelligent and educated men who are even outsiders to our society have an importance that should not be underrated. . . .

For a full appreciation of the issues involved in the sea-voyage question it is necessary to bear in mind a few well-known facts which may be thus stated:

1. For a long time past the practice of eating things condemned by Hindoo rules or custom has been pretty common in Hindoo society, but the gentlemen who have indulged in such practices have not been put out of caste. Their number is growing. They include not merely schoolboys or wild young men, not merely a few insignificant people who might be regarded as the waifs and strays of society, but also and mainly, elderly, respectable, influential gentlemen, some of whom have been recognised as social leaders. In their own private residences or those of their friends, European or Native, in garden houses, in hotels kept by Europeans or Mohammedans, on steamers, in railway refreshment rooms, numbers of Hindoo gentlemen dine in the European style, and the orthodox members of society find it convenient to connive at these practices. Demand creates supply. Hence it is we find that restaurants where European dishes are offered, are multiplying. They are set upon largely frequented streets, and near offices and theatres. Year after year, in every town in which the Indian National Congress is held, it is found necessary by the organizers to make special arrangements for those delegates and visitors who are to live in the European style. In a word, the rules as regards orthodox living are every day trampled underfoot, and the violations are in no way punished.

2. There was a time when it was considered an un-Hindoo practice to drink pipe-water. Not only is pipe-water drunk today by Hindus of unquestioned orthodoxy, but aerated waters, European wines and spirits, and medicines prepared by Europeans, are habitually consumed by large numbers of them. Bread, biscuits and confectionery of European or Mahomedan manufacture are also largely indulged in.

3. Hindu society has not been able consistently to keep out of its pale all those who have made voyages to Europe. Some of them received recognition in society, at any rate among their friends and relations; and after their death, their sons and other relations have had no difficulty in being accepted as members of society, though no *prayaschitta* [penance] had ever been performed by them.

4. Some of those that have made voyages to Europe have, on their return to this country, lived, permanently or for a time, with their relations. Many of their friends and relations have also dined with them on many occasions. Orthodox society has never ceased to recognise these friends and relations.

5. Either for purposes of business or on pleasure trips, several Hindoos have made voyages to Rangoon, to Madras, to Ceylon. Nobody dreams of excommunicating them.

6. Esteemed Hindoo gentlemen have on some occasions taken part, as host or guest, in entertainments, almost of a public character, conducted in the European

style. The names of those who dined on the occasions have sometimes been reported in the newspapers, but orthodox society has never cared to take any notice of their errors.

7. Hindoo Society has exhibited nothing like consistency, observed no definite principle, in dealing with those of its members who have made voyages to Europe. The same men that recognise them on one occasion do not recognise them on another. They dine with them today and decline to dine with them tomorrow. If they are to be excommunicated, those who have dined with them, or otherwise mixed with them in formal social intercourse on ceremonial occasions, should be excommunicated also. But the utmost that the ultra-orthodox members of the community seek to do is to omit to recognise only the travelled men, while they permit themselves to mix freely with men who have been tainted by association with the chief offenders.

What is the inference to be drawn from these facts? Obviously this, that it would not be fair or consistent to exclude from society men who had made only a voyage by sea without transgressing Hindoo rules of living. Surely it cannot be contended that a mere crossing of the sea is a grosser offence than living in a non-Hindu style, or even as gross as that. When open, or, at any rate, well-known violations of Hindoo rules of eating and drinking are connived at and excused, neither reason nor orthodoxy demands the exclusion of men who living as Hindoos had merely travelled to the West. . . . That a voyage by sea as such, does not militate against Hinduism seems to be tacitly admitted by Hindoo society by the manner in which it has been treating Swami Vivekananda's visit to America. The Swami, so far from being regarded as an apostate by reason of his visit, is being looked up to as a prince of Hindoos and the pride of Hinduism. It is inconceivable, therefore, that the sea-voyage movement should be opposed on grounds either of religion or logic. If there could be any objection to it, it would be its conservative rather than its revolutionary character. . . .

LETTER REGARDING THE MOVEMENT, 1894
Bankim Chandra Chatterjee

. . . The questions which you wish me to answer are such as are best answered by professors of the *Dharma Sastras*. I do not profess the *Dharma Sastras*, nor am I prepared to undertake the office of expounding them. But

I have no objection to offer a few observations regarding the present agitation about sea-voyages by Hindus.

In the first place, I do not believe that it is either possible or desirable to promote social reforms by invoking the authority of the *Sastras*. I had to object on the same ground to the late lamented Ishwar Chandra Vidyasagar's proposals to suppress polygamy with the aid of the *Sastras*; and I have seen no ground since then to change my opinion. This opinion I hold on two grounds. The first is, that Bengali society is governed not by the *Sastras* but by custom. It is true, that very often custom follows the *Sastras*; but as often again custom conflicts with the *Sastras*. When there is such a conflict custom carries the day.

The second reason for my opinion is that if society were everywhere governed by the *Sastras*, it is doubtful whether the result will be social welfare. You seek to collect the behests of the *Sastras*, regarding sea-voyages, and to induce society to follow them;—are you prepared to induce society to be guided by the *Sastras* on all other matters as well? One of the precepts of the *Dharma Sastras* is, that it is the duty of the Shudras to perform menial offices for the Brahmins and other superior castes;—do the Shudras of Bengal follow the precept? The *Sastras* are not a guide here. Are any of you prepared to enforce this precept? Do you think that any endeavours to enforce it will succeed? Will a Sudra Judge of the High Court leave the bench, or will the prosperous Shudra *zamindar* leave the *zamindar*'s seat, to respectfully tend the feet of the Brahmin manufacturer of eatables? By no means. Bengali society obeys a portion of the *Dharma Sastras* according to its necessities. The rest it has cast off because of its necessities. The same feeling of necessity may induce it to cast off what still remains. What good then there is in seeking to ascertain the commands of the *Dharma Sastras*?

My own conviction is that it is impossible to carry out social reformation regarding any particular practice merely on the strength of the *Sastras* without religious and moral regeneration along the whole line. This I have tried to explain at length in my work on *Krishna Charitra*. I have already stated that society here is governed by custom, not by the *Sastras*. Reforms in custom can be achieved only when there is an advance in religion and morals along the whole line. The present agitation is the outcome of the advance that has already taken place. As society advances gradually in religion and morals, the objections against sea-voyages will disappear, or if any opposition should still continue to exist, it would be powerless.

But so long as the full measure of advance is not attained, so long it will be impossible to make sea-voyages acceptable to society.

But it has also to be observed that none of us are aware of the exact measure of opposition which exists in Bengali society towards sea-voyages. I see that whoever commands the necessary means and is otherwise favorably circumstanced, does proceed to Europe when willing to do so. I have not come across a single instance in which the journey to Europe was abandoned out of respect to the authority of the *Sastras*. But I am also bound to admit that most of those who return from Europe remain outside the pale of Hindu society. It is a question whether the fault lies with them, or with Hindu society. On their return to this country they voluntarily keep away from Bengali society by adopting European habits and customs. They separate themselves from us by adopting foreign costumes, foreign habits of living, and foreign usages. Those who on their return from Europe did not adopt this course have in many instances been re-admitted into Hindu society. If gentlemen returning from Europe did generally resume habits and usages conformable to Hindu society, it is impossible to say that they would be as a body left outside its precincts.

Lastly, I have to point out that before deciding the question as to whether sea-voyages are in conformity to the *Dharma Sastras* of the Hindus, it is necessary to decide whether it is not in conformity to *Dharma* (religion) itself. Must we reject that which is conformable to religion but opposed to the *Dharma Sastras*, merely because it is opposed to the *Dharma Sastras*? Many will say that alone which is conformable to the Hindu *Dharma Sastras* is religion; and that which is not conformable to them is irreligion. I am not prepared to admit this. None of the older sacred books of Hindus say so. Krishna in the *Mahabharata* says—"*Dharma* is so called because it holds all. Know that for certain to be *Dharma*, which contributes to the general welfare." If the *Mahabharata* is not guilty of a falsehood, if he whom the Hindus worship as the Divine Incarnation is not guilty of falsehood, then that which is for the general welfare is religious. Now, are sea-voyages for the general welfare or not? If they are, why should they be opposed because they do not happen to be encouraged by the *Smritis*? . . . Sea-voyages are conformable to religion because they tend to the general good. Therefore, whatever the *Dharma Sastras* may say, sea-voyages are conformable to the Hindu religion.

NOTES

"Vindication of the Hindoos as a Travelling Nation" originally appeared as [Bholanath Chandra], "Vindication of the Hindoos as a Travelling Nation," *Calcutta Review* 46, no. 92 (1867): 391–434. "My Future Visit to America" originally appeared as Caroline Healey Dall, *The Life of Dr. Anandabai Joshee* (Boston: Roberts, 1888), 82–91. A verbatim account of Joshi's speech was published by "A Well-Wisher" as *Speech by a Hindu Lady* (Bombay: Native Opinion, 1883) (British Library, 1415.a.62.[8.]). Dall's version omitted or reworded some important passages. The original text has been restored here and is marked with brackets. I am grateful to the British Library for permission to include these passages. "May Hindus Cross the Ocean?" originally appeared as S. E. Gopalacharlu, "Sea Voyages by Hindus (I): May Hindus Cross the Ocean?," *Imperial and Asiatic Quarterly Review* 4, no. 7 (July 1892): 49–55. "The Hindu Sea Voyage Movement in Bengal" originally appeared as *The Hindu Sea Voyage Movement in Bengal* (Calcutta: J. N. Banerjee, 1894), preface, i–vi. "Letter Regarding the Movement" originally appeared as Bankim Chunder Chatterji, "Letter Regarding the Movement," in *The Hindu Sea Voyage Movement in Bengal* (Calcutta: J. N. Banerjee, 1894), 15–19. The letter was originally written on July 27, 1892.

1. Francis Bacon, "Of Travel," in *The Essays of Francis Bacon*, ed. Mary Augusta Scott (New York: Scribner's, 1908), 82.
2. The section of the household in which women were secluded.
3. Oliver Goldsmith, *Letters from a Citizen of the World to His Friends in the East*, vol. 2 (Chiswick: C. Whittingham, 1819), 97.

PART II

Critiques

Chapter Three

THE GREAT GAME

ENGLAND AND RUSSIA, 1879
India

Recent events have shown that these two powers are not on the best of terms
with each other. England distrusts Russia and thinks that the great northern Bear fondly cherishes the design of someday dethroning the British Lion
in India. . . . The bear has, no doubt, long since issued from his "frozen lair"
and filled large tracts of country with sounds of victory. But he is yet far
from the den of the lion, and the question which the king of the four-legged
race has to decide is, what is the meaning of all this stir and noise? . . . There
is considerable difference of opinion on that point. . . . We belong to the race of
bipeds and our opinion is certainly less weighty than that of the race
which possesses a couple of legs more than we have been gifted with. . . .
As a two-legged animal, we humbly think that neither the Liberal nor the
Conservative is wholly right in this matter of the bear's designs in relation
to the lion. It is known all over the world that the lion is now king in India.
But does the bear think of challenging him in his den and wresting from
him the scepter of sovereignty? The Liberal says—no; the Conservative, yes.
Perhaps the truth lies between this "yes" and this "no."

In the first place, the lion's natural place in the hierarchy of quadrupeds
is not necessarily an insurmountable obstacle in the way of the bear. The

Panchatantra tells the story of a jackal that once proclaimed himself king of the forest and enjoyed kingly powers for some time. So, what happened once may happen again. To be serious, Russia has yet to make her history. She has not yet done anything particularly remarkable in the world's history. The instinct of outward expansion is as strong in nations as it is in individuals. France has labored to possess India. Spain has done remarkable things in America to increase her power and influence. Portugal was about the earliest ambitious arrival in India. Holland and Denmark have made endeavours in the same direction, though with scanty success. The thing is, a great nation cannot help making great efforts, and the extension of empire is certainly one of those directions which such efforts take. . . .

[Russia] is now a rising power, and like all powers that are rising or are fairly in the way of rising to a great height, she is giving birth to great minds in all departments of human activity. And it is a noticeable fact that she is now particularly strong in soldiership and politico-military genius. The Turko-Russian war has brought a large number of Russian military officers to the front rank of European soldiership; whilst conquered provinces are transforming simple soldiers into ambitious military governors full of that buccaneering spirit which, as is proved by the early history of British India, produces restless activity and leads to wonderful achievements in arms and political organisation in the most unexpected directions. . . . Judging from all present appearances and the stage of national development which Russia is now passing through, it may be concluded with some degree of confidence that she will for some time give birth to men of this stamp in gradually increasing numbers. But minds of this order cannot brook restraint, they despise limited horizons, and are seldom satisfied with small or inglorious fields of action. Sandy steppes and barren plains inhabited by half-nomadic and half-agricultural communities are not theatres of action sufficiently attractive to or sufficiently glorious and dignified in the eyes of great politico-military adventurers. . . .

Side by side with this wonderful politico-military development, Russia presents the spectacle of a literary activity of which the study of India's ancient greatness forms a striking feature. Russian soldiership cannot certainly remain entirely unaffected by the enthusiasm of Russian Sanskrit scholarship, and the spirit of the Russian soldier may be profoundly stirred by the grand panorama of Indian greatness held up to his view by the Russian scholar. Commerce, again, has a value which a large empire, working with essentially expansive instincts, cannot afford to ignore or underrate; and India represents in a million-fold form the commerce of all the Central Asian Khanates taken together. That Russia should at some future time endeavor to acquire a footing in India is not, therefore, improbable. It is absolutely impossible to say that she entertains such a design at the present moment. Her past relations with England have not indeed been of a perfectly satisfactory or assuring nature. But it cannot be forgotten that England has herself done much from time to time to draw Russia into a position of apparent antagonism which she has never probably desired to take up. Whether, however, she cherishes a militant policy or not, it is perfectly clear from what has been said above regarding the economic needs of her extensive empire and the strange tendencies working in her foremost minds that an invasion of India by her at some future time is not an absolute impossibility—nay rather, is something like a moral certainty.

English liberals consider the great deserts of Central Asia to be a crushing obstacle in the way of Russia. But foreign invaders of India from Alexander the Great to Ahmed Shah Abdali have proved that arguments based upon mountains and deserts do not and cannot possess overpowering force. Human power has accomplished feats more difficult and daring than Russia's march to India over the deserts of Central Asia and the mountains of Afghanistan would in all likelihood be.

It is also argued on the side of the liberals and by writers with liberal sympathies that if Russia had really been actuated by aggressive instincts, she could have by this time annexed China to her empire. The great Cobden is said to have used an argument like this. But it seems to us to contain two errors. If Russia is not aggressive, why is she just now in Central Asia? As regards China, it may be observed that there are superstitions in war as much as in religion. And history proves that India has been an object of attraction to great minds of all times and countries—to travelers, philosophers, historians and soldiers. Somehow or other, great warriors have at all times considered it very much more glorious to conquer India than to conquer China or any other country in Asia. . . .

It is also forgotten by writers on the liberal side, that to a great power, determined to achieve a great conquest, India with her innumerable nationalities divided from each other by all that can divide nations as well as individuals, would in all probability appear very much more practicable than the vast empire of China inhabited by a wonderfully homogeneous population, obstinately fond of their independence and isolation and possessing as it were one mysterious heart, one mysterious will and one mysterious pulse. Of two populations so differently composed, the one that is heterogeneous and accustomed to foreign domination will not only yield sooner but be easier to govern than the one which is so perfectly homogeneous and possessed of a sense of national freedom marvelously intensified by a historic memory as old as the earliest human settler on the earth. Soldiers, moreover, love glory; and there is certainly greater glory in snatching a prize from a powerful competitor than in achieving a conquest alone and unchallenged on an uncontested field.

The present emperor of Russia is often pointed to by writers on the liberal side as a convincing refutation of the theories advanced on the Conservative side. We have not the smallest doubt that emperor Alexander is one of the best of sovereigns, and a sincere lover of peace. But Russia and its emperor are two distinct things, and the will of the former generally prevails over that of the latter. Besides the emperor is but an individual who may any day make room for a ruler with strong warlike instincts. And the political constitution of the Russian empire provides no guarantee for the maintenance of a policy of perpetual peace.

What, then, should England do?—quarrel with Russia? Certainly not. Russia, it may be safely assumed, has now no intention of coming to India; and even if she had, her exhaustion in the late war in Europe would undoubtedly incapacitate her for some time from engaging in a great military enterprise. But although exhausted, she has certainly power and vitality enough to undertake an expedition of the kind which England has sent into Afghanistan. And the result of a collision of this kind between England and Russia is not very likely to be favorable or complimentary to the former power. . . . All the world now sees that England has no army fit to be arrayed against the gigantic battalions of Russia. Her recent wars in the Cape and in Abyssinia have served only to bring out the weakness and inefficiency of her soldiers and generals, and the much-vaunted operations in Afghanistan are not regarded by anyone outside of the official cliques in England and India as affording anything like a satisfactory proof of a good army organisation. . . .

The fact is, of all European powers, England alone has outlived the military and long since entered upon the industrial stage of national life. England's geographical situation and her peculiar social and political development have weakened her military instincts, and nothing proves this more clearly than the influence of Manchester on both English and Anglo-Indian politics. There can be no doubt that European civilisation, in general, will go on gravitating towards industrialism. But the continental nations of Europe have had their interests mixed up with each other so closely and in such diverse forms almost from the time of the dissolution of the Roman empire, that they have been compelled and will be compelled for many years to come to stick to the military system of life for a perfect disentanglement of their respective interests. England has never been, however, so organically involved in the general European system, and she has been, therefore, able not only to work out her social problems alone and unhampered, but to make more rapid strides in civilisation than continental Europe. It is for this reason that England is now ahead of the other nations of Europe and therefore not in mental harmony with the great continental system. If she chooses to deal or come in contact with that system, she must, therefore, retrace her steps, cultivate the military instinct, and become the first-class military power that she had been in the age of her Edwards and Henrys.

It is clear from what has been said above that England has very little option left to her in this matter; because the probabilities are really very heavy of a collision between her and Russia for the sake of India. In addition to the causes at work in Russia itself, writers on the liberal side may be requested to consider whether causes are not at work in India itself, which may turn towards India eyes that are now probably looking in other directions for wealth and glory. England has failed to secure the love of her Indian subjects, and if the English administration in India goes on in the fashion it is now going on, the discontent that already exists in the country may assume a form which an essentially military power like Russia may feel tempted to regard as an opportunity. It is clear, therefore, that England would be wrong in thinking, as many of her liberal writers and statesmen seem to do, that she has nothing to fear from Russia. English liberals need only bear this in mind and take measures accordingly, and England shall remain safe and sound. The conservatives, though in the right line of political forecast, have taken a morbidly exaggerated view of the whole question, and accordingly adopted a policy which, if adhered to, will absolutely ruin England and her glorious Indian Empire. They take no note of the present condition of England and they are taking measures in relation to

Afghanistan which may involve them in a conflict with Russia, the result of which, if not entirely ruinous to England, would be in all probability fatal to her prestige in Europe and Asia.

In our humble opinion, England's best policy now and for some time to come would be to revert, if practicable, to the policy of "masterly inactivity" so long pursued by her with reference to Afghanistan, to cultivate the friendship of Russia with the view of securing a permanent alliance with her, and at the same time to reorganize and increase her military power in order that she may not be found wanting in the event of an unprovoked invasion of her Indian Empire by Russia. The military reorganization is likely to be impeded by two causes—the unwillingness of most liberal statesmen to believe that India can be at any time invaded by Russia, and, secondly, the unwillingness of the English people to submit to military service on anything like compulsory terms.

The first cause is likely to prove less powerful than the second. There are men in the Liberal ranks who do not think with Mr. Gladstone that Russia is an "innocent lamb" morally incapable of cherishing hostile designs against England. . . . But the prospect is not so clear as regards the second cause. For there the difficulty lies not in leading individual minds but in the mind of the whole English nation. We do not mean that Englishmen have lost their national valor or patriotism. But we do think that the long reign of English industrialism has weakened the military instincts of the English people and changed their ideal of valor and patriotism. But we have confidence enough in Mr. Gladstone's power over the genuine English mind to hope that this very difficult question too will sooner or later meet with a satisfactory solution at the hands of a liberal ministry animated by his marvelous patriotic enthusiasm. We now only hope that the Beaconsfield cabinet, which has so signally failed to represent England and its truest interests, will fall and make room for the adoption of a safe, sound, and truly English policy in regard to Russia and Afghanistan by the great Gladstone and his mighty phalanx of patriotic colleagues.

WHY DO INDIANS PREFER BRITISH TO RUSSIAN RULE?, 1885
British Indian Association

1. Because the English are the freest and the most liberty-loving people in the world, while the Russians are the slaves of a military caste.

2. Because the aim of British rule in India is to elevate and educate the Indian people to an equality with the English nation; while the mass of the Russian people themselves is still kept, to a great extent, in a deplorable state of ignorance and slavery by the ruling military caste.

3. Because the principles of British rule in India, as authoritatively declared, are liberal and generous, laid down by some of the noblest sons of Britain—men like Lord Cornwallis, Lord Bentinck, Mountstuart Elphinstone, Sir Munro, Lord Macaulay, Sir Metcalfe, Lord Canning—and are intended to raise the Indian people, and not to crush them down; while the iron yoke of Russia is crushing not only to the races it has conquered, as those of the Caucasus, and of Upper and Central Asia, but to the mass of its own subjects.

4. Because the *Pax Britannica* has, for the first time in recent days, afforded that opportunity for national advance and improvement which in the divisions and distractions that preceded the advent of British rule it was almost hopeless to secure.

5. Because the English people have generously established schools and colleges in India, and appointed professors to teach to the Indians all those arts and sciences which have raised England to glory and prosperity; while the Russians are suppressing their own colleges, and expelling youths from the national universities. The Russian dominant caste is afraid of light and knowledge, and would suppress everywhere all places of learning, if it could.

6. Because the British have given a free press to India, with the result that that press is already growing into a power; while the Russian government shackles its own native press, to curb which it has a highly organized press department, with its "Press" and "Censure" committees, its "Third Section," its "Preliminary" and "Subsequent" censorship, ruthlessly suppressing even the slightest expression of free and independent opinion upon its acts.

7. Because the English rulers of India deliberately seek light, and officially invite the freest criticism of their acts and measures; while the Russian bureaucracy does everything in the dark, and shuns and suppresses public criticism.

8. Because the British government admits the natives of the country to a share of power in local Administrative Boards, in Legislative Councils, and in the general civil service of the country.

9. Because, while Russian militarism has converted the students of its own colleges and universities into nihilists, ready to blow up their rulers, the Indian colleges, established by the English in this country, are yearly turning out educated and enlightened men and scholars, who most fully appreciate English rule,

are most loyal and devoted subjects of Her Gracious Majesty, ready to fight her battles, and are at the same time the most earnest reformers of their country.

10. Because it is under the benign influence of English rule, that the signs of a slow awakening of national life are seen in India for the first time in its modern history, and the continuance of the existing contact with the free and great people of the United Kingdom is expected further to train the Indian nation in the paths of national regeneration.

11. Because it is the deepest and the firmest conviction of every educated Indian that not Russia, but England, in spite of all the shortcomings, aye, and all the serious defects of its rule, is the champion of liberty, and the friend and sympathizer of subject nations.

12. Because, to sum up, the Indians appreciate English liberty, English justice, and English progressiveness, and they do not wish to exchange these good things for the Russian system of military aggression abroad and official repression at home.

The moral, therefore, is that England should never attempt, even in an indirect way, to take a leaf out of Russia's book.

RUSSIA, INDIA AND AFGHANISTAN, 1886
Dinshah Ardeshir Taleyarkhan

... It must be admitted that Russia could not have satisfied itself with its march through the wilds of Central Asia, without pushing on the confines of wealthy empires, thus rendering its influence felt. Hitherto it had struggled to conquer insignificant little States, though possessed of warlike material. Having secured these States, it now lies, or will at no very distant date lie, side by side with the leading powers in Lower Asia, and especially with the Paramount Power ruling our own country. That Russia has ever considered England an inconvenient thorn by its side in both Asiatic and European countries, and that, therefore, it has been fast descending upon the northern and north-west confines of India, can admit of no doubt. Unless England feels strong and supplants it in the neighbourhood, where it makes its stealthy marches, both Afghanistan and Persia must come below its thumb. Russia has hitherto had a good deal to fear from England. Russia has known this to its cost on several occasions, such as what it had to suffer at Crimea and the check which it received more recently in Turkey.

It seems to have moved its chessboard in another direction altogether, having failed elsewhere for the last quarter of a century. But we must view its movements towards this part of the world from another standpoint. . . .

What we, the princes and people of India, have to look to is—these near possessions of mighty powers do not form, in course of time, a mine of gunpowder underneath us, doing the teeming populations of India incalculable mischief. We shall be content to have the Russian bear as near us as may be desirable, but do not wish to see the Bear and the Lion converting the fair regions of the earth into a battlefield. We shall be glad to remain at peace with Russia, and even encourage its merchandise, but we should certainly resent its interference with our relations with the British power. Let it approach us as a kindly neighbour, but its evil eye on our peace and prosperity and our smooth-going civilization we shall damn with all our might and resolve. . . .

Of all the political questions now affecting the condition of India, that of the reported design of Russia on India is most important, deserving of the utmost consideration of all in India. The patriots of the country are parading their various grievances, in which they are not altogether wrong. If, however, they did so after fully satisfying us that they have understood the Russo-Perso-Afghan question, and that they do not think it need cause any anxiety to India, we should not blame them. But we do blame them for their want of foresight and for their tendency to waste their precious time in wholly devoting themselves to minor internal affairs, while we are not sure as to the forces now working in our foreign relations, which may or may not disturb the whole country eventually. The question of the Empire's safety does not rest in the hands of one political party in England, nor is influenced by any solitary or local considerations. To be sure of the permanent peace of India, we must not only be sure of the adequacy of our own Imperial and feudatories' forces, but of the good faith of our several Eastern neighbours and of the powerful States in Europe and Asia, who have so much to do with our parent country and its dependencies. We should like to have the name of *one* native of India directly or indirectly engaged in dealing with Indian problems, who may have influenced the public mind in a practical manner in reference to this question of the most serious import.

What our public men have to do is to persuade the Government in England to explain how India need not be anxious as to the sufficiency of the

British and Native military strength to cope with any amount of force which Russia may possibly amass on the Herat, Kabul, or any other sides of India. We have some of the highest Indian authorities declaring in the strongest terms that if Russia chose to descend upon the plains of India, British India cannot count upon even half of the military force requisite to repel it. It is a sad commentary on the doings of native patriots of India that Englishmen should seem to perceive dangers of the highest magnitude to this country, while the former have as yet failed to gain any practical idea about them. . . .

Does even a patriot of India dread what is possible to happen to our country a few years or a quarter of a century hence? The whole might of patriotism is exerted to get a handful of natives of India admitted into the civil service, to secure the free talk of another handful of us in the local municipal boards, or to force half-a-dozen native orators into the Government Councils and the British Parliament. We would move heaven and earth if the rights and privileges of landholders are questioned, or even if a sentimental grievance can be made out for the impoverished *ryot*, or an Englishman has insulted or maltreated a native.

I do not for one moment mean to say that the work performed by our patriots in India is generally such as we can afford to disregard. It is one in which the most capable and the wisest of statesmen and politicians are not unfrequently compelled to be warmly interested. All I mean to maintain is that while they profusely employ their energies in getting comparatively unimportant matters mended, they have as yet not been able even to perceive the sources of such probable dangers to India as might someday make short work of the lesser aspirations by which they are now so entirely controlled. We should all see that while learning the alphabets of patriotism as it were, we do not fail to realize the serious events now in rapid progress, which, if not practically dealt with, may land us in national disasters that may forever seal the fate of India, which now can even hope, and strongly too, to be a free and prosperous country in future. I have said that our country can now fairly hope to be a free country at some future day. But adieu to this bright hope—which Great Britain has lighted in our breasts—if ever India was trampled under the iron heels of the hungry and wily Cossacks. . . .

I cannot admit any person in India to be a faithful and a wise patriot unless he keenly feels the humiliation and disgrace now attached to his country, which Russia has covertly dared to menace. . . . I question further anyone who wishes to answer me, what number of effective naval and land forces will be available for the undoubted defence of India, should there gradually ensue a general conflagration of war in both Europe and Asia? We must not be found unprepared for any day of trouble and danger. India must somehow or other be made capable of punishing her wrongdoer herself, if possible without necessarily relying upon any great foreign help. Every patriotic prince, every patriotic subject of the Queen, whether British or Native, should exert in bringing about the reorganization and increase of our various forces. We must all call upon our Government to declare the maximum strength that would be indispensable for the Indian Empire and for the full protection of its open ports on any day of emergency; to devise measures for an increase in the imperial armies by measures of economy and investigations into the sources of various funds, used and unused; to assemble the provincial Indo-British councils and provincial native administrations with a view to ascertain the respective shares they bear in the local and general military needs of the Empire, and to recast these shares according to the means, preoccupations and extent of each administration; to fix upon the limits and manner of reductions in, or additions to, the land forces and naval strength of each of the Indian administrations, the principles of arranging the mixture of various elements of the forces of the different provinces and states, both locally and in times of war, being also settled; to determine upon the responsibility and share of Great Britain in applying these permanent measures of safety in the interests of her Empire; to fix upon a prompt method of carrying out the reforms, as may be thus settled, in each of the states and provinces; to frame a charter under which the princes, noblemen, and the ordinary subjects in India could reasonably aspire after occupying high military posts and a certain number of them, and those particularly selected, could find an immediate entrance into the military academies of England and the military services in India, the creation of such academies in India being also considered with a view to take immediate action thereat.

One may now be inclined to ask, why have the public men in India failed to request the Government to look after securing the full military strength of the Empire? I would at once reply that we have given no proof that we have understood our gravest want, our sole ambition being to call out for reductions in the military as also other public expenditures of the country.

Its growing expenditures have no doubt caused us anxiety, but the failure in grappling with the difficulty is shown in the absence of the method to be adopted in obtaining the reduction of those expenditures which legitimately call for a reduction. The failure, again, is evidenced in perceiving what expenditures, and in what directions, they need to be enhanced in an urgent manner, and what are the sources of revenue which ought to be tapped for obtaining the further funds essentially required. The policy with which we have waged our battles with the Government has been as unsound as it has proved eminently misleading. All our halcyon of security and prosperity for the country is embodied in reductions of military expenses and of the public taxes levied which we have advocated on every conceivable occasion. . . . I would ask my fellow-patriots whether they would prefer the least chance of being subject to a bloody revolution in consequence of a universal sanguinary war, or pinch themselves a little more than now with financial burdens which may at least serve to prevent violent disorders in India and a re-awakening of the terrible feuds and jealousies of old, which must upset every kingdom and drain it entirely of the resources left after the telling changes already passed through.

The public sense in India as to the fighting strength and the money reserves it should command would be ludicrous, if it were not tending towards disasters which would take one century to mend, once they were allowed to take place. Our patriots do not dream of creating a united materially powerful India on the basis I have pointed out, because they have somehow or other held to the belief that the military strength of India can even be curtailed; that the public taxation must be absolutely reduced, and not enhanced; and that the integrity of the Native States should not be touched, as if an advocacy like mine would for a moment mean that any state should be burdened with an extra farthing if it already has any force commensurate with its capacity.

When I consider the position of the Government, I deplore that it is only a little more hopeful than what the present condition of the leaders has brought about. The Government of India cannot initiate any large measure unless with the hearty co-operation of the India Office and the British Parliament. The party differences of the Government of England operate too strongly against any vigorous and far-seeing Viceroy daring to adopt a broad and independent measure of the kind India so badly needs today. We cannot expect very serious attention being paid to the question I have here touched under the temporising foreign policy of England's party administrations. . . . It is hence my emphatic opinion that the ordinary and princely leaders should unite in pressing the Government to solve our naval and military difficulties in a comprehensive and national sense so that every member and every community of the Indian Empire may patriotically contribute to our fighting strength, and each of the many national divisions of our Empire may take pride and glory in becoming its actual bulwark of strength and contributing to the stability of the Queen's benign predominance in the East. . . . I therefore earnestly implore my countrymen no more to neglect the most vital question in which their dearest interests and aspirations are immediately involved. . . .

THE NATIVE INDIAN ARMY—REFORM OR INCREASE?, 1886
G. V. Joshi

The question of Indian Native Army reform, though it cannot be ranked as one of the most burning public questions of the day, is none the less a question of vital importance to the highest interests of the country. . . . It is true that it had not hitherto received its due measure of consideration either from the native press, or from native associations; but recent events have necessarily forced this subject upon general attention, and it is time, we think, to invite the native public to a calm and dispassionate discussion of it, with a view to arrive at a workable scheme of definite reform, which might be made the basis of a common and unanimous appeal to the responsible authorities.

Approaching the question on its constitutional side, we may safely lay down the position that the Indian nation has a right to ask—(1) that the Native Army, which is in truth the very back-bone of its whole military system, and on whose loyalty and honest devotion to the British flag in the last resort, Government must depend as a provision against internal disturbance or foreign attack, should in its constitution be really a *national* army, an army of the Indian nation and not solely, or even principally, a mercenary one; (2) that the numbers and proportion of different branches of this army should be placed on a thoroughly sound footing with due regard to the needs and changing circumstances of the country, regarded both as an Asiatic government, and as a loyal dependency of the British empire; (3) that it should be maintained in a healthy state of efficiency, possessing a sufficient degree of elastic and recuperative vigour, able to withstand all danger, and equal to any exigency; and (4) that at the same time it should be administered as economically as possible, in other words, at a charge compatible with the poor condition of our national and financial resources. . . .

We have to take note on the one hand of (1) the inevitable effects of the Arms Acts in demartialising the entire population of the peninsula, and thereby striking at the root of all military self-reliance and internal defensive strength of the country, and (2) of the equally inevitable results of a regime of peace in inducing a general disinclination to military life, and a love of peaceful pursuits, even amongst the once famous military classes of the community; and on the other, we must note (1) the tendencies of the military situation in Asia, and (2) the rapidly-gathering clouds of trouble and difficulties on our North-West and Eastern frontiers, consequent on closer contact with populations, divided from us by deep differences of race and creed, of thought and sentiment, and particularly with that large zone of Mohammedan fanaticism, zone of highly excitable and explosive material, which (to quote the impressive language of Lord Salisbury's speech at the Lord Mayor's Banquet), "is always electrically charged, out of which thunder-storms may with but little notice proceed." . . .

The present state and constitution of the Native Army are thus a most important and pressing subject of legitimate inquiry. Its importance is not a whit diminished just now, because we are ostentatiously invited to dismiss from our minds all timid fears and weak anxieties on the point, and called upon to pay the Income-tax, and trust in loyal confidence in the all-seeing and all-wise omnipotence of Government to fore-see and provide against all possible human contingencies. Unfortunately, the people of India are not children to believe that an addition of some 30,000 men to the standing army of the country, carried out at a charge of two or three crores of Rupees raised by unpopular fresh taxation, would make for us quite an impregnable tower of strength unassailable, if not inaccessible, either on the side of the Indus or of the Ravi. The very vehemence of these most comfortable and gratifying assurances which are vouchsafed to us defeats their end, and makes even the credulous, seldom-suspecting, seldom-doubting public opinion of India rather suspicious on the point, and people are tempted to ask whether the whole thing can be so easily and charmingly managed.... It is much to be regretted that the public is not in possession of full or detailed information on the subject, but the broad features of the system as it exists are clear and open to our view, and we are grievously mistaken if a close analysis of them, especially in the light of the more recent developments of the situation, does not disclose a state of things, as far as the Native Army is concerned, such as to excite the gravest misgivings even in the minds of the most credulous optimists, and to justify a demand for a thorough, radical, and comprehensive reform.

Our Native Army stands, we suspect, at this day in all its essential elements of numbers, organization, and management, on precisely the same footing, on which it was placed after the Mutinies of 1857–58.... The main object which the military authorities had then in view was, how best to disarm the revolted soldiery, and make similar risings impossible in the future. This purpose and *raison d'être* not only do no longer exist, but on the other hand the source of danger has shifted elsewhere and requires all available internal strength to be utilized and knit together to ward it off. Self-complacent official optimism is, however, still swayed by the influences of an unworthy military policy of jealousy, distrust and suspicion, adopted with some show of justification immediately after the Mutinies, but for which no decent excuse can now be pleaded.... They only admit the inadequacy of its present numerical strength to meet the new requirements of frontier defence, and recommend addition to that strength as the simplest, the best and the most obvious solution of the problem; and Government seems resolved—though it has not yet thought fit to vouchsafe to the bewildered public those considerations of high policy which have led it to the resolution—to carry out this recommendation of military experts, which seems to accord so well with suggestions of its own mind....

It is our firm conviction that the whole existing military organization of the country, at least as far as the Native Army is concerned, is not what it ought to be, and requires a thorough over hauling. No merely arithmetical manipulation of the standing army of the country can furnish any solid or safe basis on which to found the true solution of the military difficulty.... Believing, as we firmly do, that the *sine qua non* of an efficient system of national defence is the soundness of its organization, and distrusting all schemes of arithmetical additions, what we ask for is a candid and honest revision and re-casting of the present arrangements, with a view to secure *reform* in the first place, and thereafter *increase* of numbers, if imperative necessity be shown to exist. "Reform the Native Army first, and increase it next if necessary"—sums up our own view of the matter.

Let us then see how the Native Army at present stands. We shall begin by examining first its composition. Here we find still in force the same vicious principle of state-craft—"Divide and rule," which was in such high favour with the military authorities of the Mutiny period. The present policy of recruiting for the army is the same old alien and jealous policy of putting together, by way of mutual check and balance, opposing nationalities, conflicting castes, and antagonistic races, and we fear if there has been any change in this respect, it is all, as far as we can see, for the worse, certainly not for the better. . . . Only last summer we saw, how in the anxieties of a threatening crisis of a serious nature on the North-Western frontier, the Government of India, with perfect confidence, and without the least hesitation, turned to Nepal and Sikkim for fresh drafts of recruits for the new battalions it wished to form. . . . Men are picked up wherever they can be found, in the country or outside it, and from whatever class, with a single eye to breadth of chest and height of stature, and the commanding officers are satisfied if they get into their respective battalions, men of the broadest chest and the tallest stature, no matter from what field they come, from Patagonia if they will, and do not further trouble themselves, and with reason as military officers, with any political considerations of State policy. . . .

Here is then, one of the most crying evils of our present system, which is doing a world of harm to our Native Army, and reform therefore, we respectfully submit, must begin here if anywhere. Our Native Army must be our own national army, ours in something more than a name. Its ranks should be filled up by none other than Indian races. It should reflect in its composition and characters the varied elements of the nation, its spirit, its loyalty, its aptitudes, and even, we would venture to add, its idiosyncrasies. . . . The material instincts of our military classes, as far as they are still alive and have been not extinguished by the effects of the Arms Act, should be turned to account by cautious encouragement, developed with care, and utilized by prudent arrangements for the purposes of national defence, and this cannot be surely beyond the resources of military statesmanship. . . .

The second fatal fault of the existing system appears to us to be the purely mercenary basis on which our Native Army has come to rest. . . . We fear, particularly looking to the new method of recruitment above referred to, men join the army less and less through prompting of noble ambition to serve the Queen Empress and their country, and share in the honors and toils of the service, and more and more, as time goes by, through the pressure of necessity and in search of bread. . . . But, on the other hand, the better classes stand aloof; all the higher prizes of the service lie beyond the reach of native ambition, and the existing system of pay and promotion for the native sepoy offer to them no sufficient inducements to enter the army. There are no honorary commissions in the army to attract into its ranks members of the military aristocracy of the country. The practical effect is that our native army is gradually deteriorating in quality from a moral, if not from a physical, point of view. . . .

The military dangers, in the hour of trial, of such a mercenary feeling getting firmly rooted in the soldier's mind, and growing deep and wide in the army, are too obvious to call for remark, and this circumstance of itself should suffice to convince sceptics of the radical unsoundness, even from a military point of view, of a system that gives rise to such apprehensions, and make them reasonable. But the political danger of such a mercenary basis of our whole organization is more serious still. . . . If the evil be once admitted and recognized, the line of reform is clear, and the remedy is obvious. . . . In one word, every effort should be made to get for the army picked men from the higher and more intelligent and independent classes of the community. . . .

We now pass on to a third feature of our existing military system. . . . Our whole military organization stands at present exclusively on the basis of a "standing" army—which forms, so to speak, the beginning, the middle, and end of the system. It has no reserve, and no support in the country of any kind to fall back upon. Such an army organization stands alone, we believe, without example in the modern world; and surely nothing can be opposed to the whole theory and practice of modern European nations, including England herself. We may go further, and venture to add that in our former history, such a standing army never existed in India. . . . After the Mutinies of 1857–58, however, this condition of things underwent a most momentous change. . . . The general disarmament of the country was carried out as a necessary measure of pacification and permanent security against internal disorder and disturbance, the old native armies of annexed States were disbanded, and the old military aristocracy of the nation was allowed, in British and Native territory, quietly to pass into the general body of the peaceful population. . . .

We have no intention to exaggerate the inherent evils and inseparable dangers of such an army organization; but we must take leave to be skeptical about its theoretical soundness or practical adequacy to meet the needs of the times. . . . We cannot believe that in a serious straggle on the North-Western or on the Eastern frontiers with a formidable military power, we can safely count on obtaining needful supplies of drilled or seasoned men from across ten thousand miles of sea. . . . In the face of these considerations, people very naturally doubt the wisdom of the prevailing arrangements in India that neglect to provide guarantees for safety by timely measures of reform against such a possible, if not a probable, contingency, and seem to take refuge in a "makeshift" addition by which no permanent advantage can be secured, but which will only entail a serious charge on the poor resources of the country. . . . A good reserve and a good militia are indispensable to our military defence, and this necessity demands, we submit, candid recognition at the hands of our responsible authorities. . . .

Now, as to the practical question, how to form such a reserve and militia, opinions may differ, and various schemes may be suggested. But there is one important factor which we cannot overlook in the consideration of this problem—we mean, the condition of the national finances; and no plan could stand any chance of being seriously considered which ignored this essential element and looked only to the military side of the question. Any feasible project that may be recommended must satisfy the condition that it does not compel a resort to intolerable taxation. On this point our ideas are briefly these: as far as the creation of a reserve is concerned, the end, we think, can be in a large measure attained without much additional expenditure, if a plan be devised by which the armies of our Native States . . . can be utilized for the purpose. . . . The disciplined portions of these armies might be drafted into the reserves, and the undisciplined levies might safely be incorporated into the national militia.

The incorporation of these armies with the defensive system of the Empire has a political and moral value of its own, which cannot be over-estimated. But even from a military point of view, the gain would be by no means small. In point of mere physique and moral fiber, these native armies are fully equal, certainly not much inferior, to the Indian native army, and if equally well-drilled and armed, there can be no shadow of doubt that they would prove equally efficient, as component parts of our Imperial army. . . . Thus, the incorporation of both these armies (English and Native), now suffered to waste their strength in a useless round of jealous watchings, with the general military system of the Empire, will be a most valuable reform in the right direction, and the moral effect of utilizing the native armies in the way suggested above would simply be invaluable, as it would confer on the whole military organisation of the Indian Empire the character it sadly lacks at present, we mean, a really *national* character.

As regards the national militia, we do not see our way very clearly towards its reconstruction, but we believe something might be achieved in this direction if the strictness of the Arms Act were relieved, and every encouragement held out to the people to act as volunteers. Certain precautions would be of course necessary at the first start, and the progress must be slow. But the whole arrangement can be carried out, we think, with much ease, at little cost, and with very great gain. . . . [The] exclusion of the native element from the volunteer system of the country is in our judgment unfair and impolitic, and furnishes a legitimate ground of complaint on the part of the intelligent classes of the community. It seems to cast an undeserved slur on the loyalty of the people, and creates feelings of suspicion and distrust where they ought not to exist, and gives rise to false and unfavourable impressions in foreign countries, near and remote, regarding the relations between the rulers and ruled in India. . . .

In conclusion, we would most earnestly beseech the consideration of Government to the point, whether, in dealing with this most vital question of Army reform, the time has not arrived for the adoption of a more liberal policy of "trust in the people" in military matters than has hitherto prevailed. A truly generous recognition of the loyal sentiments of the nation, and a statesmanlike appreciation of the military and political necessities of the new situation with which we are now called upon to deal, seem to us to call loudly for a change of policy. For our own part, while fully recognizing the fact that foreign rulers cannot afford to forget the fact of conquest, we must express our deep and strong conviction that a comprehensive *reform* in the Army organisation on lines suggested above is in the interests of both rulers and ruled, at once both more desirable and safe than an *arithmetical addition* to the existing numbers of the standing army, and if financial considerations are allowed their due weight, such a reform is the only alternative open to Government.

For, it is no use to forget that the whole question has a financial aspect, though, for obvious reasons, we have not touched upon it in the foregoing pages. Our Army budget is already ruinously heavy, and to judge from the remarks of Sir Colvin in the Financial Statement of March last, these army charges might possibly swell, in case, "apprehensions" therein fore-shadowed, "of fresh demands for further increase" in the military esti-mates, should be realized. This is a feature which Government cannot with safety ignore, for economy is the true key of sound finance, and must not be neglected in the military, any more than in the other branches of the public service. Our Army expenditure has gone up by leaps and bounds during the last 20 years of profound internal peace, from 15 ½ millions in 1865 to close upon 21 million in 1885—a charge on our "resources" already larger by no less than 6 million per annum, than the corresponding charge on the exchequer for the British army. In fact, it appears to be the largest military charge borne by any civilized country in the world, if we only except France; for on comparison we find that, while we have to pay for our mili-tary establishments more than 21 million a year, the German army costs in round figures £18,800,000, the French army about £22,800,000, the Italian Army about £7,300,000, the Austro-Hungarian army about £14,000,000, including the cost of the local militia, the Russian army about £19,000,000, while the United States army costs not more than £8,000,000. The cost of the English army itself, including the Reserve and Voluntary Forces, does not go higher than 19 million. And yet though we bear ungrudgingly and unmurmuringly a *maximum* outlay on account of the Army, as compared with the other civilized nations of the globe, we are compelled, under our present system of organisation and management, to be content with a min-imum of effective forces. For the whole of our Army, European and Native, maintained at a cost of 21 million, shows a total of men and officers not larger than 189,597—a strength manifestly inadequate to the growing necessities—internal and external—of the Indian Empire, and one which is, besides, utterly *incapable of expansion* in the hour of need for the pur-pose either of offence or defence, except by a resort to wasteful recruitment, or drafts on the English Reserve 10,000 miles away. The European nations can, in consequence of the excellence of their organisation, raise their armies at short notice to any required strength to meet the demands of national defence. For the sums above mentioned, Germany keeps an army of 420,000 men on the peace-footing, with an organisation capable of raising it to 1,300,000 in time of war; France, an army of 500,000 men, which may be increased in the hour of necessity to a total of 2 million; Italy an army of about 200,000 men, without reserves, capable of being raised to about 4,500,000; Russia, an army of nearly 800,000 men in peace, and 1,200,000 more in time of war; and Austria-Hungary an army of 270,000, capable of raising its numbers in time of war to nearly 800,000; while with our military outlay of 21 million and more, we cannot raise our army, in the hour of need and peril, even by a single battalion of seasoned soldiers, except by importation from England! This is, in our judgement, an awful fact which we must not shirk looking fully in the face. A system of army organisation—so inexcusable and dangerously inefficient, and so ruinously and extravagantly expensive—cannot certainly be described as sound and economical, and if we wish to have an efficient and economically managed army for purposes of national defence, a reform of our present system seems imperatively called for. Any addition to our present military strength, consequent on the contemplated increase of the standing Army, if unaccompanied by improvement of the system, would be sheer waste of money and resources, against which the Indian taxpayer, we submit, has a right to protest.

INDIAN MILITARY EXPENDITURE, 1891
Dinshaw E. Wacha

... In my speech at the First Congress, I submitted ample evidence of the growth of the military expenditure as culled from official Blue Books and dispatches. So I will not detain you by reciting them here. Suffice to say that, between 1864 and 1885, they had increased by five crores. Since the days of the Second Afghan War, of unhappy memory, there has been no limit to that growth. If you ask me the reason of it, I will say that it is the imperial policy of Great Britain, which is annually entailing on the poor people of India sacrifices which they are absolutely unable to bear, but which they do bear, all the same, silently, and with a sullen discontent. It is the policy of England in her relations with the politics of Central and Eastern Europe— the policy which leads to complications now and again with Turkey and

Russia, and other great European Powers—which unhappily leads to military activity or military "preparedness," so called in this country, entailing crores of wasteful expenditure. . . .

The Russian game is to gain as far as possible a footing on the banks of the Bosphorus, while England tries to thwart her in that desire. As a consequence, the former tries, whenever occasion offers, to threaten England in Central Asia. But, while Russia idly threatens us, the military tax eaters at Shimla, who eagerly pant for promotions, decorations, and kudos besides, do not leave a stone unturned, under one pretext or another, to push forward what is euphemistically called the "scientific frontier"—a visionary frontier leading nowhere, but ever plunging the country into greater and greater financial embarrassments. Scares are manufactured which could never be substantiated, and while this sort of manufactured panic is designedly created among us, they push on new schemes having for their object nothing but the conquest of wild border tribes, the despoiling them of their territories, the bribing of the recalcitrant with British rupees, and so forth. They thus carry on a warfare of external aggression under the hollow pretense of defending India against so-called attacks from without. From what I have stated you will no doubt be able to understand the import of the intense activity going on on our North-Western frontier borders since 1885, and the rapid construction of forts, bridges, and so-called strategical railways. There is a whole history of these scares and scientific frontiers, but which it is impossible for me to unfold before you on this occasion.

So I now pass on to the question of actual expenditure itself since 1885. That year was indeed a calamitous year for India. For it was the year which witnessed the forcible seizure of Upper Burma, which brought an additional step in the peerage to the Earl of Dufferin, the then Viceroy. At the First Congress we deprecated that seizure as iniquitous and unrighteous; and if you read between the lines all that has been stated in the Blue Books on this conquest, you will be fully convinced that the Congress was justified in condemning those proceedings. . . . Well, gentlemen, it was the Viceroyalty of Lord Dufferin which led to the increase of 30,000 additional troops (10,000 English and 20,000 Native), saddling India with a permanent expenditure of another two crores. It was this Viceroyalty which laid the foundation of those financial embarrassments, the consequences of which are to be seen in the enhanced duty on salt and the re-introduction of the income-tax of nearly sixpence farthing in the pound.

How fruitful are these embarrassments for evil may be further perceived in the larger amounts which India had annually to remit to England for the army services, effective and non-effective. When it is remembered that, on an average, we remit four million sterling on this account, or just one-fourth of the whole amount of the bills annually sold by the Secretary of State for India, it will be evident how much heavier this loss becomes with every fall, even of one farthing, in the exchangeable value of the rupee. But the increase is not only on account of additional troops; though it is a fact that, inclusive of the army services in Upper Burma since 1885–86, the additional burden laid on the taxpayers is equal to twenty-four crores. There are again the expenses for special defence works, strategical railways, so-called punitive expeditions, mobilization of the frontier army corps, transport service, new arms and ammunition, and so forth. It would be tiresome to treat you to a formidable table of statistics; but if you would only turn to the pages of the current financial statement under the head of "Army," you would find all the details stated. I will, however, summarize these figures for you. Thus:

	Rs.
1. Increased Army Expenditure since 1885–86	24,220,000
2. Special defence works to date	3,770,000
3. Strategic Railways to date	7,500,000
4. Frontier Expeditions to date	1,320,000
5. Upper Burma Military Expenses	10,020,000
Total	46,830,000

Add:	Rs.
6. Special defence works, balance to complete	1,230,000
7. Strategic railways yet to be completed	4,000,000
Grand Total	52,060,000

I do not think, however, that the limit of the military expenditure will be reached when the special defences are completed and the additional railways, now under construction, are built; neither do I believe, gentlemen, that Upper Burma will ever become a paying province. My fear is that there are many troubles still to be overcome there. But the Government is reckless. It is trying to heap on itself more troubles in that direction, while it is madly endeavouring to push the Eastern frontier to the very gates of Yunnan. You have but little idea of the difficulties beyond Bhamo; while the fixed intention of the

Government is to penetrate the southernmost and fertile province of China, in obedience to the call of pious Manchester for the sale of the products of its spindles and looms. Remember, gentlemen, this may soon bring the Indian Government into collision with China. And I need not again describe to you what a Chinese war in that direction may mean. It will be as disastrous and sanguinary as was the Second Afghan War or the war of the French with the people of Tonkin a few short years ago. You will thus perceive what possible embarrassments there loom in the near future for unhappy India. While your net land revenue is increasing during the last few years at the slow rate of twenty-five lakhs per annum, the net military expenditure is growing at the rate of fifty-one lakhs or at double the pace.

The *ryot* is bled in order that the military tax eater may thrive and gain stars and medals. But just think for a moment, gentlemen, how contented, how prosperous, how progressive India might have been today had she been saved this huge extraordinary extra expenditure of Rs. 54,000,000 in five years. How many productive commercial railways and irrigation canals, branch feeders and lines, which are yet a crying want in almost every province of the empire, might have been built. And what blessings these might have brought to our unhappy countrymen. How many millions might have been easily spared to arrest the growth of that gaunt famine which is devastating parts of Southern India and Deccan. Is there a doubt that all this expenditure is a pure waste—waste of the resources and the labour of the whole population? They might as well have dropped them to the bottom of the sea. . . . It is, gentlemen, recorded in black and white, in the report of the Shimla Army Commission, of which Sir Frederick Roberts was no inconspicuous a member, that the army seems to exist not for the people of India, but that the people of India exist for the army. Truer words were never recorded by an official Commission.

If, then, our finances are more or less embarrassed, and if military expenditure is the principal cause of that embarrassment, how are you to remedy this growing and uncontrolled evil? This is the practical question which it is our solemn duty to solve. . . . We must all endeavor, first, to realize the magnitude of this state of military finance. When you consider that the expenditure of a Government depends on the policy it pursues in its relations both to internal and external affairs, you will at once perceive that it is the present calamitous, nay culpable, foreign policy of the Government of India which dominates the whole condition of finance. And as the financial position of India in turn dominates all its other conditions, especially the material conditions, you will be further able to perceive how imperative is the urgency to agitate for a complete change of that policy. If our Government, therefore, adopts a wise policy you may depend on it that our finances in the near future can be more economically administered, and that the people will immensely advance in material prosperity. If, on the contrary, it persists, in spite of all remonstrances and representations, in adhering to its present fatal policy, it goes without saying that the material condition of our people will grow worse and worse, till one day some appalling disaster (which God forbid) overtakes the Government. I think, therefore, you will agree with me that it is time for us all by our persistent agitation to bring about a healthy and wholesome change in the military policy of the Government. . . .

A tone of helplessness pervades the financial statements whenever the question is referred to, as if a change in the policy could not bring about a better state of matters. In support of my statement allow me please to quote to you one or two short paragraphs. It is observed in the Financial Statement of 1886–87 as follows: "By the events of late years, in Central Asia, India finds herself almost in contact with one of the greatest European Powers, and she cannot hope to escape the necessity which the position imposes on her of increasing her military strength."[1] The question here is this: Who created the necessity? Did the people of India create it? Did they appeal to their rulers to cross the natural but impregnable boundaries of the country on the North-West, and thoughtlessly rush into the open to meet the Russians halfway? Did they say that benefit was to be derived from such a course; that India would be assured of greater external security and internal contentment? No. The people have all through condemned the procedure. They have still to be convinced of the "necessity" on which the Government grounds the increase in the military strength of the empire in a variety of ways. Gentlemen, it was the wise policy of the earlier generation of Viceroys, beginning with the ever-sagacious John Lawrence (than whom no other Viceroy has more fully grasped the true significance of confining our line of defence within the natural boundaries of the Empire), and ending with Lord Northbrook, never to cross the Indus. The weighty reasons urged in favour of this line of policy may still be read with profit in those ponderous Blue-books on Central Asia which have been published since 1864, and which have been so well summarized in that book issued by

Lord Lawrence and his coadjutors entitled "Causes of the Afghan War."[2] To go beyond our natural line of defence, gentlemen, is to court defeat. We expose ourselves needlessly and fritter away the resources and strength which we ought to conserve for the defence from within our impregnable boundaries whenever the dreaded external attack becomes a real one, which, I think, is still a remote contingency. At present we are creating an artificial ring fence in which to entrap ourselves. Just imagine what may be the result in case of a defeat. Let us assume the worst. Does it not stand to reason that the very lines of strategical railways, the very outposts and forts which we take to be our special defence works, would be in the hands of the enemies, and that these would be the very means whereby Russia would sooner become master of India than she could possibly have done had we left natural physical difficulties of the country untouched as Providence gave them to our hands? Ordinary common sense tells us that this policy is a most fatal one. It has not the merit of ordinary sagacity, let alone statesmanship. It is the maddest policy which a wise Government could be led or betrayed into adopting by its irresponsible military advisers. . . .

The whole question hinges on this: Are the trans-frontier defences required? Is it a wise policy to advance beyond the natural frontiers of India? They say it is a question for military experts. In the first place, I deny that proposition. It is a question of policy and not of experts. And on questions of policy those who have studied and given thought to them are as competent to pass an opinion as the Government itself. But, leaving this argument alone, may it be asked if even military experts are all agreed? Gentlemen, there are able military experts who have condemned the defences on which so many millions have been spent. They have demonstrated that in the long run these will prove a "death trap." . . .

I will now pass on to other experts, though not military experts, who speak with authority from the position they occupy as the responsible members of the Executive Government of India during the Viceroyalty of Earl Dufferin in its earlier period. Their names are held in the highest respect. I allude to Sir Auckland Colvin and Mr. [Courtenay] Ilbert, who have recorded a joint minute of dissent on the subject of increased troops and trans-frontier defences, which is as much remarkable for its independence as for its close reasoning and logic. . . . In fact, the sum and substance of their argument is that the increase of troops and other measures would "prove a weapon less of defence than of aggression." This memorable statement, so forcibly and tersely put, changes the whole aspect of the policy pursued by Government. . . . This being the situation, is not the following observation in the same Minute prophetical?

> We are further of opinion that the proposal is open to the objection that it may lead to the advocacy, and possibly to the adoption, of projects for the extension of our present frontier. The question then narrows itself to this: Is it the duty of the Government of India to maintain the charge on Indian revenues of a permanent addition to its forces, not required for India, but available for the purpose of extending and securing its dominion beyond India?

There are many other points which, for want of time, I must give up. But I cannot conclude this important part of my observations without drawing your special attention to the caution and forethought displayed by these two members of the Viceroy's Council as far as the financial aspect of the question is concerned. In this respect they have rendered an invaluable service to India, for which we must publicly express our warmest gratitude:

> We agree entirely with the opinion of those who hold that, as an alien people, our best claim to the regard of the people of the country, and therefore one of our main sources of security, lies in the fact that taxation is light. . . . It seems an axiom which, at the present time, it is singularly incumbent on the Government of India to bear in mind. If it was important when India had no European neighbour, it becomes much more so when she has at her frontier a Power whose agents will make the most of all our mistakes, and will bid against us, by every means at their disposal, for popularity . . .

You will thus be able to judge for yourselves from what I urged in my speech on the same subject at the first Congress, and from what I have adduced before you today, how crushing is the growing burden of military expenditure, and how uncalled for it is. It is fast increasing, and it will go on increasing, unless we are true to ourselves and legitimately and constitutionally resist further burdens in the same direction. We must agitate, firstly, for a complete change of the present unwise and aggressive policy—a policy which, under the hollow pretext of defending the Empire, secretly aims at extending its frontiers and is really courting untold disasters—in fact a policy of external aggression pure and simple. The pressure caused by the absorption of our resources, consequent on this mischievous policy, transcends in its cramping and distressing effects all other financial errors of the Government. . . . If the policy is to be persisted in, then we must demand that England shall contribute a substantial share towards the cost entailed by that policy. . . .

But, before I sit down, permit me to read a few verses from the pen of Dr. [John] Pollen, a distinguished member of the Bombay Civil Service, who stayed for some months in Russia to study the language of the country. From the intimate contact with the people there he was of opinion that there was a great deal of exaggeration and misrepresentation as to the intentions of Russia. I believe there is a great deal of truth in his observations: If Russia's political necessities goad her forward in Central Asia, is it not true that the same necessities have in times past been alleged as compelling the British to annex—first to seize Sind, then the Punjab, then Lower Burma, then Upper Burma, and so forth? For my part, gentlemen, I believe that there is not in these respects a pin to choose between the practical political moral-ity of the English and the Russians . . .

NOTES

"England and Russia" originally appeared as India, "England and Russia," *Oriental Miscellany* 1, no. 9 (December 1879): 362–71. "Why Do Indians Prefer British to Rus-sian Rule?," originally appeared as "Why Do Indians Prefer British to Russian Rule?," in *Indian Leaflets No. 10* (Calcutta, 1885). The signatories were the British Indian Asso-ciation, Indian Association of Calcutta, Bombay Presidency Association, Sarvajanik Sabha of Poona, Mahajan Sabha of Madras, Sind Sabha of Kurrachee, and Praja-Hita-Vardhak Sabha of Surat. "Russia, India and Afghanistan" originally appeared as Dinshah Ardeshir Taleyarkhan, *Selections from My Recent Notes on the Indian Empire* (Bombay: Times of India Steam, 1886), 1–62. "The Native Indian Army—Reform or Increase?" originally appeared as G. V. Joshi, "The Native Indian Army—Reform or Increase?," *Quarterly Journal of the Poona Sarvajanik Sabha* 8, no. 3 (January 1886): 13–43. "Indian Military Expenditure" originally appeared as Dinshaw E. Wacha, "Speech of Mr. D. E. Wacha on the Third Resolution, Regarding the Grievous Distress Among the People of India, and the Reforms Needed for Its Removal," in *Summary of Resolutions of the 7th Indian National Congress* (Nagpur: Indian National Congress, 1892), 22–29.

1. *Copy of Indian Financial Statement for 1886–87* (London: Henry Hansard, 1886), 10.
2. *Causes of the Afghan War, Being a Selection of Papers Laid Before Parliament with a Connecting Narrative and Comment* (London: Chatto and Windus, 1879).

Chapter Four

THE EASTERN QUESTION

THE POSITION OF TURKEY IN RELATION
TO BRITISH INTERESTS IN INDIA, 1875
James Long

... The Turkish or Eastern Question—a burning one—is gradually coming to the front, and the late happy measure of the English Government with regard to the Suez Canal will hasten the unfolding the drama of the Eastern Question and bring it to some kind of settlement. It involves, however, problems of the most serious and difficult character, which may task the highest powers of European statesmen to solve. . . . While there has been a deluge of literature on the Eastern Question, proposing all kinds of schemes, . . . India's interests have been seldom the standpoint, though the Central Asia Question, so vital for India, is linked with that of Turkey. . . .

The death-knell of Turkey is sounding, bankruptcy indicates a political crash, while England sees now that her blood and treasure so freely spent for the upholding Turkey have been utterly wasted. Turkey has borrowed £200,000,000 in twenty years, and there is nothing substantial to show for it; her independence and integrity guaranteed by treaties the result of hard-fought battles, are a dream. The Crimean War, undertaken to support the Sick Man, has rather hastened his end; for twenty years new efforts have been made to improve Turkey, but they have ended in galvanizing a corpse. . . .

The present is a favourable time to discuss this question calmly. It was felt by various Anglo-Indians at the time of the Crimean War that India's interests were not regarded sufficiently on that occasion: hence Russia, shut up in a southerly direction, in consequence of the war, pushed on the eastern slope until she now hangs on the flanks of India. I merely refer to this very difficult question in order to introduce the main point—who is to have the estate of the Turk, a now dying man? A government in the hands of trustees ceases to be a government, and foreigners are taking the helm which the Sick Man's feeble hand can no longer grasp firmly. . . .

Supposing that, with the concurrence of England, France, and the Northern Powers, Asia Minor comes under Russian rule, would not this, like any European rule, be a blessing to the millions in those regions so long desolated by Turkish barbarism? Would not the desert rejoice and blossom as the rose? Russia itself, with all its shortcomings, has made great strides in reform during the present reign, and more are in progress. . . . But whatever effects the occupation of Asia Minor by Russia may have on the inhabitants of Turkey, the question for England is, how would it affect British India? . . . The effect on England's prestige in the East would be very different according as Asia Minor was occupied by Russia with or without the concurrence of England.

With the former there would be no loss of prestige. People talk of the effect on the Mohammedans of India by England being the ally of Turkey, but it certainly was not seen in the Mutiny, when our bitterest foes were the Moslems; and nothing excited more ridicule against England among the Natives of India than when they heard that a ball was given in London to the Sultan, at the expense of the people of India, in order forsooth to conciliate the Mussulmans of India. When the fall of the Sultan comes it will have as little effect in India as the fall of the Pope's temporal power had in America. Ignorance and sectarian bitterness isolate the Indian Moslems from the Turks; besides, the different sects of Mohammedans in the East hate each other cordially, as we see with the Shia and Sunni, and are as bitterly antagonistic as Protestant and Papist in Europe. The other 200,000,000 Natives of India are too much occupied in their own concerns to be affected by a country so distant from them as Asia Minor, whereas it is from Central Asia that Russia's prestige penetrates into India, and which impresses on the Natives of India a profound awe of the Russ. *Omne ignotum pro magnifico.*[1] The buzz of the bazaar indicates a constant expectation of the advent to India of the men that have knocked down the Khanates as

ninepins. . . . The crumbling of Moslem power in Constantinople, Ispahan, Delhi, and Samarkand are signs of the times to the Indian Moslem,
who is gradually learning that the pride of six centuries of conquest is liv-
ened in the dust, that the Sultan who bears the title of *Amir al-Muminin* is
being shorn of all his power, and that the shadow of the Caliphate is going
down, as the shadow of the Great Mogul has gone down in Delhi.

The point I wish to submit is: is not Russia now like a mighty stream
whose waters you cannot easily dam up, but you may partially divert them
into another channel? In other words, the stream of Russian development
and conquest flows at present in a Central Asia direction, is dashing up
against our Indian frontier, and undermining its bulwarks, which are weak.
If that stream be turned partly into another channel, its natural one—viz.,
Asia Minor—you are saved from great evils to both Empires, or, at least, of
two evils you choose the lesser: there is less likelihood of collision from Russia's developing herself in Asia Minor than in Central Asia. Is it not safer
for England to have Russia in force on the Mediterranean, than on the
Hindu Kush and frontiers of Afghanistan? . . .

Russia is a great military Power, which in a few years will be backed by
3,000,000 bayonets. The advances it has made from the Caspian during the
last fifteen years show what it is capable of the next fifteen. Khiva went lately;
Kokand is gone; and Kashgar, a barrier to Russia's onward move towards
China, and a focus for Moslem raids against Russia, will probably be the
next to go down the stream. This will bring Russia close to Kashmir and
Kabul; within the next ten years a railway will be completed from Russia
to Tashkent, and another line will be opened from Russia to Tehran, from
which latter place extensions can be easily made to Herat; while a railway
from Russia to India itself will ere long be carried through.

What is the Indian embankment that is to stay this current? Only 60,000
European troops for the whole of India. . . . We can hold on even under
these conditions, but active antagonism to Russia means raising the European army in India to 100,000 men, to be maintained by increased taxes,
which signify increased discontent and the consequent withdrawing funds
from the development of the country. It is easy work for Englishmen in their
island home, fenced in by the ocean and defended by volunteers, to talk of
repressing Russia; but it is a very different thing in India to meet a powerful military nation on the frontiers, with tens of thousands of enemies ready
to start up behind on any favourable opportunity. . . .

The Central Asia, Indian, and Turkish Questions are, then, closely connected together in this respect, inasmuch as the former is used by Russia as a leverage to ease England's action against her in Turkey, or, as a Russian journal states it: "The diplomatic controversy is transferred from the banks of the Bosphorus to the slopes of Peshawar." A St. Petersburg paper refers to the conquest of Khiva in the following words: "A second route has been opened out to India, and England is put face to face with us, no longer at Constantinople, but on the northern slopes of the Peshawar mountain range." India is the Achilles' heel, where England is most vulnerable, though some have fancied the Russian march towards India could be stayed by neutral zones or embassies. Must not the solution of the Central Asia Question be sought not at Calcutta, but at Constantinople? . . .

LETTER ON HINDUSTAN, 1883
Jamaluddin Afghani

The main goal of the English in recent years has been to become masters of all the roads that lead to India. It is for this that they recently tried to seize the passes of Afghanistan and Baluchistan, and that is why they are trying to establish themselves in Egypt right now. The explanation for the policy followed in the East by Great Britain in this regard lies in the keen anxiety of this power toward preserving its domination over Hindustan and in its fear of seeing itself divested of its magnificent Indian realm in the not-too-distant future. It is this preoccupation, prevailing over all the others, that pushes the English down the path where they continually offend other nations, and that leads them to adopt an attitude that is well tailored to arouse the surprise and the justifiable sensitivities of all statesmen who are not English.

It is known in England, in fact, that all Indian inhabitants without distinction of race, caste, or religion—Muslims as well as the adherents of Brahma or Buddha, the princes as well as the porters—all have the same degree of hatred of foreign oppressors, and these persons are convinced that a single cannon shot, a single gunshot fired at some point on the coast or frontier of Hindustan would suffice to cause a general uprising, from Ceylon to the foothills of the Himalayas, and to persuade, within an instant, all the Indians to make common cause with the persons, whoever they may be, who will attack the English in India.

The latter are so far from ignoring the extent to which their domination is brittle, they know so well the hostile dispositions of their Indian subjects and the numerical weakness of their military forces in India and elsewhere, that they would like to morally isolate Hindustan from the rest of the world by cordoning this region by some sort of wall, by all the obstacles they place to the flow of travelers, whatever nationality they belong to, undoubtedly concerned that foreigners not discover and reveal the secret of the weakness of the English hidden under apparent power.

Constantly preoccupied with maintaining their unsteady domination, the rulers of India have nevertheless never sought the means to consolidate their power where they might be able to find such means. Far from working to win the sympathies of the people, they never ceased to offend them in all ways in their sentiments and in their interests. The English have ruled over India for over a hundred years and, since that point in the time, the Indians have been, so to speak, removed from humanity, unable to aspire to any military rank, to any political function, not even having the most sacred freedom of all: freedom of conscience. Instead of lowering taxes so that the unfortunate Indians do not work only for the taxman, and could at least save from their low earnings enough to provide for their needs, the English have destroyed the trade and industry of the natives by imports from their factories in Europe, and severed relations between India and Afghanistan, its neighbor in declaring an unjust and underhanded war against the Afghans in which, moreover, they have completely failed. . . .

Not having succeeded in Afghanistan, and on the other hand, watching the French occupy Tunisia with a jealous eye; sensing hatred grow day by day in the Indians, a hatred likely as of now to throw them into the arms of the first power that would like to attack England at the heart of its Asian possessions, the English, no doubt blinded by the dangers threatening their impotence, have just committed an error whose dual consequences will be disastrous for them in the future. This error is their recent intervention in the land of Pharaohs by cunning and deceit—the only formidable weapons of England—with the ulterior motive of extending their predominance on the other coast of the Red Sea to the provinces of Hejaz and Yemen, in Arabia, where they already possess Aden.

The first consequence of the British intervention in Egypt was to upset several European nations and especially France, who have indisputably considerable interests in the Nile Valley. . . . The second result of its intervention in Egypt, equally dire for England, is the feelings of indignation and anger that this brutal act raised all over the Muslim world, and especially among the Muslims of India. The veneration of the latter for the current sultan, and in general for the reigning Caliph, whoever it may be, is a feeling they hold in common with all believers in Islam. This veneration is in some way a dogma of the Mohammedan religion and in all mosques, every Friday, at prayer, Muslims begin by invoking Allah for protecting the days of the Sultan-Caliph.

The English have certainly not forgotten that, at the time they entered Egypt, the beginnings of an insurrection had taken place in Mirit and that the movement would have rapidly taken over the whole of Muslim India, had they not nimbly cooled people's spirits by putting out a profusion of manifestos where they declared the fight against Arabi was only because he was a rebel, and that they had entered Egypt only to obey the Sultan's order. This act has succeeded, it is true. But it would no longer have the same success if they want to reenact it, especially if the Turks, eyes wide open, became certain that England wants to annex Egypt, that is to say, the most important part of their empire in Africa, to subsequently remove Hejaz and Yemen from under Muslim authority and place these provinces under British rule. Sure of the sympathy of their fellow Indian coreligionists, the Ottomans would not hesitate, in such a case, to support the policies of a great power whose ambitious views are ceaselessly focused toward the Indies, even if they would not gain anything by this policy other than the satisfaction of ushering in the failure of a nation that is working to break up their empire.

In the world of government, it is very well known in England that the Sultan pushed to his limits would be a precious ally for the adversaries of the English in the Indies, by doing nothing more than preaching at Mecca and sending to Hindustan a manifesto bearing his name by some sheikh authorized to speak in his name. But, even leaving aside these potential combinations of Istanbul's diplomacy, the mere fact of the occupation of Egypt, which is the way to Mecca, and the secret but sure desire that the English have to extend their domination over the regions of Hejaz and Yemen, at the same time cradle and citadel of Islamism, would be enough to persuade Indian Muslims to now make common cause with any power that will invade English India.

And if only the English do not delude themselves into believing that they could, in this situation, oppose Indian Muslims to their compatriots belonging to other religions. They would be strangely mistaken. Bent for so many years under the same yoke, besieged with humiliations, plunged by the insatiable rapacity of the conqueror into common misery, all Indians, come the day of action, will be united in action, as they are today united in hatred. In support of what I have just said, how many examples and proofs wouldn't I find in the past; and without searching harder, during the great revolt of 1857, didn't Nana Sahib, who wasn't a Muslim, show himself to be a more tenacious enemy than Firoz Shah and the Begum Shah? This solidarity, this unity that I assert, may seem doubtful to those who ignore the means employed by the English to govern, administer, and exploit the Indies. In order to respond on this point, I will, in a succeeding article, reveal facts and details whose precision I hope will leave no doubt in anyone's mind.

EUROPE REVISITED, 1887
Salar Jung II

... The interest that we from India now have in the future of the Osmanli is a political and a religious interest, an interest which is growing from day to day with every improvement in the means of communication between India and Europe. During the month I spent on the Bosphorus, I had many opportunities of discussing the political position with the representatives of those different powers which are waiting and watching with evident impatience to seize the heritage of "the Sick Man." I confess however that I do not at all share the view that the doom of Turkey in Europe is sealed, and that the day of execution is at hand. True there are causes that make for disintegration, and I can well believe that the present nearly chaotic condition of the executive of the Porte and the difficulties ever placed in the way of all the necessary reforms, whether political, social, or industrial, have seriously discouraged, especially in England, the true friends of Turkey. But when the day comes, and perhaps it is very near at hand, when the alternative presented to the Sultan and to the great powers is either Russia in possession of Constantinople or that those constitutional reforms necessary to restore the vitality of the Ottoman Empire shall be undertaken by joint agreement with England, Germany, Austria and Italy—when this day does come, then right counsels will prevail, and Turkey, a country of great beauty and natural resources, and peopled by a community which, at least in the lower classes of society, is singularly brave, industrious, and law-abiding, will again assert its position, and afford as of old an effective support to the balance of power in Europe. . . .

At the same time, it would be idle to deny that, even if the possession of Constantinople itself is to become the gage of war, Turkey can no longer rely blindly on the support of England. There is a modern school of politicians inclined to assert that the system of Turkish government is so bad, the whole administration so corrupt and so incongruous, that, come what may, no nation which would preserve its self-respect can any longer remain allied to the Porte. Therefore, "Perish Turkey, England has no longer any interest in the politics of the Mediterranean." . . .

But this school is probably not very numerous, and when the crisis of the Eastern question does come, it will be impossible for England to refuse to play her part in its settlement. England has in India some 50,000,000 of Mussulman subjects, including in their mass the most warlike of the native races, the races upon whom England must chiefly rely to roll back the tide of Russian aggression; and England is not likely to forget that it was these very races who, in 1857, at the bidding of their Caliph, the Sultan Abdul Medjid, gave their united support to the British connection at that supreme moment when their defection might have cost the life of every white man and woman in India. My late father frequently assured me that the whole influence of the Caliphate was used most unremittingly from Constantinople to check the spread of the Mutiny, to rally to the English standards the Mussulman races of India, and that in this way the debt which Turkey owed to Great Britain for British support in the Crimea was paid in full. And the time may again come when the devotion of the Mussulmans to their Caliph and the shrine of St. Sofia may be not less necessary to Great Britain than in 1857. I am aware that in the Western world the religious sentiment of nations is no longer considered an important factor in politics, but it would not be wise to regard any such maxim as applicable to the East. The myriads who today in the hottest regions in the world keep for an entire month each year the fast of Ramadan—entire abstinence from all food and water between sunrise and sunset while continuing their full daily toil— the religious zeal that has endured this trial steadfastly for more than a thousand years at the bidding of the Prophet, is not likely to look on unmoved when his shrine at Mecca and his tomb at Medina have become the objective points of foreign aggression. The enlightened classes in India recognise that the rule of England has secured us against incessant internal strife, involving a perpetual exhaustion of the resources of our communities, and also that by a just administration of equal laws a very sufficient measure of individual liberty is now our birthright. We have lost, as some think, our national liberties, which after all were merely the liberties enjoyed by despots to compel their subjects to make war on one another; this so called "liberty" is denied us; but more than 240,000,000 of us have now the right to live our own lives on what lines we please, and to be subject only to the control of a known, a written law; and this being so, the one further inducement needed to keep the Mahommedan millions for ever steadfast in the British connection is the bond of a religious faith and a cherished conviction that, being the loyal subjects of the Great White Empress, we are therefore the strongest link in the natural alliance between our Queen and our Caliph, between the temporal power in India and the spiritual power that radiates from the Bosphorus. And herein is the strength and the determination of our objection to any further Russian growth in the direction of India. It is less our dislike to exchange a constitutional for a despotic rule, for we attach but little importance to mere theories of representative government; but we do all recognise that in Russia we are confronted with the natural and the unrelenting enemy of the head of our faith, and if we are destined to see Russia on the Bosphorus and the shrine of Mecca in her possession, where then may the faithful look to find the defender of their faith, the great *Amīr al-mu'minīn?* . . .

THE MUSSALMANS OF INDIA AND
THE ARMENIAN QUESTION, 1895
Khwaji Ghulam-us-Saqlain

Now that the question of the alleged Armenian atrocities is under the consideration of a Commission composed of the representative of various European powers that have shown an interest in that question, it may appear injudicious to write anything for or against either the Government which is held to be responsible for the alleged barbarities, or those persons who are responsible for the agitation which has led to the appointment of this Commission. . . . But the interest which the English government has in the Eastern question generally, and in this particular instance of the "Armenian atrocities," is much greater than, and of quite a different nature from, the interest which it would have as one of the European powers merely, or even as one of the signatory Powers of the treaties of Berlin and Paris. The interest which Great Britain has in all questions relating to the welfare and vitality of Turkey is not merely a platonic interest. England is certainly a Christian power; and as such it has, and should have, natural sympathies and antipathies; but then she is something more. She is, in one sense, the greatest Muslim power in the world. This is a phrase which has been often repeated, but few realise the true significance of this single fact.

Any person who has carefully studied the numerous elements of which the vast Empire of Britain is composed will be struck with the enormous number of the Muhammadans who owe allegiance to the British sovereign. Excluding those scattered numbers of the Mussalmans that are found in almost every English colony or possession in Africa, Asia, and in Australia, the Muhammadan population of the Indian Empire, according to the latest census, is more than fifty-seven million. So that Her Majesty is the ruler of a far greater number of Mussalmans than the Sultan of Turkey, or the Shah of Persia, or both of these together, rule.

This aspect of the question should never be lost sight of. In her dealings with other Powers, England has accordingly duties and responsibilities which no other Power has in the same degree. Here is a unique instance of an empire which comprehends almost all religions and races on the face of the earth, and which is so situated that by the very force of circumstances it cannot, and should not, adopt any policy other than that of the large-hearted and noble-minded emperor Akbar, whose vast dominions it has inherited by a series of unforeseen and fortuitous circumstances.

Now, if we except the Christian, or rather the European, element, which is naturally the governing and dominant element, the Muhammadans are, as a people, the most important portion of those innumerable masses of human beings in India that own our Queen Victoria as their rightful sovereign. Not only on account of their numbers, but also by reason of their being the most loyal subjects of Her Majesty, they form an important part of the British empire.

There is one thing more. The Indian Muhammadans are the only ones who are being largely influenced by the pressure of the civilisation of the West. They are the only followers of the Prophet who are intellectually free, and who can study any sciences and arts they like; who can expound new philosophical theories, evolve new religious speculations, or entertain new ideas of social life; and who can, in short, enter into the ewe for progress and civilisation without any hindrance. If Egypt be partially excluded, the Mussalmans of no other country but India possess the right of free speech and have a free press. All these things combine to make them more or less united, and to produce amongst them a sense of nationality and a public spirit which is in most respects new to the East.

It is true the Muhammadan of India, when compared even with other important portions of the community, are in a miserable plight, and are far from being a wealthy or prosperous people. But such is the case all over the world, the difference being only this, that in the case of the Indian Mussalmans there has been, for the last quarter of a century, a new movement and a real awakening on their part. . . . Now this education, imparted in the colleges and schools of India, is gradually producing Mussalmans who are sufficiently versed in the English language, and who study the writings of English authors and the speeches of English statesmen almost as eagerly as Englishmen themselves. . . . They can thus understand the course of English policy and the drift of European diplomacy, and they appreciate ordinary English literature as much as any Englishman who reads his morning papers and studies his monthly magazines. . . . They eagerly read and discuss whatever is said in any quarter of the "civilised world" about the Muhammadan; for the press makes them acquainted with all such matters. . . .

Now such an important portion of Her Majesty's subjects must never be omitted from the consideration of English statesmen. England, if she is fully conscious of her duty, as by far the greatest Moslem power in the world, governing in all nearly 60,000,000 Muhammadans, is bound by the very nature of the circumstances in which she is placed to widen her political horizon, to regard every political question that comes out not merely in the provincial spirit, to which some of her politicians are apt to tend. There are some questions which affect not only the feelings of the inhabitants of England, Scotland, and Ireland, but also the feelings and sentiments of innumerable muses of human beings whose sentiments, mistaken though they may be, and whose feelings, though they might not be fully understood by European statesmen, are not for that reason to be neglected and despised.

Now, of the political feelings of the Mussalmans of India, perhaps the most firmly seated is an attachment to the Mussalman powers that still exist in the world. Of the Mussalman kingdoms, Turkey is the most important, both on account of its vastness and power, and also because of the position she occupies as the guardian of Mecca and Medina, the former being the center of Islam, the latter being the adopted home of the Prophet, where he is buried. These two places are the resort of hundreds of thousands of pilgrims from all parts of Asia and Africa; and even those who cannot visit them entertain a profound reverence for these holy places of Islam. The less cultured of the Indian Mussalmans have also a dim idea that the Sultan of Turkey is somehow or other their Caliph, or religious head. This is an opinion which is hardly supported by competent authorities and traditions; but the mass of the people, not merely in India and Asia, but everywhere in the world, are despotic in their nature, and will brook no contradiction or rational correction of their notions and prejudices. . . .

I do not think that the Mussalmans of India regard themselves bound to the Turkish Empire so much that they would rise in rebellion against the English Government if, in their opinion, it took an unfair advantage of the weakness of Turkey and brought about its downfall. Such a supposition would be pronounced absurd on the very face of it by every person who has ever lived and moved amongst the Indian Mussalmans. They are loyal to England through conviction and interest. They are perfectly assured that their present position, though by no means prosperous, is very satisfactory. They are safe under the rule of Britain. Their religious freedom is secured. They have a possibility of future progress and development such as no Moslem country allows to its inhabitants. Their staunch loyalty to England cannot he doubted, and, with the exception of a few old-fashioned Englishmen, who might be still haunted by the phantom of a supposed Wahhabi insurrection, it has been universally acknowledged by the English officials in the country that the Muhammadans of India are the most loyal of Her Majesty's subjects.

But suppose that a crusade is proclaimed against the remaining Moslem kingdoms of the world . . . then it is not difficult to conceive that the loyalty of the Muhammadans will not remain unshaken. . . . We may even take another and more probable case, of English statesmen giving way before the torrent of invective and calumny which has been for centuries past directed by the enthusiastic, the philanthropic, the ignorant, and the bigoted against the "unspeakable Turk," and, joining with the Christian policy of annihilating Turkey, pursue with regard to the Mussalmans the policy of Russia; this will again produce ill-feeling and anger in the Mussalman population. . . .

No nation has a right to attribute to itself all moral excellence, and to assign to same other nation, particularly disliked, everything that is disagreeable or distasteful. But the Turks have long suffered from such unreasonable prejudices. They have a different religion, a different nationality, and their name has become in Europe a byword for all unnatural and inhuman vices. . . .

Granted that there are many shortcomings, and even perverse principles, in the Turkish system of government, two questions naturally arise. Do these things exist nowhere but in Turkey, and have no other government and no other people in the world, or even what is called the civilised world, any such faults? And do the gentlemen who constantly declaim against the Turkish Empire sincerely desire that it should reform its system of government and make a real internal progress, unchecked and unhindered? . . .

Of the two questions mentioned above, I wish to briefly discuss the latter question first—Whether the critics of the Turks earnestly desire the amelioration of the condition of those various races that own the sway of the Sultan? If they do, they certainly do not adopt the best method to effect their ends. I do not deny that these gentlemen are honest in their intentions and sincere in their professions of benevolence and philanthropy; though the benevolence is somewhat partial and the philanthropy somewhat mixed with something other than love. Yet they either fail to recognise or knowingly shut their eyes to the fact that, on the whole, Turkey has been steadily trying to reform its old abuses and to change itself according to the requirements of the age. This change towards improvement is observable in every department. . . .

The other question is this: Are the abuses complained of in Turkey such as exist in no other part of the world, and is the Turkish system more decidedly corrupt and cruel than the system of any other Christian government in the world? If this fact should be conclusively settled against Turkey, then indeed there would be strong reason for condemning a government which suffers such barbarities to be perpetrated, and allows such laws to mist in its dominion as are entirely foreign to the civilised sense of the world, and wholly given up by every other state. But no statesman, even no ordinary politician, who knows enough of the general character of the different governments, not to say of the world, but of Europe only, will venture to make any such sweeping assertion. No one, however strongly prejudiced he may be against Turkey, can deny that the severe and oppressive despotic system of Russia, according to which system half the European continent is governed, is in no way less lenient, less barbarous, or more humane than the corresponding Turkish system. The world cannot easily forget the late heartless expulsion of hundreds of thousands of Jews. Men were driven from their homes, where they had lived for centuries, their property was confiscated, and they were driven out in absolute poverty, and pushed forcibly on into other reluctant countries. It is impossible to calculate the amount of human suffering brought about by this expulsion; yet the collective humanity of civilised Europe was hardly powerful enough to save one Jew from being expelled from his native place. . . .

The Mussalmans of India, informed by the vernacular papers of all these contemporary events, take notice of these facts, and generally look upon all such professions of philanthropy and human sympathy as hypocritical pretensions. No doubt they are wrong in their sweeping condemnation, which is owing to their not being fully acquainted with the political ideas and principles current in Europe, and with the methods in which the Europeans express their opinions. But though they may be erroneous, they are excusable. Any man of common understanding, not gifted with an extraordinarily subtle and discriminating conscience, would fail to find any reason why laws and practices in a Christian country should be passed over in silence, while similar laws and practices, which entail even lesser evils, when found in a neighboring Moslem kingdom, should be denounced from all public places, from the senate, the pulpit, and the platform. In such cases there must be either a strong religions antipathy, or racial hatred, or both; and if so, the humanitarian gentlemen come down almost to the level of vulgar agitators and the bigots who excite the religious animosities of the masses.

I do not mean to say that the Turkish system is even comparatively perfect. There are, indeed, grave errors of principle, as well as of detail, in the administration. The most important and perhaps the greatest grievance is the absolute suppression of the liberty of the press. The fact that no paper or book can be published or brought into the country without passing through the severe ordeal of being inspected and "corrected" by a very watchful and ruthless licenser is shocking to the minds of men who have been brought up in the midst of a free press and free discussion. . . . But the Mussalmans of India naturally suppose that the English public have no right to denounce Turkey for its suppression of the liberty of the press before they exert themselves to give a free press to the Christians of Russia, by inducing their Christian ally to grant that right to its subjects. When we consider that it was only a few years back (1878) that an Act was passed by the Governor-General of India in Council to take away the liberty of the native press, an Act which was repealed by the truly sympathetic Viceroy, Lord Ripon; and when we see that even now not a few Englishmen of India, who are known as the Anglo-Indians, loudly desire to suppress the liberty of the native newspapers, we ought to be a little more lenient in condemning the Oriental government of Turkey. . . .

Such considerations produce anger and contempt in the minds of the Mussalmans, who repose even less confidence in the partial philanthropy of interested politicians than the diplomats have in the political treaties. It was a few days ago that I heard some leading Muhammadans saying in perfect good faith, without thinking themselves cynical in expressing such sentiments, that treaties between unequal powers are only so much wastepaper! The stronger always consider them worthless, in so far as they are in favour of the weaker powers, while any terms in favour of the stronger power are most sternly enforced by that power. . . . Such an unfavourable idea of the Europeans formed on the part of their Asiatic fellow-beings, however partial and erroneous that idea may be, is much to be regretted. I have tried here to prove that, if such ideas are held by a large number of the Indian Mussalmans, they are not wholly to be blamed; and that Englishmen also contribute to the formation of such prejudices. . . .

If the British and the Irish people, either Conservative or Radical, calmly think over the great responsibilities which they have, as the rulers of the greatest Empire now existing in the world, and if they clearly appreciate their duty as the rulers of the greatest Moslem community in the world, they will not be carried away by racial or ecclesiastical prejudices. They will calmly and impartially judge before they condemn or agitate against any Moslem power or kingdom with which sixty million of their fellow subjects have strong sympathies. . . .

THE CALIPHATE, 1897
Syed Ahmed Khan

. . . [T]hose who possess and govern a country and have the power to enforce and keep alive the rules of faith and can through their strength and resources defend the country against its invaders, can be regarded as Caliphs or deputies of the Prophet: provided that they are gifted with the virtues and manners of the Prophet and follow the dictates of the religion and possess external and internal holiness. . . .

It is possible from this point of view that Mahomedan sovereigns of a country may regard themselves as Caliphs: but they are Caliphs or Sultans of that country *alone* which they rule and of those Moslems *only* who are their subjects. They are *not* Caliphs or Sultans of that country or of those Mahomedans who are neither their subjects nor are governed by them; because it is necessary for a Caliph that he should be the ruler of the country, able to give orders of punishment and retaliation and to enforce them; that he should be the defender of the faith and that he should protect the country and its people from their enemies and maintain peace and order within. So that if a Moslem sovereign does not possess such power and cannot exercise such authority in a particular country he cannot be and cannot be called the Caliph over that country or its Mahomedan inhabitants.

In deciding the question whether the Sultan of Turkey is the Caliph or not, some people urge that he is not a Quresh; while those who think him to be a Caliph do not believe in the correctness of the tradition which requires the Caliph to be of the Quresh descent. Setting aside all these controversies and even taking for granted that the Sultan of Turkey is the Caliph, we say that if he is the Caliph, he is the Caliph only in that country which he governs and for those Mahomedans only who owe him allegiance; he is the Caliph only in that country in which he can inflict punishments of death or retaliation and maintain the laws of religion; he is not Caliph in that country over which he does not hold the supreme authority and control; in which he can neither give orders for death or retaliation nor can he maintain the faith nor can he protect its Mahomedan inhabitants. Not fulfilling the conditions necessary for the Caliph he cannot be the Caliph over that country or its Mahomedan inhabitants.

We, the Mahomedans of India, are the subjects of the British Government under whose protection we live. The Government has given us peace and allowed us all freedom in religious matters. Although our English rulers prefer the faith of Christ yet the Government presents no difficulties to a Christian who comes to Mahomedanism, as it does not prevent Mahomedans becoming Christians. The Christian Missionaries have nothing to do with the Government. As they are wandering about preaching their religion so are hundreds of Mahomedans delivering public sermons on Islam. If a Mahomedan becomes a Christian, there is, on the other hand, always some Christian converted to Islam. So that the English Government has given to us Mahomedans who live as subjects under their protection, enough liberties in matters of faith. Over and above that, under the English government our lives and property are safe, and we enjoy all the rights concerning matrimony, divorce, inheritance, and wills, gifts and endowments which Mahomedan law allows us, even when Christian judges have to decide upon them; because Christian judges are obliged to decide according to the law of Islam, so it is our religious duty to remain faithful to and well-wishers of the English Government and not to do or say anything practically or theoretically inconsistent with our loyalty and goodwill to that Government.

We are not the subjects of Sultan Abdul Hameed Khan nor does he possess any authority over us or over our country. He is no doubt a Mahomedan sovereign and consequently we sympathize with him as Mahomedans—happy for his happiness and grieved at his troubles—but he is *not* our Caliph either according to Mahomedan law or Mahomedan religion. If he has the rights of a Caliph he has them only in the country and over the people that he is the master of.

History also proves that whenever a Mahomedan sovereign assumed the title of Caliph his Caliphate extended only to the extent of his dominions and his subjects. A country beyond the range of his government had nothing to do with his Caliphate, Imamate and Sultanate. . . . Now, there were in the Mahomedan world three permanent, independent and powerful Caliphs—the Abbaside Caliph in Baghdad, the Allyite Caliph in Egypt and Abdul Rahman Nasir and his successors in Andalusia. Each of these three Caliphs regarded himself the Caliph of the country which was under his control. In the court of each there were *Kazis* and *Muftis* who administered Mohammedan law under the orders and directions of their respective Caliphs in their own particular country. In the Court of the Abbaside Caliphs of Baghdad the Hanafi law was followed, and in the Fatimite Government of Egypt the Ismailia law was in force; while in the courts of the Caliphs of the Umayyad dynasty of Andalusia the Maliki Mohammedan law was acted upon. The *Kazis* and *Muftis* regarded the claims to Caliphate of every one of these Caliphs to be lawful within their respective dominions.

From these accounts it is clear that Sultan Abdul Hameed Khan is not and cannot be the Caliph for us Mahomedans who are the subjects of the British Government. . . .

Some people say that it is necessary that the Imam or Caliph in every age be one for the Mahomedans of the whole world and therefore they regard the Sultan of Turkey such a Caliph for the whole Mahomedan world. But they are quite mistaken in holding such a view. Their assertion that for the whole world there should be one Caliph is neither proved from the Holy Koran nor from any tradition. None has ever ruled the whole world and perhaps none will ever rule in future. The Mahomedans inhabit various portions of the globe and when they live in a country where the Sovereign is not Mahomedan then over those Mahomedans there can be no Mahomedan as their Caliph or the Imam of the time (the word Imam is taken to mean the same thing as the word Caliph). Moreover their assertion contradicts the teaching of history. We have already stated that there have been three Caliphs living at the same time who have been looked upon as lawful Caliphs by the *Kazis* and *Muftis* then inhabiting their respective territories. . . .

It has been argued on the authority of some traditions that it is incumbent upon every Mahomedan to know and swear allegiance to the Imam of the age. Though these traditions also are not genuine and trustworthy; yet we do not dispute about this matter and supposing them to be genuine we say that it is the duty of every Mahomedan to know the Caliph under whose Government he lives and swear allegiance to him. By swearing allegiance we mean to affirm loyalty and faithfulness and every one should obey him whose subject he is. This does not require that even those who do not reside in his dominion as his subjects should own fealty. In short, no Mahomedan sovereign is Caliph for those Mahomedans who do not live in his dominions.

A MOSLEM'S VIEW OF THE PAN-ISLAMIC REVIVAL, 1897
Rafiuddin Ahmad

The last decade of the nineteenth century is an important epoch in the history of Islam and its followers throughout the world. After three centuries of social and political decadence the Moslem world seems, at last, to have awakened to its sense of danger and responsibility. Signs of Islamic revival are observed everywhere, and though, in many cases, these signs only indicate Moslem unrest, it may fairly be inferred that some common feeling is universally shared by the followers of the Prophet at this particular time. What is this feeling? . . . If I may venture to guess, it is a perception of reasonable and probable dangers to Islam and the Islamites engendered by the Greco-Turkish war and the attitude of Christendom towards Islam during recent years. It is an assertion of the natural feeling of self-preservation and self-respect. What events have caused this perturbation in the Islamic world? The most important event of the present century concerning the Moslem world is the change in the traditional policies of England and Russia with respect to the treatment of the Eastern question. England, which has been hitherto known in the Islamic world as the ally of Turkey, has denounced her alliance with that country; while Russia, the ancient and mortal enemy of Turkey, and the traditional defender of the Christian races in the East, has become the protector of the Sultan and friend of the Moslems all over the world. The other events are the following.

The Armenian question is responsible for many evils. It started in England as a humanitarian protest against the massacre of Armenian Christians at Sasun. As such it had the sympathies of the educated Moslems of India, and even of Turkey. By degrees, however, it assumed, in the hands of designing Christian ministers, imbued with a secret hatred of Islam, and Forward Liberals inebriated with party fanaticism, an anti-Islamic character. For months, a section of the British press indulged in vituperation and vehement denunciation of the Turkish race, Moslem law, and the head of the Mohammedan faith. . . . The echo of the furious denunciations of Islam and its Caliph in England reached all parts of the Mussulman world, and the Faithful began to discuss whether the so-called humanitarian protest in Christendom was not really a crusade against the power and the prestige of their religion. . . . The result was that Abdul Hamid, who was becoming unpopular with young Moslems both in and out of Turkey, three years ago, on account of his coercive policy, began, when fighting single-handed with the Christian Powers of Europe, to be gradually recognised as a patriotic hero of Islam. It became a question of Islam *versus* Christendom.

Hardly was the Armenian question settled, or rather put off, when the Cretan question assumed its mutest form, owing to the filibustering expedition of Greece into that island. Two things in connection with the Cretan question excited the indignation of the Islamic world: the cold-blooded massacres of the Moslems by the Cretan Christians when the latter got the upper hand through the assistance of the Greeks. The incident reminded them of the treatment reserved for their fellow believers in the Turkish empire, in the event of the Crescent losing its ascendency over its Christian subjects. Secondly, the fact that Prince George of Greece was allowed to land troops in Crete under the very eyes of the admirals of the Great Powers, while the Sultan, the legitimate owner of the island, was prevented from sending any troops to quell a rebellion in his own territory. The incident clearly showed to them the injustice of Christendom towards Islam. Here, again, it was England who took the lead in defeating the proposals of Turkey. . . .

The above-mentioned are some of the leading events which have caused no little commotion in the Mussulman world. But it may, not inaptly, be asked—What is the importance, political and commercial, of this Mussulman world that European nations should bother themselves about its feelings? . . . The total population of the Moslem world approximately is 270 million. The political and commercial advantages derivable from the above-mentioned millions of human beings can be more easily imagined than described. Their organisation, if brought about, would be formidable, and their moral support is not to be despised.

Some explanation is necessary as to how these Moslem communities, separated from each other by the width of the ocean, and scattered all over the world among peoples diametrically opposed to them in religious no less than in political matters, can possibly be brought together to deliberate on topics affecting themselves and their religion. What chance, it may be asked, is there for the Moslem of Java to meet his fellow-believer of Algeria, or for the inhabitant of Kabul to embrace the inhabitant of Constantinople at the same time and at the same place, for interchange of views? . . . In Mecca, the true capital of Islam, will a student of theology, ethnology, and politics annually observe the Chinaman, the Indian, the Malay, the Afghan, the Persian, the Algerian, and the Turk, freely mingling and discussing together, all guided by the language of the Arabian Prophet. Here every Moslem daily repeats and hourly practices the favorite maxim of the founder of Islam, "All true believers, ye are brethren unto each other." . . . During the last three years the one all-absorbing topic of conversation among the *Hajjes* has been the dangers to the Caliphate, the Holy Shrines and Islam itself, owing to the menacing attitude of Christendom towards the Caliph. They know not much of all the Powers that constitute

Christendom, but every one of them knows or has heard about England and Russia. Possibly they know little of the power and influence of these respective countries, but they have always believed that England is the friend and Russia the enemy of the Sultan of Islam. During the last three years various reports have given them to understand that the two Christian powers most concerned with Islam have changed places; that Russia has become the friend and England the enemy of the Caliph. . . .

The growing change in Islamic feeling towards England is most deplorable. It is harmful both to England and to the Moslems themselves. It is harmful to England, because she is the greatest Moslem power upon earth; because she has intricate political and commercial relations with all Moslem states; and because she has a dangerous rival in Asia, who looks upon England's difficulties as her opportunities in every part of the world. No European nation knows the value of Moslem goodwill more than Russia. She is studiously detaching Moslem sympathy everywhere from Great Britain and is losing no opportunity of making herself popular among the followers of the Prophet. . . . But this activity of Russia and her ostentatious display of friendship towards Islam must not blind us to the merits and faults of the real policy of the two Christian nations towards Moslems. . . . Nobody knows it better than Abdul Hamid. It does not require much political study to know that the real aim of Russia is to take Constantinople, if possible, without fighting. . . .

The policy of England, on the other hand, has always been to check the aggression of Russia in the south-east of Europe, by supporting Turkey. Consequently, her best interest is to have a strong Turkey. What does England desire? That His Majesty the Sultan should introduce real reforms in his empire, remove at least the most dangerous causes of disaffection among his subjects, and otherwise improve his government in order to prolong its existence as a civilised State in Europe. Twenty years ago, Lord Beaconsfield made England believe that Turkey would reform her administration, provided sufficient time and peace were given her. Today England is of opinion that Turkey will not improve herself, and that therefore she should cease to support her.

Which of the two policies will the real well-wishers of the Turkish empire favour? Undoubtedly the policy of England. Nine out of ten intelligent Moslems pine for reforms consistent with the integrity of the empire. The Sultan has for the time being joined hands with Russia. But on calmer reflection

His Majesty must see that the step which he has taken will, at best, only make him a vassal of Russia, and gradually result in the absorption of his country by the Slav. That policy must be changed. I have always deplored the attacks in the British press upon the Caliph. Equally do I deplore the recent outburst of ill-feeling towards England in the Turkish press. I have stated that England could not afford to dispense with the sympathy of Islam; neither can the Moslem world afford the permanent hostility of England. It is the duty of all thoughtful Moslems to bring home to the Caliph the evils of his present policy. It is their duty also to impress upon the ministers of the Queen-Empress to re-establish cordial relations between this country and the Islamic world. . . .

NOTES

"The Position of Turkey in Relation to British Interests in India" originally appeared as James Long, "The Position of Turkey in Relation to British Interests in India," *Journal of the East India Association* 9 (December 1875): 179–209. "Letter on Hindustan" originally appeared as Sheikh Jamaluddin Afghani, "Lettre Sur l'Hindoustan," *L'Intransigeant*, April 24, 1883. Translated here by Sravya Darbhamulla. "Europe Revisited" originally appeared as Salar Jung II [Mir Laiq Ali Khan], "Europe Revisited II," *Nineteenth Century* 22, no. 128 (October 1887): 500–10. "The Mussalmans of India and the Armenian Question" originally appeared as Khwaji Ghulam-us-Saqlain, "The Mussalmans of India and the Armenian Question," *Nineteenth Century* 37 (June 1895): 926–39. "The Caliphate" originally appeared as Syed Ahmed Khan, "The Tehzib-ul-Akhlak— the Caliphate," *Aligarh Institute Gazette*, September 11, 1897, 26–32. The essay was subsequently reprinted as "The Sultan and the Caliphate," *Pioneer*, September 19, 1897. The essay prompted an anonymous rebuttal by "Truth" titled "The Sultan and the Caliphate," *Pioneer*, September 25, 1897. Khan's reply was published as "The Law of Jehad," *Pioneer*, September 28, 1897. "A Moslem's View of the Pan-Islamic Revival" originally appeared as Rafiuddin Ahmad, "A Moslem's View of the Pan-Islamic Revival," *Nineteenth Century* 42 (October 1897): 517–26.

1. A Latin phrase meaning "the unknown appears magnificent." See Tacitus, *Complete Works of Tacitus*, trans. Alfred J. Church and William J. Brodribb (New York: Modern Library, 1887), 1.30.

Chapter Five

FREE TRADE

A VOICE FOR THE COMMERCE AND MANUFACTURES OF INDIA, 1873
[Bholanath Chandra]

. . . I want humbly to raise a voice for the commerce and manufactures of India. It is altogether a novel attempt that I propose to make—one among "things unattempted yet in prose or rhyme." Let me break ground by analyzing and criticizing the opinion current about India's unprecedented prosperity under British rule. . . . In a lecture, on the "Industrial Economy of India," delivered by Mr. Beverley at the Canning Institute in 1870, it has been remarked that

> the trade of India on an average of the last five years is upwards of 86 million pounds sterling. A hundred years ago, under the fostering care of the East India Company, it was scarcely two million. In the face of these figures will anyone presume to say that the country has suffered from its connection with the British rule?[1]

. . . Nothing is more common to hear than remarks in this strain upon the thousand and one benefits derived from "British administration," and the great material prosperity of India therefrom. But how far such remarks are well-founded, is a question which has never been raised and subjected to the least scrutiny or examination before the tribunal of public opinion. . . . Looking from the English standpoint, the state of things now certainly contrasts favorably with all previous instances of the kind, and the conclusions arrived at are incontrovertible. This is one way of viewing the matter. But let us shift our ground to the native standpoint. The scene is changed. The prospect wears a different character altogether. It is denuded of all its charms. There is no greater or more pernicious fallacy than that which lurks in the proportion of India's "unparalleled prosperity" under the present regime. I admit the increase of the national harvest. I admit the expansion of trade—the high figures attained by our exports and imports. But I take leave to doubt that their net results have been at all favourable to our nation. . . .

India, described from a native point of view, presents a very different picture from the India presented in Budgets, Blue-books, official reports, and the works of officially-inspired writers. . . . Far from appreciating the immense change in the state of things around them, they question the merit of the commercial policy which has hitherto been at work, and regard it as an insidious evil which has noiselessly effaced all their arts and crafts, and brought on an abject dependence upon foreign industry. . . . Nothing is more sensibly felt by them now-a-days than that the so-called trade of their country, is, properly speaking, no trade of India. Between a trade carried on *bona fide* by the Indians, and a trade carried on by the Europeans, they make a broad distinction. They have discovered that the so-called trade of India benefits only a few foreigners, and not the mass of their nation; and they refuse to place any more confidence in the official assurances. . . . The true criterion to judge by of the prosperity of India, is the degree in which the natives of the country are found to participate in the proceeds arising from its several sources of income, and the store of capital accumulated in their hands. The principal sources of a country's wealth are its labour, its agricultural and mineral produce, its own independent manufactures and commerce, and its territorial revenue, or offices. From none of these sources of national income, excepting that of labour, does any native derive more than a nominal advantage. . . .

The enormous expansion of Indian commerce under British rule, is a phrase which finds frequent employment in the speeches and writings of men in this country. But the term *Indian* made use of has no meaning at all, and makes the phrase altogether absurd and deceptive. It may have a meaning in the mouths of the Anglo-Indians, who carry on that commerce, and reap all its benefits. It has no meaning whatever in the mouths of the natives, who take no part in that commerce. Surely that commerce ought not rightly to be called Indian, which is not carried on by the Indians themselves, which does not accumulate and circulate capital in India, and which does not contribute to its enrichment. . . .

The only fact about which there can be no dispute, is the growth of a demand for certain articles, such as jute, oilseeds, and opium, which did not exist before, and under which demand those articles are now extensively cultivated and produced. This is, strictly speaking, development of Indian agriculture, and not expansion of Indian commerce. India has a home-trade of its own, but not any maritime trade. The profit of her commodities ceases to India the moment they are sold off in the port of shipment. They no more bring any return to a native, but to the foreign shipper. There is scarcely a native merchant or ship owner, no native voyager or supercargo, no native Insurance office, no native Bank, and no native agency in foreign markets, the operations of all which machinery can truly be said to constitute Indian commerce, and from which can accrue any real prosperity to India. The Indians have long retired from the sea, and the carrying trade that was once in their hands has passed away into those of the Europeans. . . .

Considered in a true commercial light, many of the exports of our country, are "not exchanged in the course of barter, but . . . taken away without any return or payment whatsoever."[2] The trade in our best raw-silk, indigo, lac-dye, shell-lac, and tea, is carried on without any purchase and payment. Those staples are grown or manufactured and taken out of India by foreigners, who retain all the profits in their country. . . . Instead of a flow of money into the country, there is a continuous undercurrent of drain. This drain first set in from the time when "the East India Company kept aside a portion of the Indian Revenue" for their commercial investments. Money then passed out through a single channel, but it now pours away through a thousand outlets. Far from prospering, our country evidently suffers from its export trade, "what is tantamount to an annual plunder"[3] of some £25,000,000—the sum made by the balance of trade due to her. . . .

No untruth is more strenuously sought to be impressed upon our minds than that we form an agricultural nation. Such a misrepresentation is impeached and scouted by all history. From time immemorial India has never been a consumer of foreign goods and manufactures. She is the cradle of all the principal arts which minister to the well-being of mankind. The rest of the world is her pupil in them. It is she who manufactured for other nations, while none manufactured for her. But by a mischievous inversion of that order of things, she is now a dependent upon foreign looms and forges for her supply. Her own rich mineral resources lie neglected, while she buys iron and copper from other countries. Her own raw cotton is all taken away from her, while she has to buy back the self-same cotton in the shape of made material. Every civilized country in the world is now striving to develop its own independent industry, while one manufacture after another is being crushed out of India under the destructive system of our ruling power. The arts and manufactures of a country form to it an important source of wealth. Without them, there is no digestion and assimilation of the gold and silver flowing into it from outside commerce. They disappear in a receding ebb tide from its dependence on foreign industry. . . .

There remains now the item of revenue to gauge the prosperity or decline of India. True, her territorial revenue has now reached a figure which it never did at any time in its past history. In the most palmy days of the Moguls, it was 32 crores. It now exceeds 50 crores—a sum raised only by the first-class Powers in the world. But the revenue of a country is never fructuous without a recognition of the give-and-take principle. Here only the first and better half of that principle is followed. Money is raised from the people of which only an infinitesimal portion ever finds its way back again into their hands. The chief and lucrative posts are all filled by Europeans, who are gorged with public money. The natives ask for bread, and receive a stone. It is the European civil service, the European army, the European justices, engineers, doctors, schoolmasters, clergymen, railway-proprietors, and fund-holders that almost wholly absorb and eat up the vast sum, leaving at the most but a tithe for the natives, who are soured at the small share of the loaves and fishes of the State falling to their lot. . . . Look at the enormous remittance of 16 crores of rupees for the Home Charges, annually draining and disappearing from the country never to return to it again. . . .

Nor has much profit accrued to our country from what I may term the secondary sources of a nation's income. The learned professions make a rich field, but from which it is the Europeans who gather the largest harvest. It is they who keep to themselves the most valuable appointments, enjoy the largest practice, and charge the heaviest commissions and fees. No native lawyer, attorney, schoolmaster, editor, litterateur, engineer, artist, or doctor has yet turned a rich man. The banks are all in the hands of the Europeans. The principal brokers are Europeans. The railways belong to European companies. The gas company is European. The public architecture is built and repaired by Europeans. The public advertisements and printing are given to the Europeans. The very university courses are published by European booksellers. The very Native Hospital is being erected by European builders. In India, which way you turn, it is the European making money that meets the eye. There is no room or verge for the natives—no prize, patronage, or prospect for them. They are studiously kept in the background—at arm's length—and beyond a certain range of the rich preserves of the heaven-born. This *world is made for Caesar*. . . .

The only sources from which India derives an undoubted profit, are labour and land. The labour market remains intact to her children, uninvaded by the foreigner. They owe this non-interference, however, not to the tender mercies of a paternal Government, but to the *Indian Sun*, that keeps out all *Saheb* diggers, bricklayers, and coolies, from the land. Our laboring classes are now decidedly in better circumstances than in the days of impressment and scanty wages. The *Banias*, or moneylenders, also form a class that is the creation of the British regime. Our landowners, too, are, many of them, monied men. If there is any class to represent the wealth of our country, it is the *Zamindars* and *Talukdars* who have thrived under the Permanent Settlement. . . .

Thus, with the exception of land and labour, there is no other source—agriculture, commerce, banking, manufactures, office, or profession, from which there accrues any increment to the indigenous estate and national wealth of India, to justify the prevailing opinion of its growing prosperity. Instead of accumulation of capital, there is a depletion. Instead of aggrandizement, there is decay. The *Kohinoor* is gone. The treasuries of the ancient Princes of the land have been emptied. The hoarded wealth of ages has disappeared. . . .

There is as little truth in the current opinion of India's prosperity, as in that of its being "a burdensome possession to the British crown." The power and prestige of England are all from that possession. . . . There is unquestioned moral and intellectual elevation under British dispensation, but no *material prosperity*. . . . In the light of facts shed upon the subject, the small value of the commercial statistics commonly cited, is well seen. They prove the existence of prosperity upon paper, but not in reality. In the face of the drain pointed out, will anyone presume to deny that the country has not suffered from its connection with the British nation[?]

It is time to dissipate the error involved in the opinions forming the settled creed of the country and governing the public mind. Upon the exposition of their fallacy depends the prosperous future of India. I have referred to all, the principal points for consideration, with as much brevity as is consistent with a clear and intelligible demonstration. But it is the particular object of this paper to examine in detail the questions of India's commerce and manufactures, and to advocate a change of the Indian commercial policy—a policy that should abolish all duty upon the exports to enable behind-hand India to compete with more intelligent nations, and that should levy an increased rate of duties upon the Imports to rescue her arts and industries from ruin, and give to the country, which has been robbed of its liberty, a true and substantial glory in exchange.

It is not a little surprising that a matter of such high importance from fiscal considerations, as the restoration of our commerce to its ancient basis, and the revival of our manufactures, should never have suggested itself to the mind of any portion of our community. . . . The silence of the European community in general, interested as it deeply is in maintaining the existing commercial not less than political *regime*, is the most natural thing in the world. . . . But I am surprised at the supineness and negligence of the natives themselves, to whom it has occurred never to discuss the question and expose the fallacy of the declarations and doctrines of their rulers. To this day they have not entered a protest against the policy which has brought on the decadence of their trade and manufactures and reduced them to an abject dependence on foreign looms and forges. So little are they interested in the study of commercial politics, that there is scarcely anybody among them who has ever given a thought to the matter and brought home to his mind the fact of his living in a state of double slavery. They take no pains to gather any commercial statistics from the actual state of things around them and ascertain the actual fact. They never inquire into the condition of our weavers and calculate the annual loss to our country from the decay of its large cotton-industry. The idea of a Native Chamber of Commerce to protect their commercial interests, has not yet entered into anyone's head. Our young men all go to England either for the Civil Service, the Medical

Service, or the Bar. No one goes to attend the lectures at the Royal Institution, or the Royal School of Mines, London, or enter any of the schools of practical engineering or useful arts, or learn iron smelting at Birmingham, or cloth-weaving at Manchester. There is a universal craving only for the profits of office—no inclination for mercantile or manufacturing pursuits. The educated natives have not yet got over the prejudice of their ancestors against trade—still thinking it less honorable than quill-driving. They are pleased with a few casual bonbons or lollipops in the shape of a High Court judgeship, or Foreign Office attacheship—contemptuous crumbs to Cerberus or reluctant sacrifices to a vague apprehension of the Nemesis of Injustice. Barren Rajaships and Rai Bahadurships make them content and turn them away from their duties to the nation. They struggle for semblance of worth and neglect the substance. I do not find them wanting in shrewdness, but I cannot overlook the weakness which makes them so easy victims. This is partly traceable to their antecedents, and partly to the defective system of their mere book-reading education. . . . It is high time for them to direct their attention towards the substantial interests of the country—towards the attainment of those materialistic improvements, without which our progress can never be solid, and our nation can never get to "a status co-equal with that of the civilized and superior nations of the earth." . . .

The native English [and] vernacular papers, should preach for the founding of independent native banks, native companies and corporations, native mills and factories, and Native Chambers of Commerce in the Presidencies. They should denounce the insensate practice of preferring foreign goods to home-made manufactures. They should inculcate the discipline of self-denial, and the cultivation of patriotic sentiments. They should collect and compile details of Indian urban life, to draw public attention to the helpless condition of our weavers, blacksmiths, and mechanics. They should point out the enormous and unceasing drain upon the profits of Indian labour, to show that the country is growing poorer year by year, and thoroughly expose the statistical delusion of the authorities. They should sedulously strive for the subversion of the policy, which, in addition to our political slavery, has steeped the country also in an industrial slavery. . . .

Not one of our platform men has ever come forward to expatiate upon the all-important theme. It has never been broached in native literature—never been treated of in any native magazine. It has never been the grievance of a public memorial—never been made the occasion for a monster-meeting. The nation is busy only in acquiring brainpower. It minds not its material needs. Such is either the blind ignorance or profound apathy prevailing amongst the natives towards a subject, to which their attention ought to be diverted from all other channels—which should be "the ocean to the rivers of all their thoughts"—which should appeal not to their self-love only but also to their patriotism; particularly if the formation of themselves into a recognised nation be at all their ambition.

THE COMMERCE AND MANUFACTURES OF
INDIA—ANOTHER VIEW, 1873
Kissen Mohun Malik

I have carefully perused the article in the last number of this periodical entitled "A Voice for the Commerce and Manufactures of India." This voice is not a novelty, but a mere echo of that clamour which at the present moment is raised by several unpracticed theorists throughout this country and even in England.

Many loudly deplore the loss of our trade in Indian cotton manufacture, and evince a wish for its restoration, which is the offspring of an unprofitable over-zeal. This show of patriotism reminds me of the well-known fable of "the cats and the mice"; but none I see, practically speaking, dare hang the bell by suggesting even the plausible means for attaining that desirable end. That India once enjoyed exclusively the boon of this once flourishing branch of our commerce, none can deny. In those days of yore, she had no rival, weak or formidable, to compete with. She had all the advantages of a monopoly, which as a general rule, can never be lasting to doomsday. Take, for instance, the monopoly in this region of the late East India Company, which was knocked at the head by the English Parliament after it had existed for fully 200 years. To that monopoly were our weavers chiefly indebted for the consumption of their manufactures. In bewailing the extinction of the Indian trade in cotton piece-goods, we may as well bewail the loss of the Company's monopoly and pray for its revival. . . .

This writer as well as others ascribe the cruelty of depriving our weavers of their bread, to commercial and political handicapping of the English, but they seem to be totally unmindful of the real cause of that disaster. It was no intrigue or unfair play on the part of the British Government or merchants that ruined our trade in cotton goods, but in truth it was the power-looms of Great Britain and the best quality of the cotton produced in the United States which killed this trade in Bengal, not all India, as I shall show hereafter. The unrivalled superiority of the most valuable fiber of America at once enabled the Manchester millers not only to produce cloths of unexceptionable qualities, but to lay them at outports at costs which proved highly tempting to customers of all classes. These cloths were sought after with the greatest eagerness, and this in the face of a rapid increase in their imports: our own cloths, which theretofore had cost three to four times as much as the price paid for English goods, made room for the latter. For instance, a piece of 39 yards 7 lb grey shirting could lately be had for 4 Rs. 8 annas. per piece; whereas a piece of Bengal cloth of similar texture and dimension, if such Bengal ever produced at all, could hardly be procured for less than 15 Rs. a piece, or 6 annas. a yard at the least. As to the comparative qualities of the two species of cloths, I cannot help stating here candidly, though somewhat to the disparagement of our country's manufacturers, that our Indian cotton goods were generally of a deceptive make and character, while the English, especially in earlier days, were even and smooth from one end to the other. Poor souls whose comfort in the cold season was formerly basking in the sun in the morning, and warming themselves in the evening by the side of a fire made of dry leaves, were afterwards in a position not only to cover their indecency, but to cover their whole frame with the products of Manchester. Thus, millions of the poor are benefitted, whilst a few thousand weavers suffered by the influx of foreign goods. Well, gradually then, our own manufactures, as a matter of course, died a natural death. What I say here is not a hearsay, a mere hypothesis, or an exaggeration, but is the result of personal experience.

Unfortunately for the artisans of Bengal, supineness and the total absence of that energy which behooves them, especially when they have to contend with foreign invasion of rival articles, are their characteristics. For these reasons they evidently slackened themselves in their perseverance to keep up their trade with greater care and assiduity. Had they acted with a moral courage, they might have still retained in their hands some portion of the trade now almost totally annihilated. They were then more independent and not in need of foreign encouragement, and might have to some extent sustained their position.

From the appearance in these markets of a new and a powerful rival, the Madras weavers had cause to share a similar fate with those of Bengal, but it is no little praiseworthy to the former to hold out yet, in their honest occupation both at home and even in a country whose products have shoved out of market those of Bengal. . . . If the Bengal manufacturers should have suffered from such dodges, Madras must have suffered likewise; but no, the misfortune so bitterly complained of in sympathy with the Bengal weavers, has independently of what I have observed before, visited them from scientific inventions and natural incidents, as well as the incomparable wealth of Great Britain; advantages which Bengal never possessed for warding off that misfortune. The writer of the article under review says:

> If India's manufacturing power was so great in times of misrule and anarchy, when genius had little encouragement, and labor a scanty reward, how many times more would that power have increased under the security of life and property we now enjoy, under increased intelligence, increased energy, and increased prosperity.[4]

Now he runs down the English and gives them credit in the same breath. He talks of "misrule" and "anarchy" of the former dynasty, and with some degree of candour unconsciously expresses his gratitude to none but the British Government "for our increased security of life and property, increased intelligence" and so forth. All I can make of this assertion is a desire for transferring the gigantic power of England in cloth-making to India, and to give all the prestige now enjoyed by Manchester and Glasgow to our Dhaka and Shantipur.

The writer perhaps is not aware of the attempts heretofore made, not by natives of Bengal but by men of that august nation to which we are indebted "for our increased intelligence, energy and prosperity" to manufacture cotton piece-goods at places not far from Calcutta. All their combined efforts failed, though millions of rupees were sunk in the undertakings. The fact is that cloths made in this part of India do not and cannot generally pay by reason of the absence of those advantages which England possesses over other countries. Germany lately attempted with the aid of her powerful machinery to compete with Manchester by importing here her own cotton twist, and soon after gave way to the more economical and more useful twist of England; though every encouragement was afforded by our Government by the removal of differential duties on foreign goods. Even the United States attempted to trespass here upon Manchester, but failed at last, though she possesses an ascendency over all other countries in respect to the production of cloths with her own cotton on the spot. In 1859–60, the year before the Civil War in America, she had sent us her cotton goods of the value of Rs. 5,43,280, and in 1869–70 Rs. 31,824 only, whereas from Great Britain alone we imported in the last-mentioned year cotton piece-goods of the value of Rs. 8 crores and 12 lacs.

I have already said that all cotton-growing countries depend upon the manufactures of Manchester. A few years before the American War when cotton wool was cheaper and the produce of Manchester was inexhaustible, her customers at home and abroad were unable to take up her enormous stocks. England then openly expressed a wish for the discovery of another world for consuming her vast produce. In the face of such an all-absorbing power of English manufacturers any attempt on the part of our Bengalis at cloth-making under a renewed activity and with the support of English skill, English machinery and English capital, would be preposterous in the extreme.

One word more on this subject, and I have done with it. . . . The Manchester millers and merchants, as well as our English importers here, are content with almost a nominal profit. It would therefore be a fruitless attempt on the part of the manufacturers here to undersell them. It is urged by many that the saving of transit and other incidental charges to which the imported goods are subject, is a sufficient inducement for a fair trial in this part of the country; but in fact, as experiment has shown, the advantage of manufacturing in Bengal is more than counterbalanced by those numerous drawbacks which counteract a successful issue. The cost of the block and machinery, the heavy charge of keeping the engines in good repair, the extravagant expense attending the maintenance of a European establishment, the impossibility of getting at raw cotton of a superior quality at a moderate cost, and above all, the interest upon the capital which will have to be borrowed, would tell seriously upon the concern. To any individual of practical experience these drawbacks are enough to discourage him at once.

By heedlessly laying blame at the door of England for destroying our piece-goods trade, we may as well find fault with her for shutting out of foreign markets our once extensive trade in Benares Sugar, with China for throwing into the shade the bulk of our raw silk, and with Germany for interfering with our saltpeter. Common sense ought to teach all non-commercial theorists that cheap goods of one country supersede those of another when they are comparatively higher in value. Now there are several of our staples which are most in favor with customers in other parts of the world, and their exports have increased and consequently their prices are high. To protect them from being encroached upon by rival countries I ventured to recommend an extension of cultivation in order that we might lay our produce at a more tempting price. I was, therefore, of opinion, as I still am, that agriculture is our only resource. If we have lost our export and home trade in Bengal cotton piece-goods to the extent of, say 3 crores of rupees, we have since produced articles of a value of five times that amount for export only.

Rice	3 Crores
Jute	1½ Crores
Linseed	1½ Crores
Opium	6 Crores
Tea	2 Crores
Indigo	2 Crores

How far our landholders, agriculturists and laborers of every denomination have severally benefitted by the extension of the produce of our soil, I need scarcely dwell upon. It is very justly and truly observed by some journalist that out of the total profit derived from our products, 5 per cent only is left to the exporter, if anything at all. To any impartial observer, the increase in our export trade is glaring enough not to admit of the loss of our commerce in Bengal cotton manufactures having been by far compensated. If a section of the Bengal populace has suffered in one department, they have in common with several others reaped rich harvest in other divisions of our traffic. To say that England pockets 10 crores of rupees by importing here piece-goods of that value, is to ignore that she has had to pay us by far more than that sum by taking off our hands commodities of various descriptions too numerous for detail. We do not pay her the equivalent in coin, but in kind, nay receive from her more than she does from us.

I have recommended our enlightened natives to "wield the plough." I now more confidently aver that in our agricultural pursuits solely depends the prosperity of our countrymen. In these unpropitious times, such as are engaged in trade frequently are crossed by adverse results. Those who labor under the bondage of servitude are hardly in a position to meet both ends. Being so situated, what can be more desirable for us than to take to an honorable and independent profession which holds out to us at all times the brightest prospects for acquiring that prosperity which we are fruitlessly hankering after by unprofitable pursuits? Let us produce articles by means of extended cultivation and bring them to market at reduced costs, and we shall never be in want of customers to purchase them of us at remunerative rates. . . . Application is all that is necessary, and in course of time, as energy and enterprise shall hold out an encouragement, ample will doubtless be the reward for all labor and expense for bringing those lands under cultivation. Let us act prudently and in harmony with those under whose rule and protection it has pleased Providence to place us, and we shall not fail to prosper and be happy. But it is much to be pitied that talking at random against power and policy is becoming a chronic disorder with the more enlightened of our present generation. . . .

A FEW THOUGHTS ON THE POVERTY OF INDIA, 1897
P. Ananda Charlu

. . . The two directions . . . in which most men would in the first instance look for the causes that have impoverished India, are to detect what has told on the tiller of the soil and what, on the skilled workman. Taking the latter first, they will see that India received free trade with open arms, and her industries have become extinct; but a great many, if not all of the other countries of the world, not less enlightened than Great Britain, have seemingly listened to the siren voice of what is nicknamed protection and they have marvelously piled up wealth, with their industries, which were nowhere at one time, multiplying and expanding, so as to threaten even England's ascendancy in almost every mart on the globe. This palpable antithesis has led not a few cultured Indians to swear against free trade and denounce it as the main author of India's industrial misfortune of the present day. That under these circumstances, the uncultured mass of

Indians, witnessing heaps of their skilled workmen out of employ or eking out, at best, a miserable hand-to-mouth existence, should mutter bitter curses—though inaudibly—against the saviour of England's commercial greatness is therefore only too natural.

Having regard to this spreading opinion against free trade, it is incumbent on anyone who wishes to speak on the poverty of India to examine that opinion and pronounce his conclusions without mincing matters, to the best of his lights. Let me at once declare that I am a firm, conscientious and loyal adherent of free trade. No one who is capable of thought or even is capable of understanding a plain, fundamental principle could possibly take up an attitude of opposition to the universally intelligible dictum that an imported article when not taxed, i.e. when imported under free trade, would be available to the consumer, cheaper than when it was taxed i.e. when the consumer got it, with the addition which the importer would make to its price by distributing the tax he pays, over the articles, so taxed. This is the fundamental principle of free trade and so far, it must be perfectly intelligible to the cultured and the uncultured alike. . . .

The Indian consumer may, from the boundless charity that is within him, prefer that when he himself is not hard pressed, the skilled workmen in his own community should be properly fed and clothed, so that these may have their customary living, may not starve and be thrown on the State, on the country and on foreign charity. If the State represents the aggregate of the charitable consumers, it will check all invasion which might have a contrary result. This, in effect, may amount to taxation of imported articles and be, in reality, an indirect tax, falling on the consumer in the shape of an enhanced price. But then, *ex hypothesi*, the consumer submits to it, out of consideration for the well-being of a mass of his own country's skilled workmen. How does it clash with free trade? Such presumably is the plea for what the countries, other than England, have been doing all along and it appears to me to be a good enough plea. Their policy has indeed been stigmatised as a policy of protection. It all depends on the point of view. It may produce the same result as protection but may not emanate from any desire to favour protection.

In every enlightened country, which has a government of its own, the State represents the people and reflects the ideas and sentiments of the people. The British government represents the British and the British government of the day, in adhering to free trade, reflects the ideas and wishes of the British—the actual tax-payers—in that direction. . . . In this respect the people of this country are at a tremendous disadvantage. Our British masters have not yet contrived for India a governmental machinery the voice of which may be the expression of the voice of the people, i.e., their charitable sentiments and patriotic self-denials, for the general good of the entire community to which they belong. I do not say that, when this becomes an accomplished fact, all will be well. But this I venture to assert that till this consummation were achieved, the poverty of India would not be sensibly diminished and the advancement of her people would not but be seriously retarded, despite our railroads, telegraphs, post office and the other paraphernalia of modern civilization. The people are unable to make their government realise what their wishes are. The educated among them are brusquely set at naught; and the rest are set down as incapable of thought. The consequence, in the meantime, is that the impression is abroad that the innocent free trade has ruined India's industrial interests and that the British rule is responsible for it. . . .

But is free trade really responsible for our customary industries having withered? Is it not, far rather, a change in the tastes of the people—be it for better or for worse—and the inevitable competition between handiwork and machine-power? I have not here in Calcutta the necessary materials to explain, by means of figures, wherein lies the cheapness of the one and the costliness of the other. This must, however, come home to people at large from the fact that the machine-made articles of apparel have been steadily making headway.

There is further an element, contributing, not unoften, to the cheapness of these articles, which is not generally known. Great capitalists in Great Britain as elsewhere own extensive industries, carried on through machinery and hosts of specially skilled workmen. If these workmen are once disbanded, they are difficult to be again got together. But if, in obtaining his money's worth from these workmen, any manufacturer finds on his hands any great surplus i.e., more than is needed in the markets to which he has access, three courses are open to him. He must either disband the workmen or pay them for being idle or pay them for making articles, particularly cheap. The first course is obviously suicidal. The second is sheer wastefulness. As to the last, though it is not altogether free from entailing loss on the manufacturer, it certainly has the advantage of reducing the weight of his loss. . . . The bearing of these seemingly irrelevant remarks, is this: viz., that we are subject to goods such as these coming into the country in floods and selling at marvelously cheap prices. Thus, in the face of this doubly overpowering encroachment of European manufactures it is idle to hope that, for the benefit of our hosts of weaving population, all these cheap fabrics should be studiously and artificially kept out of the country and from meeting the prevailing altered tastes which, be it wisely or unwisely, have created a demand for them.

From this point of view, it might strike one, at the first blush, that the movements, here and there preached and here and there given practical effect to, to induce our people to confine themselves to indigenous (*Swadeshi*) articles of clothing as far as possible are abnormal efforts, notwithstanding that they betoken humanitarian feelings of the noblest type. To my mind they are perfectly intelligible and perfectly sound, as I understand free trade. These movements fall well within the principle I have already ventured to set forth viz., that if the consumer, deliberately and with his eyes open, would consent to buy the dearer article or even one particular sort of article in preference to another cheaper or of the same value, he does it by free choice and out of humanity to hosts of his own countrymen, whom he would benefit and befriend, both from an unselfish charitable nature and from the selfish dictates of a wish to escape future taxation for preserving them from starvation and death.

While therefore I look with unqualified approval, upon the patriotic *Swadeshi* movements and insist upon their spread, as self-denying but transitory efforts for the good of an appreciable section of the indigenous population, I am clearly of opinion that it would be leaning against a slender reed to rely upon them alone, or even mainly, for the industrial salvation of this country. They are good enough as concomitants. But they fall far below the mark as permanent and perennial sources of our industrial development, which, to be progressive, must be natural, not heroic merely; for it is not everybody who will take away his eyes from the self and submit to large and continual orders on his generosity and purse. It is a truism that no country prospers which does not move with the spirit and the tendencies of the times. While you are in Rome you must be like a Roman, is a [saying] which has a far wider application than appears on the surface. Unless our endeavours are, so to speak, on up-to-date lines of improvements we are doomed to lag behind, go to the wall and die out industrially—even if the much-maligned free trade were turned out of doors. The public taste, like the public mind, is essentially variable with the varying fashion and exigencies; and the exigencies of the present day and a perception of comforts and conveniences, hitherto unknown, accentuate the need to suit ourselves to the altered conditions. It seems to me therefore that the tweed, the surge and the broad-cloth are bound to form the staple material, at least with the dressy upper ten in our country, and it is therefore a factor that should never be left out of account in all our considerations and projects of our industrial development. In a word, what we want is not revival but regeneration—not that the defunct and dying industries, famous as of old, should be set on foot so much as that others should be started, utilising the machine-power of the day in imitation of Europe and Japan. . . .

But what is relevant in this connection is that, so far as our nascent industries are concerned, they cannot outrage free trade, if her concessions are carried out in fidelity by those who are responsible for the well-being of India. . . . I know and I freely confess that factory laws have been enacted for India, which are utterly uncalled for and have only been the result of crocodile tears, shed elsewhere for our mill-hands. That these and such as these are harmful—and gratuitously harmful—to our rising mill and other industries, I do not hesitate to admit. But the fact remains that they are frauds in the name of humanitarianism and free trade and not the legitimate outcome of free trade principles. Let our effort be, not to disparage the claims of free trade, but to expose her false friends; and let us, in season and out of season, press for a full and unqualified recognition of two most important doctrines which free trade unreservedly grants. The first of them is that, for purposes of necessary taxation, tariff duties are perfectly legitimate, even although they result in indirect competition or produce effects, such as follow from an active policy of protection. The second of the doctrines I have referred to is that a moderate degree of protection is rightly admissible, where the industries are yet young; for free trade is but free fight and how can there be sense in allowing a free fight as between a tender stripling of a lad and the studied robustness of a gymnast.

What is of vastly greater importance than quarrels with the free trade and injuries inflicted in her name is for us to reform ourselves and take to turning to our account the almost illimitable potential wealth of the country. . . . Now, having regard to this limitless store-house of raw materials, how does it come about that, like Tantalus, we are starving in the midst of plenty? It is want of union between wealth and talent, between the purse and the brain. It is, to use the simile of a Sanskrit poet, the want of peace and harmony between the mother-in-law, the goddess Lakshmi, and the daughter-in-law, the goddess Saraswati. This want of combination between the two potent agents of wide spreading good has yet a deeper cause. It is the want of mutual trust and want of adequate and dignified conception of labour. The perfect confidence, with which people of the West put their funds in the hands of the bankers or of directors of great industries and the unruffled composure with which they contemplate the use and the fruitfulness of their money are yet mere ideas in our country. So penny-wise and pound-foolish we are and such confirmed believers in a bird in hand being [better than] two in the bush, that, till quite recently, our staff for managing undertakings costing lakhs, did not cost us quite half a hundred a month. A radical change in these respects is bound to bring us untold wealth and put us on a career of prosperity which neither free trade, true or false, nor other, real or fancied, causes of disturbance could seriously and materially affect. . . .

NOTES

"A Voice for the Commerce and Manufactures of India" originally appeared as [Bholanath Chandra], "A Voice for the Commerce and Manufacture of India," *Mookerjee's Magazine* 2, no. 7 (March 1873): 79–121. "The Commerce and Manufactures of India—Another View" originally appeared as Kissen Mohun Mullick, "The Commerce and Manufactures of India—Another View," *Mookerjee's Magazine* 2, no. 8 (May 1873): 202–11. "A Few Thoughts on the Poverty of India" originally appeared as P. Ananda Charlu, *A Few Thoughts on the Poverty of India: A Paper Read at the Anniversary Meeting of the Chaitanya Library* (Calcutta: Juno Printing Works, 1897).

1. *Report of the Canning Institute for Sessions 1868–69 and 1869–70* (Calcutta, J. M. Gomes, 1868).
2. *Ninth Report from the Select Committee Appointed to Take Into Consideration the State of the Administration of Justice in the Provinces of Bengal, Bahar, and Orissa* (London: J. Debrett, 1785), 30.
3. *Ninth Report from the Select Committee*, 30.
4. [Bholanath Chandra], "A Voice for the Commerce and Manufacture of India," *Mookerjee's Magazine* 2, no. 7 (March 1873): 116.

Chapter Six

RACISM

INDIAN FOREIGN EMIGRATION, 1893
Mahadev Govind Ranade

No object of national economy is more directly practical in its bearings upon the prosperity of the people than the question of providing expansive and remunerative labour facilities commensurate with the natural growth of the population. The Report of the Famine Commission has emphatically drawn public attention to the fact that

> at the root of much of the Poverty of the people of India, and the risks to which they are exposed in seasons of scarcity, lies the unfortunate circumstance that Agriculture forms almost the sole occupation of the mass of the population, and that no remedy for present evils can be complete which does not include the introduction of a diversity of occupation, through which the surplus population may be drawn from agricultural pursuits, and led to find their means of subsistence on Manufactures, or some such Employment.[1]

There can be no doubt that the permanent salvation of the country depends upon the growth of Indian manufactures and commerce, and that all other remedies can only be temporal palliatives. At the same time, it is admitted that this diversity and change of occupation is a very arduous undertaking. It presupposes a change of habits, it postulates the previous growth of culture and a spirit of enterprise, an alertness of mind, an elasticity of temper, a readiness to meet and conquer opposition, a facility of organization, social ambition and aspiration, a mobile and restless condition of capital and labour, all which qualities and changes are the slow growth of centuries of freedom and progress. It is the object of Associations, like those under the auspices of which we meet here today, to promote and facilitate this change and diversity of occupation, but it is clear that, as a present remedy, there is but little hope of relief in this direction. A vast majority of the surplus poor population of an agricultural country can only be naturally fitted to work as agriculturist labourers, and the slow development of our manufactures, borne down as they are by the stress of foreign competition, cannot provide at present the much-needed relief of work suited to their aptitudes. Inland and overland emigration, the overflow of the surplus population from the congested parts of the country to lands where labour is dear and highly remunerative, can alone afford the sorely needed present relief. . . .

Inland emigration, however, cannot be, in any way, compared in its volume, or in its immediate and remote bearings on national prosperity, with foreign emigration to the British and French and Dutch colonies beyond the seas. I propose in this paper briefly to give a summary of the history and progress of Indian foreign emigration. Few people are aware of the comparative magnitude of this relief, thus afforded to our surplus population, and of the magnificent field for extension which is opening before our vision in the possibilities of the future. In this respect, the expansion of the British empire in Africa is a direct gain to the mass of the population of this country. The permanent opening up of the heart of Africa and of the central regions of Australia would not be possible or advantageous even to the indomitable resources of British skill and capital, if it did not secure the help of the unlimited and intelligent labour and skill of Indian emigrants. Of course, there are difficulties in the way, as there will be difficulties in the way of all great enterprises. But the certainties of the future are too imperative to be much interfered with by these present dangers and inconveniences. The tastes, habits, temperaments, and prejudices of our people have acquired an inveterate force which makes it no easy task to adapt themselves to new surroundings, and yet if the old thraldom of prejudice and easy self-satisfaction and patient resignation is ever to be loosened, and new aspirations and hopes created in their place, a change of home surroundings is a standing necessity and a preparatory discipline, whose material and moral benefits can never be too highly estimated. . . .

The first question we have, therefore, to consider in this connection, is the extent of this foreign emigration and the localities to which it has spread. The localities where Indian coolies emigrate are Mauritius, Natal, Jamaica, Trinidad, St. Lucia, Grenada, St. Vincent, St. Kitts, the Fiji Islands, British Guiana, French and Dutch Guiana, the French Possessions of Martinique, Guadeloupe, Reunion, the Danish Island of St. Croix, Ceylon, and the Straits Settlements. In 1874, the Government of India appointed a special officer to report upon the question of coolie emigration from India. That Report gives a detailed account of the condition of these settlements, and I shall first try to summarize its leading features, and then bring down the information to more recent times, with the help of such official publications as were made available to me.[2]

Mauritius

Mauritius is the largest, I am speaking advisedly, of our Indian colonial settlements.... The Indians were 1,50,000 males, and about 1,00,000 females, out of a total population of 3,60,000 souls. More than two-thirds of the population of the Island is thus of Indian origin.... The indentured Indian adult Coolies get, besides their rations and houses free of rent, five to seven rupees a month, and have to work six days in the week, and nine hours each day. Medical care is free of charge and there is a free return passage provided at the end of the term of five years.... The total amount of savings brought by the returned coolies was Rs. 32,394 in 1890. In some previous years, this total was as high as Rs. 1,40,000, Rs. 1,03,000 and Rs. 1,23,000 in 1886, 1887, and 1888 respectively. The savings in Deposit Banks to the credit of the Indian coolies resident in the colony show an average of Rs. 16,50,000 during the three years 1888–1890....

British Guiana

... In 1838, the first importation of 400 Indian coolies took place. In 1844–45, the number of Indian coolies imported was 4,616. Between 1850 and 1870, about 65,000 Indian coolies were imported, out of whom 7,000 returned to India during the same period. In 1871, the total population of the colony was two lakhs, out of whom 43,000 were Indians.... The fact that there are thousands of Indians who do not care to return to India, even after a stay of fifteen or twenty years, goes to show that, on the whole, these Indian settlers are well-off in the colony. . . . About 2,820 Immigrants who returned between 1839 and 1869 brought with them 95,000 dollars to India. . . .

Trinidad

. . . The total population of the island in 1856 was 68,000, of whom 4,000 were natives, and about 2,000 Africans, and 4,000 Indian coolies. In 1871, the Indian immigrants had increased to nearly 23,000 souls. . . . On completion of the five years' term, a certificate of industrial residence is given, and after ten years, a man is allowed free passage back to India, or he may in lieu thereof, claim a ten acre grant of Crown land. . . . A large portion elect to remain in Trinidad when they are entitled to free passage back to India. Those who go to India take large sums of money with them, and not a few return back to Trinidad. . . . The annual remittances to India by Trinidad coolies range from £15,000 to £23,000. Since 1869, about 1,168 Coolies have received their land allotments of ten acres each, 1,475 have each received a five-acre allotment, and about 3,100 took their £5 bounty in lieu of return passage. The total population in Trinidad in 1891 was 71,533 of whom nearly 55,000 were coolies. . . .

Jamaica

. . . Indian immigrants were first introduced in 1845. In the first three years, about 4,000 Indians were imported into the colony. . . . In 1871 the number of Indian coolies was nearly 10,000. . . . After the indentured term of five years is over, the Indian coolie is free to follow any calling he likes. . . . After ten years' residence, the immigrant becomes entitled to a free passage, which he may commute by accepting a grant of ten acres of Crown land. . . . The total number of Indians in the colony in 1892 was 14,000, of whom 4,100 were working under indentures, and 10,000 had completed their ten years, and were working as free labourers. There were 667 Indian depositors in the Savings Banks, and the amount to their credit was 14,054 dollars. . . .

Natal

Immigration into Natal first commenced in 1860. Since that date 50,101 Indian immigrants entered Natal. Out of this total number, 5,172 died, 7,115 returned to India, and 4,552 left the colony otherwise, in thirty-two years. . . . After retiring from the position of labourers, many Indians take up Crown land and grow sugarcane on their own farms. . . . The children of the coolies live and thrive better in Natal than in India. The death rate is lower, and the general state of health is better. . . . They generally form a prosperous and orderly section of the population of Natal. . . . Their reputation for reliability and Industry is thoroughly established, and without them the industry of the colony could not be carried on. . . . As might be expected, there must be, in the nature of things, considerable conflict of interests between the Indian traders and the White population, and things apparently have gone from bad to worse during the last few years. . . .

. . . This completes our review of the British, French, and Dutch colonies and possessions to which, during the past fifty years and more, the surplus labour of India has been exported. Taking a general view of the question, it will be seen that foreign emigration from India represents a large and most important interest. As the result of the past fifty years of protected emigration, as many as 12,00,000 of people are to be found scattered throughout these settlements. The popularity of foreign emigration is evidenced by the following facts which can be gathered from the Reports: (1) The number of emigrants has been steadily increasing. (2) The proportion of women to men is also more favourable in recent years than it was in the first half of this period of fifty years, 1842–1892. (3) The number of those who return back to India has always been smaller than those who left each year. (4) Among those who return to India, a good many re-emigrate with their families, (5) Of those who go out of India as indentured labourers under contract, nearly one half settle in these colonies as free labourers. (6) Of those who so settle, a small proportion acquire land of their own, or become traders, or pursue other callings, indicative of their attainment of a higher social status. (7) Notwithstanding the severity of the laws against desertion and absence from work, the Indian coolies thrive remarkably well, and acquire habits of thrift and independence for which they are not much noted during their residence in India. (8) The wages earned are from two to three times those obtained in India, and the climate appears generally to agree with the Indian settlers and their families. (9) Their general prosperity is fully attested to by the large remittances they make to this country, and the savings they bring with them when they return, as also by the increase of their deposit accounts in the local Savings Bank.

Of course, there are difficulties and obstructions in the way. Without a strict enforcement of the Protection Laws in their interest by the Government of India, the coolie emigrants would not be able to hold their own against the greed of their employers, the Planters, who are not generally noted for their humanity. The magistracy and the government machinery in these colonies, being entirely in the hands of the White population, are not very impartial in their treatment of the Indian settlers, and there is not much scope allowed for the independent growth of the coloured races. Notwithstanding these disadvantages, there can be no doubt that the system of Protected Emigration has, on the whole, been very beneficial, and that it will, in course of time, lead to further developments in the interest of the Indian settlers in those colonies, at least, where, as in Natal, Trinidad, Mauritius and British Guiana, the Indians already represent a considerable proportion of the population.

The most hopeful feature of this stream of foreign emigration is represented by the fact that the higher castes of Hindus occupy no small place among those who emigrate. . . . Out of nearly 47,000 people who emigrated from the Port of Calcutta during the three years, 1889 to 1891, about eleven per cent were Mohammedans, and eighty-nine per cent were Hindus; and out of this eighty-nine per cent, less than forty-five per cent were low caste people, and the rest were artisans, agriculturists and Brahmins and men of the higher castes.

. . . In connection with these twelve lakhs of people settled in foreign parts, if people in Bombay, or Madras, or Calcutta would venture to go out of their usual track, they could easily establish thriving Agencies in all these ten or fifteen colonies, where such a large number of Indians are settled, and are presumably well off. . . . The schoolmaster, the doctor and the lawyer, the artisans of all classes, and even the priests of different sects, have here a most favourable field for their operations and enterprise among people who are their kith and skin, and on whom sympathy would never be wasted. The Government of the Queen-Empress extends its common protection to us and to them, and the Government of India is most conscientiously alive to its duty of protecting the interests of these Indian settlers. If we could send out our young men to these possessions of the Crown, they will surely be able to earn their living, and do a great deal of practical good. A little organization and some enterprise are alone needed for utilizing this vast force which lies scattered about in distant possessions. It is with a view to rouse interest in the welfare of these people, and enable us to do our duty by them, that I took up this subject for this year's Conference, and I shall be amply rewarded, if among those who hear me, the merchants, manu-facturers, traders, and representatives of different Provinces, any one or more feels himself moved by the spirit of enterprise and sympathy, and is led in consequence to cultivate better relations of trade and industry with these twelve lakhs of people established in foreign parts.

INDIAN SETTLERS IN SOUTH AFRICA, 1895
G. Parameswaran Pillai

. . . We discussed last Saturday many questions of Imperial importance affecting the interests of the people of India. We laid bare the hopeless con-dition of our finances and traced it to the abnormal growth of military expenditure. We exposed the reckless way in which frontier expeditions are constantly undertaken in this country and insisted on the cost of these expeditions being shared between England and India. . . . These, gentlemen, are all questions affecting the interests of the people of India in India. But deeply conservative and averse to travel as we are said to be, some of our brethren have ventured to emigrate to distant lands in quest of fresh fields and pastures new, and I hope you will bear with me if I entreat your atten-tion for a moment to the condition of our brethren in those distant lands. I wish to invite your attention, gentlemen, particularly to the condition of our brethren in South Africa, for it is they of all others that stand in sore need of our sympathy. Ladies and gentlemen, it is rather hard that as if our own growing grievances in this country were not sufficiently numerous, we should have to add to our burden by ventilating the grievances of those who have settled in other parts of the globe; but it is impossible for us to be devoid of that fellow-feeling which makes us wondrous kind and to forbear extend-ing our hand of fellowship to our suffering countrymen in South Africa. I have therefore very great pleasure in moving the proposition entrusted to me:

That the Congress deems it necessary to record its most solemn protest against the disabilities sought to be imposed on Indian settlers in South Africa, and it earnestly hopes that the British Government and the Govern-ment of India will come forward to guard the interests of those settlers in the same spirit in which they have always interfered, whenever interests of their British-born subjects have been at stake.

I presume you have formed some idea of the ill-treatment of Indians by the European settlers in South Africa from the Indian and English newspapers particularly during the last few months. But to arrive at a clear understanding of the exact nature of the disabilities to which our countrymen are subjected in South Africa, it is necessary for us to go back to the history of the question. After all, gentlemen, we have not to go far back. As I understand that others, who will follow me, will deal with the condition of our brethren in Natal and other British colonies, I shall confine my attention to the condition of our countrymen in the South African Republic.

Curious as it may seem, the history of this question dates from that very year which saw the birth of the Indian National Congress. It is but eleven years old. While a few of the more patriotic and more prominent of our countrymen were putting their heads together for the first time in Bombay for organizing the means whereby they could bring into public prominence the political grievances of their countrymen, the European settlers in South Africa were engaged in forging a fresh link to the chain of their sufferings. According to Article 14 of the London Convention of 1884, all persons, other than natives, conforming themselves to the laws of the South African Republic (a) will have full liberty with their families, to enter, travel or reside in any part of the South African Republic; (b) they will be entitled to hire or possess houses, manufactories, warehouses, shops, and premises; (c) they may carry on their commerce either in person or by any agents whom they may think fit to employ; (d) they will not be subject in respect of their persons or property or in respect of their commerce or industry to any taxes whether general or local other than those which are or may be imposed upon citizens of the said Republic. According to this Convention, gentlemen, Indian settlers were entitled to the same privileges as Europeans, as the former were not natives of the place, and only natives of Africa were subjected to restrictions with regard to habitation and trade. But it soon dawned upon the White population of South Africa that it was unsafe to extend the same privileges to Asiatics and particularly natives of India. Evidently, gentlemen, when the London Convention came into existence they thought the yellow races of India were beneath contempt—too insignificant to be noticed, but they soon found that the Indian settlers, by their growing numbers, their thrifty habits and their genius for trade, were making life a little bit unpleasant to them, and the white settlers set up at once an agitation for excluding Indians from the privileges they enjoyed.

The London Convention, as I have already observed, excluded only natives of Africa, but the authorities of the South African Republic proposed to amend the Convention by confining it to all persons "other than African natives or Indian or Chinese coolie immigrants." This suggestion was submitted to Lord Derby, the then Secretary of State for the Colonies, for approval by Sir Hercules Robinson, the High Commissioner, and Lord Derby, in a weak moment, permitted the Volksraad to legislate on the lines suggested.

The result was that the Volksraad immediately imposed several disabilities on the Indians. The Indians were prevented from acquiring citizenship in the Republic; they were prohibited from owning landed property; those who settled in the Republic were required to register themselves by paying £25 within eight days of their arrival in the colony and the Government reserved the rights of assigning to Indians special streets, wards and locations for habitation. These were indeed hard conditions and Lord Derby soon discovered his mistake, and after an elaborate correspondence on the subject, the Volksraad amended the law by permitting Indians to buy property in wards or streets by reducing the fine of £25 to £3 and by stipulating that in confining Indians to locations the Government was guided solely by sanitary considerations. . . . The result was that an immediate attempt was made by the South African Republic to confine Indians to locations not only for the purposes of habitation, but also for purposes of trade. This was indeed ruinous to the Indians and their constant complaints led to the submission of the question to an arbitrator, Mr. Melins de Villiers, Chief Justice of the Orange Free State, by the British and the South African Governments. In this matter, the Indians were not consulted by the British Government and Mr. Villiers happened to be a man with strong prejudice against the Indians. And his decision curiously enough, instead of settling the points in dispute, finally reserved them for decision to the judicial tribunals of the South African Republic or in other words left the Indians to the tender mercies of the judges of the South African Republic, who were even stronger in their prejudices against the Indians. . . . Finally, Mr. Chamberlain, the present Secretary of State for the Colonies, was appealed to. In September last, Mr. Chamberlain, while expressing his sympathy with Indians and hoping that their undoubted industry and intelligence and their indomitable perseverance would suffice to overcome any obstacles in their way, declared that the legal and international questions in dispute were closed. . . . But with due deference to him, I do not think the matter is closed even from a legal and international point of view.

I maintain that Indians in the Republic are not bound to accept the decision of Mr. Villiers for three reasons, first because they were not consulted in the matter of the choice of an arbitrator; secondly because the prejudice of Mr. Justice Villiers against the Indians was well-known and his appointment was protested against by the Indians at the time; and thirdly because Mr. Villiers has omitted to decide the points referred to him. It is interesting in this connection, gentlemen, to ascertain the ground on which a crusade of the nature I have described is being led by the South African Republic. Well, the ostensible ground on which Indians are thus treated is that from a sanitary point of view it is not desirable that they should live with the White population. With regard to this charge against them, gentlemen, several eminent doctors have certified that the Indians and their surroundings are as cleanly as the White population and their surroundings. The real reason of all this agitation is strong competition in trade. Indians, owing to their simple habits and economic living, are able to carry on a very successful trade much to the prejudice of the White population. It is indeed a matter for regret that Indians should be made to suffer on account of their perseverance and industry and if the English Government would take the same interest in Indians that they take in the treatment accorded to Englishmen in other parts of the globe, I am sure there will be no room for complaint. The Indians owe all their sufferings to the fact that Lord Derby and others failed to treat Englishmen and Indians on a footing of equality. Whatever may be said of the past, it is fervently hoped that the Government of India and the British Government would keep a keen watch over the treatment of Indians and resent any attempt on the part of the South African authorities to deal with Indians in a way unsuited to their status and condition in life, and their position as subjects of Her Britannic Majesty. . . .

GRIEVANCES OF INDIAN SETTLERS IN SOUTH AFRICA, 1896
Mohandas K. Gandhi

I am to plead before you this evening for the 100,000 British Indians in South Africa. . . . A large majority of this number are people from Madras and Bengal. Apart, therefore, from the interest that you would take in them as Indians, you are specially interested in the matter. . . .

South Africa is indebted to the colony of Natal for the presence of the Indian population there. In the year 1860, when in the words of a member of the Natal Parliament, "the existence of the colony hung in the balance," the colony of Natal introduced indentured Indians into the colony. Such immigration is regulated by law, is permissible only to a few favoured states, e.g., Mauritius, Fiji, Jamaica, Straits Settlements, Demerara and other states, and is allowed only from Madras and Calcutta. As a result of the immigration, in the words of another eminent Natalian, Mr. Saunders, "Indian immigration brought prosperity, prices rose, people were no longer content to grow or sell produce for a song, they could do better." The sugar and tea industries as well as sanitation and the vegetable and fish supply of the colony are absolutely dependent on the indentured Indians from Madras and Calcutta. The presence of the indentured Indians about sixteen years ago drew the free Indians in the shape of traders who first went there with a view to supply the wants of their own kith and kin; but afterwards found a very valuable customer in the native of South Africa.... These traders are chiefly drawn from the Bombay Memon Mohammedans and owing to their less unfortunate position have formed themselves into custodians of the interests of the whole Indian population there....

These Indians have now spread all over South Africa. Natal ... contains a European population of 50,000, a native population of 400,000, and an Indian population of 51,000. Of the 51,000 Indians about 16,000 are at present serving their indenture, 30,000 are those that have completed their indenture, and are now variously engaged as domestic servants, gardeners, hawkers and petty traders and, about 5,000 are those who emigrated to the colony on their own account and are either traders, shop-keepers, assistants or hawkers. A few are also school-masters, interpreters and clerks. The self-governing colony of the Cape of Good Hope has, I believe, an Indian population of about 10,000 consisting of traders, hawkers and labourers. Its total population is nearly 1,500,000 of whom not more than 400,000 are Europeans. The rest are natives of the country and Malays. The South African Republic of the Transvaal ... has an Indian population of about 5,000 of whom about 200 are traders with liquidated assets amounting to nearly £100,000....

The grievances of the Indians in South Africa are twofold, i.e., those that are due to the popular ill-feeling against the Indians and, secondly, the legal disabilities placed upon them. To deal with the first, the Indian is the most hated being in South Africa. Every Indian without distinction is contemptuously called a "coolie." . . . We cannot safely walk on the footpaths. A Madrasi gentleman, spotlessly dressed, always avoids the footpaths of prominent streets in Durban for fear he should be insulted or pushed off. We are the "Asian dirt" to be "heartily cursed," . . . we are described in the Statute Books as "semi-barbarous Asiatics, or persons belonging to the uncivilized races of Asia." We "breed like rabbits" and a gentleman at a meeting lately held in Durban said he "was sorry we could not be shot like them." There are coaches running between certain places in the Transvaal. We may not sit inside them. It is a sore trial, apart from the indignity it involves and contemplates, to have to sit outside them either in deadly winter mornings, for the winter is severe in the Transvaal, or under a burning sun, though we are Indians. The hotels refuse us admission. Indeed, there are cases in which respectable Indians have found it difficult even to procure refreshments at European places. . . .

This feeling of intense hatred has been reproduced into legislation in the various states of South Africa restricting the freedom of Indians in many ways. To begin with, Natal, which is the most important from an Indian point of view, has of late shown the greatest activity in passing Indian legislation. Till 1894 the Indians had been enjoying the franchise equally with the Europeans under the general franchise law of the colony, which entitles any adult male being a British subject to be placed on the voters' list, who possesses immoveable property worth £50 or pays an annual rent of £10. . . . In 1894, the Natal Legislature passed a Bill disfranchising Asiatics by name. We resisted it in the Local Parliament but without any avail. We then memorialized the Secretary of State for the Colonies and as a result that bill was this year withdrawn and replaced by another which, though not quite so bad as the first one, is bad enough. It says that no natives of countries (not of European origin) which have not hitherto possessed elective representative institutions, founded on the parliamentary franchise, shall be placed on the voters' roll unless they shall first obtain an exemption from the Governor in Council. . . . The object of this measure is not political. It is purely and simply to degrade the Indians in the words of a member of the Natal Parliament, "to make the Indian's life more comfortable in his native land than in Natal." . . .

The very fact that, at present, there are only 250 Indians as against nearly 10,000 European voters shows that there is no fear of the Indian vote swamping the European. . . . If there is any real danger of the Asiatic vote swamping the European, we should have no objection to an educational test being imposed or the property qualifications being raised. What we object to is class legislation and the degradation which it necessarily involves. We are fighting for no new privilege in opposing the Bill, we are resisting the deprivation of the one we have been enjoying. . . . Up to the 18th day of August, 1894, the indentured immigrants went under a contract of service for five years in consideration for a free passage to Natal, free board and lodging for themselves and their families and wages at the rate of ten shillings per month for the first year to be increased by one shilling every following year. They were also entitled to a free passage back to India, if they remained in the colony another five years as free labourers. This is now changed, and in future, the immigrants will have either to remain in the colony forever under indenture, their wages increasing to 20 shillings at the end of the 9th year of indentured service, or to return to India or to pay an annual poll-tax of £3 sterling, equivalent to nearly half a year's earnings on the indenture scale. . . .

The letters from Natal informing me of the Royal sanction to this Bill ask me to request the Indian public to help us to get emigration suspended. I am well aware that the idea of suspending emigration requires careful consideration. I humbly think that there is no other conclusion possible in the interests of the Indians at large. Emigration is supposed to relieve the congested districts and to benefit those who emigrate. If the Indians instead of paying the poll-tax, return to India, the congestion cannot be affected at all. And the returned Indians will rather be a source of difficulty than anything else as they must necessarily find it difficult to get work and cannot be expected to bring sufficient to live upon the interest of their capital. It certainly will not benefit the emigrants as they will never, if the Government can possibly help it, be allowed to rise higher than the status of labourers. The fact is that they are being helped on to degradation.

Under such circumstances I humbly ask you to support our prayer to suspend emigration to Natal, unless the new law can be altered or repealed. You will naturally be anxious to know the treatment of the Indians while under indenture. Of course, that life cannot be bright under any circumstances;

but I do not think their lot is worse than the lot of the Indians similarly placed in other parts of the world. . . . An indentured Indian after he becomes free is given a free pass. This he has to show whenever asked to do so. It is meant to detect desertion by the indentured Indians. The working of this system is a source of much irritation to poor free Indians and often puts respectable Indians in a very unpleasant position. . . . An Indian immigrant who loses his free pass is, as a rule, called upon to pay £3 sterling for a duplicate copy. This is nothing but a system of blackmail. The 9 o'clock rule in Natal which makes it necessary for every Indian to carry a pass if he wants to be out after 9 p.m., at the pain of being locked up in a dungeon, causes much heart-burning especially among the gentlemen from this Presidency. You will be pleased to hear that children of many indentured Indians receive a pretty good education; and then wear as a rule the European dress. They are a most sensitive class and yet unfortunately most liable to arrest under the 9 o'clock rule. . . .

But, gentlemen, you have been told lately by the Natal Agent-General that the Indians are nowhere better treated than in Natal; that the fact that a majority of the indentured labourers do not avail themselves of the return passage is the best answer to my pamphlet, and that the railway and tram-car officials do not treat the Indians as beasts nor do the law courts deny them justice. With the greatest deference to the Agent-General, all I can say as to the first statement is that he must have very queer notions of good treatment, if to be locked up for being out after 9 p.m. without a pass, to be denied the most elementary right of citizenship in a free country, to be denied a higher status than that of bondman and at best a free laborer and to be subjected to other restrictions referred to above, are instances of good treatment. And if such treatment is the best the Indians receive throughout the world, then the lot of the Indians in other parts of the world and here must be very miserable indeed, according to the common-sense view. . . .

The fact that the indentured Indians as a rule do not avail themselves of the return passage we do not dispute, but we certainly dispute that it is the best answer to our complaints. How can that fact disprove the existence of the legal disabilities? It may prove that the Indians who do not take advantage of the return passage either do not mind the disabilities or remain in the colony in spite of such disabilities. If the former be the case, it is the duty of those who know better to make the Indians realise their situation and to enable them to see that submission to them means degradation. If the latter be the case it is one more instance of the patience and the forbearing spirit of the Indian nation which was acknowledged by Mr. Chamberlain in his Dispatch in connection with the Transvaal arbitration. Because they bear them is no reason why the disabilities should not be removed or why they should be interpreted into meaning the best treatment possible.

Moreover, who are these people who instead of returning to India settle in the colony? They are the Indians drawn from the poorest classes and from the most thickly populated districts possibly living in a state of semi-starvation in India. They migrated to Natal with their families, if any, with the intention of settling there, if possible. Is it any wonder, if these people after the expiry of their indenture, instead of running to face semi-starvation as Mr. Saunders has put it, settled in a country where the climate is magnificent and where they may earn a decent living? A starving man generally would stand any amount of rough treatment to get a crumb of bread. . . .

This, too, should be borne in mind that in making his statement, Mr. Peace has not taken into account the free Indian trader who goes to the colony on his own account and who feels most the indignities and disabilities. If it does not do to tell the Uitlander that he may not go to the Transvaal if he cannot bear the ill treatment, much less will it do to say so to the enterprising Indian. We belong to the Imperial family and are children, adopted it may be, of the same august mother, having the same rights and privileges guaranteed to us as to the European children. It was in that belief that we went to the colony of Natal and we trust that our belief was well-founded. . . . Quoting statistics to prove the prosperity of the Indian community is quite unnecessary. It is not denied that the Indians who go to Natal do earn a living and that in spite of the persecution.

In the Transvaal we cannot own landed property, we may not trade or reside except in specified locations, which are described by the British Agent, "as places to deposit the refuse of the town without any water except the polluted soakage in the gully between the location and the town." We may not as of right walk on the footpaths in Johannesburg and Pretoria, we may not be out after 9 p.m. We may not travel without passes. The law prevents us from travelling first or second class on the railways.

We are required to pay a special registration fee of £3 to enable us to settle in the Transvaal, and though we are treated as mere "chattels" and have no privileges whatever, we may be called upon to render compulsory military service. . . .

The Orange Free State has . . . passed a special law whereby we are prevented from trading, farming or owning property under any circumstances. If we submit to these degrading conditions, we may be allowed to reside after passing through certain humiliating ceremonies. We were driven out from the State and our stores were closed causing to us a loss of £9,000. And this grievance remains absolutely without redress. The Cape Parliament has passed a Bill granting the East London Municipality in that colony the power to frame byelaws prohibiting Indians from walking on the footpaths and making them live in locations. It has issued instructions to the authorities of East Gripuinland not to issue any trading licenses to the Indians. The Cape Government are in communication with the Home Government with a view to induce them to sanction legislation restricting the influx of the Asiatics. The people in the Chartered territories are endeavouring to close the country against the Asiatic trader. . . .

Thus, we are hemmed in on all sides by restrictions. And if nothing further were to be done here and in England on our behalf, it is merely a question of time when the respectable Indian in South Africa will be absolutely extinct.

Nor is this merely a local question. It is as the London *Times* puts it, "that of the status of the British Indian outside India." "If," says the *Thunderer*, "they fail to secure that position, (that is of equal status) in South Africa, it will be difficult for them to attain it elsewhere." I have no doubt you have read in the papers that Australian colonies have passed legislation to prevent Indians from settling in that part of the world. It will be interesting to know how the Home Government deal with that question.

The real cause of all this prejudice may be expressed in the words of the leading organ in South Africa, namely, the *Cape Times*, when it was under the editorship of the prince of South African journalists, Mr. St. Leger: "It is the position of these merchants which is productive of no little hostility to this day. And it is in considering their position that their rivals in trade have sought to inflict upon them through the medium of the State, what looks on the face of it something very like an injustice for the benefit of self." Continues the same organ:

The injustice to the Indians is so glaring that one is almost ashamed of one's countrymen in wishing to have these men treated as natives (i.e., of South Africa,) simply because of their success in trade. The very reason that they have been so successful against the dominant race is sufficient to raise them above that degrading level.

. . . We believe also that much of the ill-feeling is due to the want of proper knowledge in South Africa about the Indians in India. We are, therefore, endeavouring to educate public opinion in South Africa by imparting the necessary information. With regard to the legal disabilities we have tried to influence in our favour the public opinion both in England and here. . . . What is required in India has been well put by the *Moslem Chronicle* in a forcibly written leader:

> What with a strong and intelligent public opinion here and a well-meaning Government the difficulties we have to contend with, are not at all commensurate with those that retard the well-being of our countrymen in that country. It is therefore quite time that all public bodies should at once turn their attention to this important subject to create an intelligent public opinion with a view to organize an agitation for the removal of the grievances under which our brethren are laboring. Indeed, these grievances have become and are day by day becoming so unbearable and offensive that the requisite agitation cannot be taken up one day too soon.

I may state our position a little more clearly. We are aware that the insults and indignities that we are subjected to at the hands of the populace cannot be directly removed by the intervention of the Home Government. We do not appeal to it for any such intervention. We bring them to the notice of the public so that the fair-minded of all communities and the press may, by expressing their disapproval, materially reduce their rigor and possibly eradicate them ultimately. But we certainly do appeal, and we hope not vainly, to the Home Government for protection against reproduction of such ill-feeling in legislation. We certainly beseech the Home Government to disallow all the Acts of the legislative bodies of the Colonies restricting our freedom in any shape or form. . . . It may not be amiss to quote a few passages from the London *Times* articles bearing on the question of intervention as well as the whole question generally:

The whole question resolves itself into this. Are Her Majesty's Indian subjects to be treated as a degraded and an outcaste race by a friendly government or are they to have the same rights and status as other British subjects enjoy? Are leading Muhammadan merchants who might sit in the Legislative Council at Bombay, to be liable to indignities and outrage in the South African Republic? . . .

Gentlemen, Bombay has spoken in no uncertain terms. We are yet young and inexperienced, we have a right to appeal to you, our elder and freer brethren for protection. Being under the yoke of oppression we can merely cry out in anguish. You have heard our cry. The blame will now lie on your shoulders if the yoke is not removed from our necks.

GRIEVANCES OF INDIAN SETTLERS IN SOUTH AFRICA, 1898
G. Parameswaran Pillai

Mr. President, Ladies and Gentlemen—I have very great pleasure in moving the resolution:

> That this Congress deplores the invidious and humiliating distinctions made between Indian and European settlers in South Africa, a prominent instance of which is afforded by the recent decision of the Transvaal High Court restricting Indians to "locations," and appeals to Her Majesty's Government and the Government of India to guard the interests of Indian settlers and to relieve them of the disabilities imposed on them.

Ladies and Gentlemen, four years ago at the last Congress held in this city when for the first time in the annals of the Congress we took into consideration the condition of our countrymen in South Africa, they were struggling in Natal against an attempt to deprive them the franchise, and in the Transvaal against an attempt to consign them to locations. Today, they are struggling for their very existence. Very many important legislative changes—changes seriously affecting the well-being and prosperity of our countrymen—have taken place during these four years in South Africa. In Natal, not only have they been deprived of the franchise—the right to vote at Parliamentary elections, which they enjoyed in common with all others till 1894—by an arbitrary law which places Indians in the category of persons who are "natives of countries which have not hitherto possessed elective representative institutions founded on the Parliamentary franchise," but several other disabilities of a miscellaneous character have been imposed on them.

In the first place till 1896–97, the law in Natal which applied to Indian labourers who immigrated into Natal enabled them to return to their homes after their period of indenture was over; and if they continued to serve for another term of five years they became entitled to a free passage. But at present, the law in Natal denies absolutely the right of free citizenship to the laborer however long he may serve the country; if he chooses to remain in Natal after his period of indenture is over, either he should enter into further periods of indenture or take out licenses annually at a cost of £3. The Indian laborer who wishes to live in Natal has to choose between perpetual bondage and an odious poll tax.

In the next place, Ladies and Gentlemen, after the recent agitation which I am sure all of you remember, the agitation on behalf of our countrymen which Mr. Gandhi so generously and courageously took up and carried out in this country, the Government of the colony of Natal went the length of passing three Acts, restricting further the rights of our countrymen to enter Natal for purposes of trade, travel or residence. One is known as the Immigration Restriction Act, another is said to be a Quarantine Act, and the third an Act referring to licenses issued to traders. The most extraordinary thing about these Acts is that in none of them is there a single word to indicate specifically that Asiatics, or Indians for the matter of that, are excluded from the colony or that their rights are restricted. But there is not the smallest doubt that all these Acts have been passed with the sole and solitary object of restricting the immigration of our countrymen into Natal. . . .

Let us now see, Ladies and Gentlemen, what has happened in the Transvaal. In that Republic, as I have said, our countrymen were struggling four years ago against an attempt to confine them to locations. It is necessary for you to understand what these locations are. They are places outside the town where the refuse of the town is deposited and buried; and our countrymen are compelled to reside in these places amongst dung-heaps. Four years ago our countrymen protested against the decision of the Transvaal Volksraad to make them reside in locations and appealed to the Secretary of State for the Colonies, and the Right Hon'ble Joseph Chamberlain promised to accord a generous consideration to the question; but the courts of law in the Transvaal have decided that it is necessary in the interests of the colony at large that Indian settlers should reside in locations, and the Transvaal Government have notified that all Indians should remove to locations within a specified time. Such, Ladies and Gentlemen, is the miserable plight of our countrymen in Transvaal at the present moment.

I need not recount all the other restrictions which are imposed on our countrymen. They are sufficiently well known to you. In certain colonies they have not the right to travel in 1st or 2nd class railway carriages. In some places they are not even permitted to walk on public footpaths. In one colony they dare not appear in any public street after 9 p.m. In another colony, it is criminal for Indians to be found in possession of native gold. In one colony they have to provide themselves with travelling passes.... These restrictions are sufficiently serious in themselves—sufficiently serious to justify my statement that our countrymen in South Africa are at the present moment struggling for their very existence.

But they are threatened with still greater dangers. Not satisfied with what they have done, the South African states are thirsting for more. It is the cry of the son of the horseleech, "give" "give." The latest news from Natal is that Progressive Leagues and Anti-Asiatic Committees are being formed with a view to prevent the Indians from acquiring land in that colony. Memorials and petitions have been addressed, and the Government of Natal have promised a very careful consideration of the question. What is more serious still is Mr. Schreiner, the present Premier of the Cape, intends convening a Conference of all the South African states with the object of taking common action with a view to prevent the immigration of Indians! Now, Ladies and Gentlemen, can anything be more dangerous to our countrymen than this promised brotherhood of mischief?

Now is the time when we ought to go to their rescue. I think it is necessary that while we are struggling for our rights in this country, we should not forget those countrymen of ours who have emigrated to other lands in search of fresh fields and pastures new. Well, the situation is all the more serious when we remember that in this matter we have received very little help or encouragement from the authorities either in this country or elsewhere.... Not only has the Viceroy deserted us and the Right Hon'ble Joseph Chamberlain who promised us assistance given us up, but I doubt also whether any help will be forthcoming from ... the Secretary of State for India who has characterized us as a nation of savages. Savages of course must be happy to live in locations and I do not think Lord George Hamilton is the sort of man from whom any help may be expected.

Nevertheless, it is necessary that we in Congress assembled should take some steps to see that our countrymen do not suffer in the way they are suffering in South Africa. And why do they suffer? Not because they are uncleanly as some say, not because they are not fit to be associated with, not because they are immoral or untruthful but because they are thrifty, they are industrious, they are persevering, they are hardworking, and as traders they are in a position to save more money than the white settlers. There is keen competition between the European and the Indian settlers, and trade jealously is at the bottom of this unfortunate affair. What shall we do in these circumstances? Are we to stand apart and see our countrymen ruined in South Africa? The rescue of our countrymen is not altogether hopeless. Our hope is centered in the Proclamation of Her Majesty the Queen-Empress. Her Majesty has declared, in no indistinct terms, "We hold ourselves bound to the natives of our Indian Territories by the same obligations of duty which bind us to all other subjects; and those obligations, by the blessing of Almighty God, we shall faithfully and conscientiously fulfil."[3] . . .

I think it is a standing disgrace that in this age of enlightenment and progress, toleration and freedom in the British colonies in South Africa, self-governing or directly belonging to the Crown, the colonies which are independent or over which the British exercise some sort of authority—it is a shame and scandal that we, Her Majesty's beloved subjects who are competent enough to compete with her English subjects in Great Britain and enter the House of Commons, should be treated as an inferior order of beings fit only to be hewers of wood and drawers of water to the domineering White population in the colonies.

NOTES

"Indian Foreign Emigration" was originally read at the 1893 Industrial Conference in Poona. It later appeared as M. G. Ranade, "Indian Foreign Emigration," in *Essays on Indian Economics: A Collection of Essays and Speeches* (Madras: G. A. Natesan, 1906), 130–69. "Indian Settlers in South Africa" originally appeared as G. Parameswaran Pillai, "Statement on Resolution IX: Indian Settlers in South Africa," in *Report of the Eleventh Indian National Congress* (Poona: Arya Bhushan, 1896), 103–6. "Grievances of Indian Settlers in South Africa" was delivered on October 26, 1896. It was subsequently reprinted as Mohandas K. Gandhi, "Grievances of Indian Settlers in South

Africa," in *Speeches and Writings of M. K. Gandhi* (Madras: G. A. Natesan, 1922), 1–29. "Grievances of Indian Settlers in South Africa" originally appeared as G. Parameswaran Pillai, "Statement on Resolution XII: Grievances of Indian Settlers in South Africa," in *Report of the Fourteenth Indian National Congress* (Madras: G. A. Natesan, 1899), 88–91.

1. *Report of the Indian Famine Commission*, pt. 1 (London: Her Majesty's Stationery Office, 1880), 175.
2. *Report on Coolie Emigration from India* (London: Her Majesty's Stationery Office, 1874).
3. Proclamation of the Queen to the Princes, Chiefs, and People of India, Allahabad, November 1, 1858.

Chapter Seven

THE OPIUM TRADE

LETTERS OF A HINDOO, NO. V, 1841
A Hindoo [Bhaskar Pandurang Tarkhadkar]

... I take up my pen to announce to you that I am in the land of the living, lamenting, as usual, the fate of my countrymen in this world, and that of yours in the world to come. . . . How could you dare hope that all your enormous crimes which you have politically committed and do still commit in the world in the broad day light of God's ubiquity will be pardoned in Heaven? To expect these favors at the hands of the Almighty, after being guilty of such enormities, is, in my humble opinion, nothing but a downright mockery of the impartial and equitable disposition of our Heavenly Father. . . . In bringing forward all your political villainies to the public notice; and, in order to convince you that I do not complain against you without reason, I put down the following circumstances as best illustrative of your knavery and political cruelty.

I shall in the first place, prove by most undeniable arguments that the war which you are now waging with the Chinese under pretense of certain injuries you have received from them, is beyond doubt quite unlawful. The origin of your dispute with the Chinese arose from your pertinaciously carrying on the opium trade, notwithstanding the emperor's having repeatedly and distinctly declared it an illegal and contraband traffic. Now I ask you what plea can you set forth to justify this your infringement of the Emperor's orders, who was the lawful sovereign of his country, and, consequently, his orders were as imperative on you as they were on his own subjects? But every principle of regard and respect for national law has no weight with you, when such principle interference in your views of enriching your country, and supplying it with all the luxuries that you can lay hold of, without your being in the least at the necessity of paying silver from your own pockets for them. You are well aware that, the large supply of teas and other Chinese peculiarities which are now imported into Great Britain, without costing you anything, is purely owing to the opium trade, which, if stopped, you cannot get them without paying hard cash. Self-interest is all in all to you, and to secure it you would do anything; you would let go their national good name and civilized character to the devil; you would trample upon every principle of honor and justice, and would not fail even to sacrifice a few hundred lives.

If impartially viewed, the High Commissioner Lin was quite justified in confiscating the contraband article from Captain Elliot, which he was compelled to do to preserve his country from the universal depravity and viciousness to which they were abandoned by the rapid progress the use of opium was making among them, as he had no other remedy left him to resort to suppress this nefarious traffic on the face of your strenuous efforts by every unfair means to force the trade upon them. What authority had you to send a poisonous substance to the dominions of a foreign king in spite of his repeated injunctions not to do so? Nay, you would not stop here, but send a large army to threaten him to submission, to ask compensation for your surrendered opium, and to secure a trading port to carry on your treacherous operations notwithstanding your being the aggressor. Now, my good friend, Mr. Editor, I ask you, where is your integrity and good sense which you so much boast of—ugh! Such are your empty boastings and pratings. What barbarities and deeds of the blackest dye are you not guilty of? When Chnsan was stormed, almost the whole of the inhabitants deserted their homes and emigrated to a distant country; now figure to yourself what serious an inconvenience they must have been put to, and how distressed they must have been at their being deprived of the peace and tranquility which they have for nearly four thousand years uninterruptedly enjoyed.

The Chinese are a timid but benevolent people. You have often times received the most distinguished marks of kindness and generosity on the part of their emperor, who has pardoned the grossest offences on your part and extended his clemency to you at a time when it was in his power to have punished you very easily. You will recollect that, how many times long before the commencement of the present war your beastly sailors have committed acts of violence and war on the Chinese; but why, how many times have you, the intelligent and sober part of your community, been detected in smuggling opium, yet your crimes have been pardoned; whereas a thousand Chinese have suffered martyrdom for those very offence. In commercial point of view, you have, I dare say, derived the most substantial benefits from China, but you would close your eyes on all these things, and would only show your eagerness to take advantage of the generous feelings and weakness of the Chinese, and try to undermine them by every means in your power. The most ancient, richest, and the proudest monarchy in the world is being rendered the poorest and humblest of all the countries on this earth, by a race of mankind who call themselves the most enlightened and philanthropic of all the human race. China seems to share the same fate as the once mighty but now unhappy Hindustan. Alas! The world is treacherous, and indeed the most treacherous are always the most prosperous. . . .

BRITISH OPIUM POLICY AND ITS RESULTS, 1880
Shoshee Chunder Dutt

. . . It is difficult now to ascertain when opium first became an article of consumption in China. The Native States of India which began the cultivation earliest appear always to have appropriated their produce partly for home consumption, and partly for export to the neighboring districts. In Bengal very little of the drug was manufactured at this period; but there is no doubt that a part of the produce, inconsiderable as it was, found its way to China and Malacca; and it seems very probable that this comprised all the opium contribution of India to foreign countries at the outset. The system was subsequently improved on behalf of the East India Company at the suggestion of Col. Watson, by Mr. Wheeler, the Vice President of Bengal in 1773, when the monopoly of the drug was assumed. The Government venture first sent out was very inconsiderable, and before 1780 the number of chests exported rarely exceeded two hundred.

It was in this last-mentioned year that a depot of opium was established by the East India Company in the China waters, on board of two vessels in a bay to the south of Macao, known by the name of Larks' Bay. But here the traders met with so much annoyance from the Chinese officials and the pirates that they were obliged to send out, in 1794, a ship properly armed and exclusively laden with the drug, and to station it permanently at Whampoa, ten miles below Canton, as a fixed depot for the sale of opium. This arrangement was successful, and, in 1796, the number of chests sent out rose to six hundred. It had unfortunately also the effect of alarming the Chinese Government, which had hitherto admitted the drug as medicine, in which character it was entered in the tariff of Canton, but which was now found to be no longer applicable to it. The introduction of the drug into China was for the first time authoritatively interdicted in 1796. Its evil effects in the country had already developed themselves, and the Emperor decreed that those found guilty of smoking it were to be pilloried and bambooed, and the vendors and smugglers subjected to the still severer punishments of banishment and death....

The present practice of growing the poppy and preparing opium in Bengal through the agency of Government officers was introduced in 1797, when the export was augmented at once from six hundred to four thousand chests, remaining fixed at the latter figure for about twenty years.... Up to this time there had been no competition of Malwa opium, the provinces of Central India having been kept in perpetual alarm and confusion by the Pindaris and Mahrattas, which left no room for the development of agriculture. On the termination of the war of 1818–19, Malwa was ceded to the British Government, and with the restoration of order and security, the cultivation of the poppy in it was widely extended.... The aggregate exports of opium in 1830–31 amounted to 19,416 chests, namely, from Bengal 6,560, and from Malwa 12,856....

In 1839, a special commissioner, Lin, was appointed by the court of Peking to deal with the question vigorously, and was vested with sufficient powers to enforce the prohibitory orders already in existence. He commenced his task by the publication of a warning addressed to his own countrymen, which has received the credit of being a State document of great ability.... Then followed overt acts of great stringency, one of the first of which was the seizure of twenty thousand chests of opium belonging to the English and other merchants, which he threw into the sea. Various other measures of persecution against the merchants were also resorted to, and that led to the first China War, commenced in 1840, and concluded in 1842, which at the time was by some regarded as the Opium War, while others called it a war in defence of free trade, but which public opinion has since more correctly designated as the war in defence of free trade in opium. . . . [The] immediate effect was a multiplication of armed smuggling clippers all over the coastline of China, for extending the surreptitious trade, which now assumed all the importance of a recognised business. . . . Every facility has thus been acquired for pushing on the trade with vigour, and the British Government has not been backward in taking advantage of the circumstance. The annual supply now, we have seen, amounts to about ninety thousand chests, which brings to Her Majesty's coffers in India a net profit of about £6,000,000. At this moment the import of opium in China is equal to, if it does not exceed in aggregate, the value of all other English imports taken together. . . .

Of course, the trade thus fostered could not have increased or assumed its present dimensions but for the active connivance of the officials in China. It is said that so universal was the desire there of securing a sufficient supply of opium, that many of the emperors successively, and almost all the great dignitaries of the State, winked at its introduction; and this assertion is entitled to belief from the safe internal transit of the drug all along, after it was surreptitiously landed. . . . The English policy has always been more intelligent and intelligible. The revenue realized by the monopoly retained by the Government of India is very considerable, and has the beauty of being raised, not from the producing country, but from the foreign consumer of the drug produced. . . .

We view the question first in its commercial aspect, because that, we think, will be best understood by all classes of Englishmen. It is the opium policy of Great Britain primarily that has estranged China from Europe and prevented the natural course of trade by embarrassing it. China was not so closed to foreigners in ancient times as it was till recently, that is, before it was forced open with an armed hand. . . . The first of the European powers that appeared in China were the Portuguese, who were followed by the Dutch and the English; and the perpetual hostility which was kept up between these different parties only established the necessity of excluding them all from the country in the estimation of the Chinese Government. The alarm was completed when opium appeared on the scene. From that time the Chinese ceased to believe in the integrity and rectitude of the foreign dealers, and if they continued their intercourse with them at all, it was only because it was not in their power to do otherwise.

Of all Europeans the English have always stood in the worst position in China, only on account of this traffic and the bickering it has given rise to. The petition of Hsu Nai-chi especially referred to this, by stating that "while all the nations of the West have had a general market open to their ships for upwards of a thousand years, the dealers in opium were the English alone."[1] It was also remarked by Hsu Ch'iu, that "while in their own country no opium was smoked, the barbarians yet sought to poison therewith the people of the central flowery land."[2] The measures, moreover, by which the trade was furthered were not, as we have seen, at all times very straight-forward. The British flag was treated with respect till, by its own conduct, it ceased to deserve it, and we all know that opium was the spark that exploded the mine on the occasion of the first war with China.

Viewed then in this aspect only, the loss to Great Britain from her opium policy is very great. The market of China is an extensive one for the sale of her general merchandise, and that market, even though it has been compulsorily opened, is still, to a great extent, inaccessible to her on account of this traffic. It is true that China herself prepares all the articles she needs for local use; but it is simply absurd to imagine that Manchester, which undersells the whole world, could not vie with the Chinese in products of fair trade. Woolen manufactures of all kinds, broadcloths, camlets, and other stuffs of the same descriptions, are already in great requisition in China; the demand for cotton piece-goods, such as white and grey shirt-ings, English drills, and tea cloths is still greater; and the Chinese are such exact judges of quality that it is not at all likely that they would shut their eyes to the superior manufactures of Great Britain merely from a prejudice for their own. From Eastern countries they take nothing but rough produce, simply because their own manufactures are much superior to those of the places in their immediate neighbourhood; but they are already purchas-ing largely from Great Britain and America all articles which they cannot produce as cheaply and well. A taste for these articles had of course to be created, and has been created already to a great extent. But China will never fully open her market to British goods till her distrust of the importer of opium is removed. . . . The withdrawal from the opium trade will also act beneficially in another way. At present the consumption of opium contracts the means of the Chinese to purchase more largely the comforts and conveniences of civilised life. This is true of the alcohol-drinker in England, and in this respect the result in both places is alike. The removal of the impediment would necessarily make general trade more free.

We now come to evils of greater magnitude—namely, the moral evils to which the traffic in opium has given birth. . . . No demonstrative evidence of statistics is available to settle definitively the important question at issue, but that the effects of opium-smoking are baleful enough is certain from the very serious attention the matter has always received from the Chinese Government. That Government has at all times and uniformly prohibited the use of the drug in the country, regarding the indulgence as a vice, and not either as a harmless luxury or a necessary stimulant; and there is no doubt that it has always been sincere both in its opinion and its prohibitions. . . . There is no doubt that the habitual consumers cease to be thrifty, active, honest, and useful members of society, which the Chinese in ordinary course usually are; and this has been most generally attested to by Chinese writers, both official and otherwise. . . .

Nor is the argument that opium is the only national stimulant of China, and should for that reason be allowed to remain so, absolutely or nearly accurate. The national stimulants of the country for the last four thousand years have been tea, tobacco, wine, and spirits. Opium-smoking in it, to any considerable extent, is only of recent growth—scarcely more than a century old. . . . The desire has been excited throughout the land, and the demand has kept pace fully with the supply. The average dose used is about twenty grains weight per man per day but ranging from ten to one hundred grains; and the ninety thousand chests exported from India, leaving aside the home-grown drug, necessarily provide a regular supply of poison for nearly fourteen million souls. We give the statistics as we find them; but the reader will remember that the morality or immorality of the traffic is not affected by its extent. It is just or unjust alike whether it demoralizes one million men or fourteen million. . . .

We have established, with sufficient clearness we think, that the opium monopoly, as it now stands, cannot be defended either on moral or political grounds. Its only defence is the one commercial plea of large profits realized from a foreign country, to the great relief of the people of India. For the sake of these profits the British Government has nearly for a hundred years designedly and deliberately contravened the law of a foreign State to sell interdicted poison among its subjects, and, persisting in this course, has eventually compelled that State to legalize the trade, so far as the imposition of an import duty on the drug has done so. . . . The morality of the course it has pursued does not admit of defence, nor has the British Government itself ever ventured to defend its policy on moral grounds. The wisdom of its position is, if possible, still less defensible, seeing as we do that, while every part of the world is now mutually open for traffic and friendly communication, China has, on account of this unfortunate traffic mainly, shown no disposition to be equally friendly to us, and that all the concession she has made in this respect has been extorted from her by the one unanswerable argument of force. And yet, this was not at all times the deportment of China, as is usually supposed. In ancient times, before the Mohammedans came to India, there was constant communication between the Hindus and the Chinese, both by sea and land, and there existed a royal road to connect their respective countries through the passes of Assam. Even the Arab merchants were allowed to trade with China freely before the merchants of Europe arrived there with their contraband drugs. . . .

We have noticed already where the real difficulty of the question lies. If the opium monopoly is given up, how is the money now derived from it to be recouped? The Government in India will and must stand out for an undiminished revenue; the people of India already complain loudly of being over-taxed. How then are the two ends to be brought together? The abandonment of the monopoly will not, we have shown, injuriously affect the *ryot* in the slightest degree; the cultivation of his lands with other crops will yield him at least as much as, if not considerably more than, the amount he now actually receives by cultivating the poppy. But to the Government there will be the immediate loss between the revenue realized under the present system and that which a prohibitive duty, like that now in force in Bombay, would yield. Approximately calculated this, even if the cultivation does not decrease, will amount to about £1,128,000.

It will be yet more when the cultivation shrivels up and causes a diminution in the number of chests to send. All this will be India's loss—loss to the people if they have to make up the deficiency in taxes. It is here, therefore, that the shoe pinches. The gain to Great Britain herself by the abandonment of the monopoly must, sooner or later, be immense; that is, as soon as it succeeds in removing from the Chinese all his suspicions of the red-haired barbarian, and induces him in perfect good faith and friendliness to open out the whole of his country fully for the purposes of traffic. This consummation cannot be doubted; it would be unreasonable not to expect it: and then the woolens and cottons of Great Britain, which have already pierced every other quarter of the globe, will have another immense field to permeate, from which they are now in a great measure shut out. But what will be England's gain will be India's loss. How is that loss to be made up? Give up the monopoly and realize the difference of revenue by taxing the people of India, will be the prompt suggestion from all sides. But can that suggestion be carried out?

One thing is certain, namely, that no fiscal consideration can justify the British Government in continuing to inflict on China the grievous evil that the diffusion of opium in that country has given rise to. No Government ought to make private vice a source of public revenue; and to this principle may be added another equally correct, that no part of the revenues of India ought to be realized from a foreign country. Such a revenue, under the best circumstances, could only be precarious, and no revenue can be more precarious than the opium revenue now actually is. It is not impossible that it may vanish all at once when it can least be spared. There is a forecast already of what China may do in despair. The effect of its sudden cessation would be exceedingly perplexing. Is it impossible to devise means for the timely prevention of such embarrassment?

This is a purely financial question which need not be discussed in this essay at all. We have referred to it simply that our other observations may not be misunderstood. India cannot be taxed further without aggravating the perplexities of her present position; there must be no jump from the frying-pan into the fire. The prospective gain by the opening out of China will be not India's in the remotest degree, but Great Britain's alone. This should induce Great Britain to deal liberally with India and give up all the indirect earnings now derived by her from the latter in a thousand different ways, which would more than fully cover the loss of her opium revenue. The abandonment of the opium policy of Great Britain absolutely requires the fullest justice being done to the Indian Empire, and when that is conceded the two ends of the account will easily meet.

THE DEATH TRAFFIC, 1881
Rabindranath Tagore

We have never before heard such a revolting story of "Thuggism," as is contained in this book by Doctor Theodore Christlieb, which lies before us for review. A whole nation, China, has been forced by Great Britain to accept the opium poison, simply for commercial greed. In her helplessness China pathetically declared: "I do not require any opium." But the British shopkeeper answered: "That's all nonsense. You must take it." Both the hands of China were tightly bound. Opium was forced down China's throat with the help of guns and bayonets, while the British merchants cried, "You have to pay the price of all the opium you take from us." . . . Such a method of carrying on business and accumulating wealth can only by courtesy be called by the name of traffic. It is sheer brigandage. . . .

This poison of opium, eating at the vitals of one of the greatest and oldest countries of Asia, has been spreading like an infection over the whole body politic. It has been killing slowly by inches mind and body alike. A strong nation, like Britain, is using its strength to sell death and destruction to a weak nation, and thus make profit; though the profit made is pitiably insignificant compared with the vast destruction wrought. If we trace the history of the way in which this traffic was introduced, it is enough to arouse indignation against Great Britain and pity for China even in the hardest hearts. When we read the history of unnatural and inhuman bloodshed in war, we have simply a feeling of horror mingled with that of wonder. But, in the Indo-China opium traffic, human nature itself sinks down to such a depth of despicable meanness, that it is hateful even to follow the story to its conclusion. . . .

China is becoming poorer every day, because so much money is being drained out of the country for opium alone. In the year 1872, China bought opium worth £4,261,381. This proved an excessive drain on her resources. We read that those who become addicted to the drug, are so degraded that they will sell their own children and their own wives. One of the Chinese addicts has recently said that all the bamboos of the Southern Hills (which are used for making pens) could not exhaust the story of the woes caused by opium and all the waters of the northern sea could not wash away its stains. In this way, owing to the selfishness and greed for money on the part of Great Britain, the millions of the Chinese people are drifting towards political and social destruction. It would appear that the British people are not really moved by the promptings of religion, but only by those of money. This is what they call "Christianity," in the nineteenth century after Christ!

Once an American missionary went to the city of Kaifeng, and he was turned out by the people. They said to him: "You have killed our Emperor, demolished his palace, brought poison to destroy us, and now you want to teach us religion!" . . . This distrust of all foreigners has gone so far, that, owing to this curse of opium traffic, the Chinese do not want to construct railways in their own country for fear lest the opium should spread into the interior. They fear that with the increase of trade in opium the foreigners will invade their country. This fear is so strong, that the Chinese Government has not ventured to develop the mines, except those of coal and iron to some extent, lest they should have to employ the foreigners and thus increase the foreign trade. The English people are really sustaining a great loss in moral prestige owing to the utter distrust with which the Chinese have begun to regard them. The English trade also has actually suffered in the long run through this short-sighted and immoral opium policy.

We have written at length about the effects of the opium traffic in China and the hostility of the Chinese. Now let us consider the evils that have been done to India itself by this opium traffic, which the British have been keeping up. A large part of the Indian revenue is obtained from this opium traffic. But as the traffic is a fluctuating one, there is a universal fear on account of the dependence of revenue on this uncertain quantity. Furthermore, the cultivation of Chinese opium is increasing. At the same time, there is a strong feeling growing up in China among the people against the use of opium altogether. Thus, the cultivation of the home-grown opium in China is on the increase, while the actual consumption is likely to decrease. These factors will make the Indian revenue from opium more variable than ever.

Furthermore, the cultivation of an opium crop requires highly fertile land, where good grain crops could be produced. In 1877–78 one million men died of famine in Bengal alone. Yet the half a million acres, which are now employed in opium cultivation, could easily supply the food for a million men and save them from starvation. Dr. Wilson declared in Parliament recently that the cultivation of opium in Malwa had done such harm to other crops, that twelve lakhs of people had died of starvation in the neighboring parts of Rajputana. It would almost seem as if the whole of Rajputana were going to commit suicide owing to the growth of the opium habit. It is hard indeed to think of such a brave and chivalrous people becoming stolid and inactive, lazy and lifeless. Whereas the ancient kingdom of Rajputana was a kingdom of noble dreams, the present kingdom of Rajputana is a kingdom of dull sleep. Such a great people has become of so little worth! . . .

If the Chinese Emperor can say that he could never stoop so low as to make money out of the sin and suffering of his subjects, why cannot the English, who pride themselves on their Christianity, declare that they will never cherish the idea of gaining wealth at the expenses of the sin and suffering of a great people like the Chinese? But we know well this "Christian" nation! These "Christians" have exterminated the aboriginal Americans. By their "Christian" method, they confiscate "heathen" lands, whenever their covetous eyes fall upon them. . . . It has become well known, all over the world, how the British Christians treat those who are weak and helpless. Their one desire is to spurn them and to beat them down. It is written in the Christian scriptures, "If anyone smite you on one cheek, turn to him the other also." When the English Christians tempted the Chinese Emperor with a big revenue to be obtained by killing his own subjects, the Emperor refused. He would not do a thing so despicably mean. Doubtless, what this non-Christian Emperor did was a slap on the face of the Christian English. Unfortunately, it had no effect.

ON THE OPIUM QUESTION, 1882
Srish Chandra Basu

I beg to offer a few remarks with regard to the opium question . . . which has been rendered the butt of ignorant and biased opposition by the Antiopium Society formed in England, composed of distinguished personages including twenty-three members of parliament and several peers of the realm. This question embraces so many tangled knots of political economy and heads of political and historical information, that an ordinary layman like myself feels conscious incapacity to conceive the same; but having regard to the fiery agitation actually gaining ground all over England against the Indian opium revenue on grounds of imputed immorality, and considering the very influential parties that have taken it up, who may, it is not improbable at no distant date with ministerial or other political changes, gain ascendancy upon the council of the nation, it is high time for all representative public bodies, nay every individual interested in the welfare of the country, competent or incompetent, to agitate the matter, since agitation is the soul of success. . . .

To meet the wishes and gratify a mere idle sentimentalism of the fanatical crusaders, the suppression of opium cultivation and manufacture in India and the consequent withdrawal of the Indian drug from China, would entail upon the state a loss of revenue varying from 7 to 9 million a year, a revenue that is raised without the operation of the least and slightest pressure upon the pockets of the miserable tax-payers of India, a revenue that strengthened the hands of the Indian Government to carry out various beneficial reforms and improvements in every department of the state viz., telegraph, education, post office, administration and public works, without which it would have been impossible to carry out these beneficial reforms as mentioned by Sir Alexander Arbuthnot, the late member of the Viceregal Executive Council. The surrender of such a fertile source of income being opposed to sound economical principles for the sake of a mere sentiment, as held by Major Baring in his remarkable Budget statement, which is an able vindication of the Government policy, the question resolves itself into one of policy and expediency. If financial considerations do not justify the Indian Government to abandon such a revenue without the imposition of an equivalent taxation, political considerations of the first moment should equally forbid the adoption or substitution of any direct taxation which had been found by experience to be unsuited to the habits and customs of the people, and circumstances and nature of the country as it is always attended with hardship, inconvenience and oppression.

If the reduction of expenditure be urged as the means to enable the Government to sacrifice this revenue . . . anybody having common sense enough will perceive that such an enormous revenue cannot be recouped by the reduction of expenditure in the existing staff of the administrative machinery, without the greatest detriment to the administration of justice, as was made clear in Lord Ripon's Budget speech whose noble utterances on the occasion of the Budget debate have filled the Indian public with an assurance that the adoption of legislative or political measures of any kind should be rendered subordinate to the interests of the Indian people, in direct contrast to those of Lord Lytton, who on the occasion of addressing a Manchester audience declared that since the English people are centuries in advance, the administration of Indian affairs must be carried on in accordance with English ideas, and English policy, and not in consonance with native feelings, native wants and wishes.

Admitting for argument's sake that financial considerations may justify the surrender of the opium revenue, the question arises—would the abolition of the opium trade of India with China bring any amount of possible good to the Chinese and effect their moral regeneration as urged by the agitators? The natural inference from the existing state of things would be that there is no possibility of reforming the Chinese by the withdrawal of exportation of the Indian drug into China, since their own cultivation of poppy combined with importation from Persia, Turkey, and the Mozambique, would easily enable them to satisfy their demand for the drug. In addition to this, there is a very powerful obstacle standing in the way of their so-called reformation. They had become so much addicted to the habitual use of opium, that imperial edicts issued by the Chinese government failed to suppress the practice, a result however which was attended with benefit to the Chinese as it served gradually, wherever opium smoking prevailed, to completely entice them away from the use of their native ardent spirits, the effects of which have been found to be worse and more injurious to health than those of opium in whatever form taken. Opium, if taken in moderate quantities, has been found to be conducive to health, in the opinion of eminent medical authorities including Dr. Moore of Bombay. This fact will however appear from enjoyment of robust and well-built constitutions and chivalrous and romantic temperament by the Rajputs, the people of Gujarat, Kutch, Kathiawar, Central India, and the Sikhs who are all addicted to the habitual use of opium, as conclusively argued by Sir George Birdwood, who holds that it would be most unfortunate if the Chinese were led back to the use of the native ardent spirits, productive of more injurious effects on their constitution in consequence of the abolition of opium manufacture in India. So much for the effects of the habitual use of opium by the people of the East which suffices to meet the objections raised by the agitators on moral grounds. Taking all these facts into consideration it goes to prove that none of the arguments adduced from political, administrative and moral points of view holds good to substantiate the position taken by the fanatical agitators. . . .

NOTES

"Letters of a Hindoo, No. V" originally appeared as A Hindoo [Bhaskar Pandurang Tarkhadkar], "Letters of a Hindoo, No. V," *Bombay Gazette*, September 16, 1841, 262. "British Opium Policy and Its Results" originally appeared as Shoshee Chunder Dutt, "British Opium Policy and Its Results," in *India Past and Present* (London: Chatto and Windus, 1880), 343–98. "The Death Traffic" appeared as Rabindranath Tagore, "The Death Traffic," *Sino-Indian Journal* 1, pt. 1 (July 1947): 109–16. The essay, a review of Theodore Christlieb's *The Indo-British Opium Trade*, was originally published as "Chine Maraner Byabasa" in the Bengali periodical *Bharati* in May 1881. "On the Opium Question" was delivered at the British Indian Association on April 10, 1882. It was subsequently reprinted as Srish Chandra Bosu, "Speech on the Opium Question," in *Public Speeches of Babu Srish Chandra Bosu Sarvadhicari* (Calcutta: Peary Mohan Mookherjee, 1897), 14–18.

1. Heu Naetse, "Opium: Memorial to the Emperor Proposing to Legalize the Importation of It," *Chinese Repository* 5, no. 3 (1836): 140.
2. Heu Kew, "Memorial Against the Admission of Opium," *Chinese Repository* 5, no. 9 (1837): 402.

PART III

The Great Debate

Chapter Eight

TO LEARN FROM THE WEST

INDIAN VIEWS OF ENGLAND, 1877
Nagendra Nath Ghose

... Some of you may happen to remember that about two years ago Sir Henry Sumner Maine delivered a lecture at Cambridge on the following subject "European Views of India: The Effects of Observation of India upon Modern Thought."[1] It was his object in that lecture to ... show the baselessness of the current English assumptions of the dullness of Indian life and the barbarism of Indian races and Indian institutions and held up our country not in the light of an English dependency—not as a field for English enterprise or as a playground for frolicsome Englishmen, but simply and solely as a scientific study. In this paper I attempt to look upon England as a scientific study. I endeavor to point out how utterly untenable are some of the assumptions so frequently made by our countrymen concerning the character of the English people and English institutions, and what there is in English ideas and English life which we can study with profit to ourselves. . . .

I know from experience that few even of the most highly educated of our countrymen are able to appreciate the really characteristic differences between ideas Eastern and ideas Western. The only differences that are recognized are material differences—differences in wealth, physical strength, costume, and so forth. Convulsively, indeed, attention is directed to the

social customs and institutions of Europe but only for the sake of amuse-
ment and self-gratulation. Interesting details in the reports of divorce cases,
scurrilous articles in periodicals, amusing incidents in sensational novels
are all assiduously studied with no other object than that of finding support for some foregone conclusion and with no other result than the con-
gratulation of self on having been born in a country with such precious
usages as ours. Anything like a patient, unbiassed examination of facts is
seldom attempted, and even of the facts that obtrude themselves into notice
a rational explanation is never sought. . . .

Much of the difference in the opinions and the beliefs entertained by the
two peoples is due to the difference in their religions. It has become the fashion now with a certain class of persons to look upon all religions with contempt. To have an abhorrence of religion and everything religious is held
to be an indication of superior wisdom. It may be that none of the religions
now professed in the world are built on a basis of sound philosophy or are
even consistent with themselves, it may be that there are more profitable
investments of time than the employment of it in religious contemplation;
but the fact cannot be gainsaid that nothing has a more powerful influence
in determining the conduct of individuals as well as of nations than their
religious convictions. . . . I am not concerned in proving the superiority of
any one religion to another. I should be abusing my privilege if I were to
read to you my speculations on the relative merits of religions so far as they
treated of matters supernatural. But in my endeavor to find an explanation
of some of the vital differences between the moral doctrines of the East and
those of the West and between the principles upon which their respective
social institutions have been founded I cannot help noticing some of the
characteristics of Christianity on its intellectual and its ethical sides.

One of the most prominent features of Christianity is its rationalism.
Christianity won its triumphs not by rousing men's fears, but by appealing
to their reason and their healthy moral Instincts. It did not compel its vota-
ries to ignore or to disbelieve physical truths; it was rather built up on their
strength. It did not avoid free discussion, it rather invited scrutiny. It did
not propagate itself by the sword, it rather preached peace upon earth and
good-will to man. It is this rational, liberal spirit of Christianity that has
prevented it from crystallizing into that rigidity which would make it
unsuited to a civilized age, and has prevented its usages from that degen-
eration which, in earlier stages of civilization analogy induces. . . . It is

likewise this rational spirit of Christianity that has prevented Christian nations from finding an abiding comfort in recollections of past achievements and forgetting the true end and aim of human activity—progress. . . . I cannot forget history so completely as to say that Christian nations have never acted irrationally, that they have never hindered the free growth and spread of science, and that religious persecutions have never had the sanction of their name. But everything is liable to abuse; and so is Christianity. . . .

Quite as important is the characteristic that it made the performance of duty a virtue of the highest order. The idea of duty is entirely foreign to all ancient systems of ethics except only one. . . . The idea of duty originated with the Stoics, but even the Stoics conceived the highest virtue to consist in living according to nature and in approaching as nearly as possible the ideal "wise man." The true conceptions of duty, individual responsibility, and moral obligation were, if not introduced, at any rate perfected by Christianity. The nearest approach to the moral doctrines of Christianity was made in India by Buddhism. But Buddhism ultimately succumbed to Brahmanism, and even during the time that it was predominant its doctrines were never looked upon as practical rules of conduct. . . . If we Indians can abate a little of our morbid vanity, if we can be so generous as to read history and human nature aright, we shall find the unpleasant fact forced upon us that people in the West have a clearer and a stronger sense of duty than we as a nation can be said to possess. . . .

Even from a practical or worldly point of view the superiority of Christianity to the Hindoo religion is manifest enough. A religion out of which has arisen the institution of caste, which "reconciles itself with ancient forms of worship, and with new ones when they become sufficiently prevalent,"[2] which dictates it as a duty to marry and have children, and a compliance with whose rules makes emigration impossible is certainly no less fatal to material prosperity than to moral advancement.

History may be laid under contribution to afford an explanation of some of the moral characteristics of the two nations I am speaking about. . . . The one fact that I need remind you of is, that while England has always been independent, our country has been for centuries under foreign domination. The consequence is that all those qualities which liberty fosters, e.g., courage, candour, independence, public spirit, patriotism are part of the instinct of an Englishman; they are the most prominent traits of his character and are perceived by the discerning foreigner almost at a glance. But a native of this country—I am not speaking of exceptional instances, but of the bulk of the people—can only come to be possessed of those qualities only after a very careful training and a very rigid self-discipline.

Before I conclude this, what I might call speculative, portion of my address I ought to point out with what qualifications and reservations I wish my remarks to be accepted. And first, let me observe, that what I have said of England is true in a great measure of all other Christian countries in the world: that the same may be true of certain exceptional men or classes of men in India, and *is not* true of every individual Englishman. . . . Nevertheless, the great fact is there—that not only in all national movements and in all combined actions but even in humble individual occupations the English people display their sense of duty in an unmistakable manner. . . . The sense of duty is part of what [Herbert] Spencer would call his "organized experience." It is the inheritance of his race.

Secondly, I ought to caution you in regard to what I have said already and what I shall say hereafter that my remarks ought not to be understood in a too literal sense. If I am applauding any European or condemning any Indian custom I must not be taken to mean that the European custom is open to no objection whatever, and that it is never departed from by Europeans; or that the Indian custom is totally irrational and indefensible, and that it is rigidly adhered to by the entire Hindu community without exception. If, therefore, I employ none but universal propositions, it is for reasons of convenience. . . .

In describing to you the distinctive qualities of Englishmen and the modes of English life, the order I shall adopt is to treat first of the individual; secondly, the family; and lastly, the society. . . .

The ideas which prevail in this country concerning the attributes of Englishmen are not infrequently as grotesque as they are erroneous. The Englishman is ordinarily supposed to be made up of all that is hard and harsh in human nature. . . . Not that he is not credited with some redeeming virtues such as energy, independence, strength of will, steadiness; but of the softer elements of human nature he is supposed to be totally devoid. The amiable sons of the East claim a monopoly of feeling for themselves. . . . First, then, let me ask, is it reasonable to presume the absence or the dearth of all kind and generous feeling among a Christian nation—a nation, moreover, whose liberal and beneficent laws, whose deeds of philanthropic heroism, whose accomplishments and achievements in literature and in science, in arts and in arms challenge the admiration of the world. . . . There is one fact in regard to Europeans in general and Englishmen in particular, which we should do well to remember if we wished to form a just estimate of European character. That character may be described in one word—business-like; and this business-like character of the Englishman is the fact we ought always to remember. He takes good luck and ill-luck alike in a business-like manner. . . . Success and unsuccess he takes as they come in a cool, philosophic spirit. He must do his duty whether fortune favours him or not. . . .

To family life or, to use a more definite and more intelligible expression, to home life belongs an importance which is very seldom recognized or felt. . . . Speaking broadly, it may be said that society makes a man what he appears to be; his home makes him what he really is. Society may compel him to put on a certain costume, to obey its own rules concerning its own institutions (such as marriage, etc), to observe *its* rules of etiquette, and perhaps also, to profess that religion and practice that morality which *it* considers best. But such obedience may not spring from the heart. The spiritual life must be shaped by some other agency, and that is the home. . . . And if this is so, is it not strange that our countrymen should have so decided opinions of English character and English life, knowing so little as they do of English home-life? The domestic scandals that appear from time to time in newspapers no more represent ordinary English domestic life than the chilly days of an Indian winter represent ordinary Indian weather. . . . Health, industry, rational and regulated amusements, order, harmony, quiet—these are the most appropriate words to remind us of the normal features of an English household. . . . There are no unseemly manifestations of temper, no obstreperous expressions of grief or joy. Contrast with this a Bengali household (which may be taken to represent Indian households in general). The number of its inmates, the diversity of their interests, the utter absence of punctuality and method in its arrangements, its ceaseless tumult—all combine to make it unworthy of the sweet and sacred appellation of home. These characteristics are not superficial defects which can be removed by a little care and discrimination. They are defects inherent in its nature. . . .

Our legislators, our social reformers, and our would-be social reformers seem to think that little more is required for the complete education of the people of this country than good colleges and good textbooks. Such a supposition is unwarranted by facts and unwarranted by principle. Our colleges have sent forth multitudes of men who can make speeches, write books, argue points of law and cure diseases, but few indeed are the men who can be said to be completely educated, to have acquired, that is to say, accurate conceptions of their duties in life. Let us not forget the reality in the dazzle of its show. Observe the man who elicits general applause by an elaborate and eloquent speech before a public assembly or in a court of law, or him who instructs an audience of hundreds of men by his luminous scientific lectures and his successful scientific experiments, or him who, day after day, or week after week, discusses the most intricate questions of politics and political economy with admirable ability and fairness—observe the same man, I say, in his home as the head of his family, how he behaves towards his female relations, how he brings up his children, how he treats his servants, how he values education, what his ideas really are in regard to honesty, moral courage, liberty and toleration, and then say if he has not yet much to learn from Christian Europe.

In regard to English society there is in our country a wide-spread idea—*belief* I should call it—which requires more than a passing notice. The belief is that English society is not governed by a very rigid code of morality, that it attaches no value to purity of life. The extravagant assertion is not seldom made that scarcely a continent man or woman can be found in England. The sweepingly general character of the charge, the confidence with which it is brought, the reluctance which is displayed to examine any evidence to the contrary, point to the existence of a fixed idea, a deep-rooted prejudice, an indifference to truth, certainly not creditable to men who are said to have received a liberal education. . . .

Public morality, also, is a great deal more elevated in Europe than in our country. Proofs of this are found in the transactions of everyday life, and nowhere more clearly than in the gigantic commercial transactions of Europe. Such a large and elaborate system of commerce would be impossible if men had not confidence in those with whom they dealt; mutual confidence could not have been inspired if proofs of honesty had not been given, and it could not be continued if strict good faith were not observed in all dealings. . . .

There is one other fact concerning English society which deserves mention, and that is its coherence. In spite of the somewhat repulsive character of English men in general, their society has a coherence, a solidarity—quite unknown among us. This appears all the more strange when we remember that there are many reasons why there should be in our society as strong a sense of unity as any that can bind men together. Unfortunately, however, many things that ought to happen in our country do not, as a matter of fact, happen. . . .

It was not my intention to appear before you as an apologist for English ideas, English customs, English institutions and everything, in fact, that is, English. I am quite as well aware of the defects of the English people and English institutions as the most Anti-Anglican of my countrymen; and I might have without much difficulty filled my pages with invectives against those defects. But of such invectives we have had enough in our country. . . . And all this has been done not by way either of learning or teaching correct principles of morality, or the true laws of order and progress, not by way of cautioning us against any impending social catastrophes, but only to gratify some of the worst impulses of human nature. The amount of mischief which this frothy rhetoric has done is incalculable. Popular attention has been diverted from facts full of valuable instruction and riveted upon matters which feed the popular fancy and feed the popular vanity too. The consequence has been that in spite of the efforts of the English legislature, and in spite of the spread of English education, our country still continues to be governed by ideas long since exploded, and is still replete with institutions fatal alike to order and progress. Whatever the defects of the English people may be, there is no questioning the fact that they are one of the most advanced and one of the most powerful of nations. They may be inferior in some respects to some European nations; but all the Christian nations are so immeasurably in advance of us, that we may safely leave out of our calculations those infinitesimal quantities which must represent the superiorities and inferiorities of one Christian nation to another. He, therefore, who would keep out of our view the sterling excellences of European nations and the manifold agencies to which those excellences are due, who would, with sweet seductive stories of what we once were, make us forget what we now are, who would explain away the facts of Indian and of European history by attributing them all to Chance and would suggest to us a course of indolent ease, insolent swagger and giddy vanity—such a man as this would deserve to be called not a patriot, not a lover of his Motherland, but the most insinuating of her enemies, the basest of her betrayers. We have been deluded too long, and grievously have we paid for our delusion. It is high time for us now to wake from our dreams and to "purge and unscale our long-abused sight at the fountain itself," not indeed of "heavenly radiance," but of the deceitless radiance of realities. . . .

THE SHAME OF BHARAT, 1879
Bankim Chandra Chatterjee

Why is Bharat not independent? Why has Bharatvarsha been without independence for so long? Most people say that it is because Indians are impotent. Europeans perpetually mouth the phrase "effeminate Hindus," which is precisely what the shame of Bharat is. And yet it is the same Europeans who praise the strength and courage of Indian soldiers. It was the might of the effeminate Hindus that enabled Kabul to be conquered. Truth be told, it is with the assistance of the same effeminate Hindus that they have subjugated Bharatvarsha. Whether they acknowledge it or not, they have been vanquished several times on the battlefield by the self-same effeminate Hindus, Marathas, and Sikhs.

But no matter how mighty the modern Hindus consider themselves, there can be little doubt that they are far inferior in this matter to their ancient predecessors. Being under the yoke of others for centuries could not but have diminished their strength and valor. There are many reasons to conclude that the inhabitants of ancient Bharat were considerably powerful before being vanquished by other nationalities—they did not lose their independence because of frailty.

We admit that it is no easy matter to accept this line of argument, and that unearthing sufficient evidence is difficult. It would have been possible to resolve this debate on the basis of ancient history alone, but unfortunately, unlike other nations, the people of Bharatvarsha did not chronicle their own achievements. There is no history available of ancient Bharat, and therefore the glory of the martial achievements of the people of those times has been obliterated. The texts that remain in the form of the Puranas contain nothing by way of genuine history. Those of them that are extant are so suffused by unnatural and superhuman exploits that it is impossible to determine what really took place.

Fortunately, there are two references to the wars fought by the people of ancient Bharatvarsha in volumes composed by historians from other lands. The first of these is to the war fought by the Macedonian king Alexander or Sikander in Bharatvarsha during his journey to conquer the world. Accomplished writers, none of them Hindus, have proclaimed the outcome of this war. And second, Muslim historians have recorded the accounts of all the military initiatives taken by members of their faith to conquer different parts of Bharatvarsha. However, it must be declared at the outset that the possibility of such witnesses being partial to one of the combatants was high. It is because humans are painters that lions are portrayed as the vanquished in paintings. There are very few historians who are willing to adhere to the truth by acknowledging the shortcomings of their own nation and singing the praises of the enemy. Leave alone the relatively obtuse Muslims blinded by conceit, even the erudite European historians who are far more devoted to the cause of the truth are nevertheless so conspicuous for this flaw that perusing their writings is on occasion an utterly loathsome experience. Therefore, no event in history can be interpreted correctly unless the accounts of historians representing both sides of a conflict are available. The military prowess of the people of ancient Bharatvarsha cannot be determined on the strength of the narrations of vain Muslim writers who are antagonistic to other religions and fearful of the truth. Be that as it may, the following two observations have both been drawn from the works of ancient Muslim historians. First, the people of the Arab realms conquered the world, vanquishing every country they fought a war against to establish an empire of unparalleled proportions. However, they were defeated by and expelled from only two countries, France in the West and Bharat in the East. The Arabs conquered Egypt and Syria within six years of the Muhammad's death, Iran in the tenth year, Africa and Spain in a year each thereafter, Kabul in the eighteenth year, and Turkey eight years afterward. But despite assiduous efforts that lasted three hundred years, they were unable to capture Bharatvarsha. It is true that Muhammad bin Qasim conquered Sindh, but he was defeated in Rajputana and forced to leave, with the Rajputs recapturing Sindh shortly after his death. The world-conquering Arabs could not extend their empire to Bharat. According to Elphinstone, the invincibility of Hindus sprang from their unshakeable love for their religion. We term it military skill or martial prowess. The Hindus' love for their religion is intact even today. Why then have they languished in a state of defeat and subjugation for seven centuries?

Second, when a newly created nation intent on conquests is situated in proximity to an ancient state, the older one is often annexed by the younger entity. The Romans in ancient Europe and the Arabs and Turks in Asia were the very embodiments of nations intent on conquering others. Every nation that has come into contact with them has been forced to submit. None of them has proved as indomitable as the Hindus. We have already mentioned the swiftness with which the Arabs vanquished Egypt, North Africa, Spain, Persia, and Kabul. We can cite examples of a small number of even more illustrious empires that met similar fates. The Romans invaded Greece for the first time in the year 200 BC, after which it took a mere fifty-two years for the Greek kingdom to be annihilated. The renowned state of Carthage engaged in battle with the Romans for the first time in the year 264 BC. By 164 BC, that is to say, within one hundred years, it was destroyed by Rome. Thereafter, the Roman Empire was invaded by the Turks in the first part of the fourteenth century and was crushed by 1453 AD—in just fifty years, in other words—at the hands of Mohammed II. The Western Roman Empire, the very standard bearer of a valorous nation, was attacked by Goths for the first time in 286 BC and then vanquished in 476 AD, within 190 years of the first Gothic Rebellion. Bharatvarsha came under the attack of Arab Muslims for the first time in 664 AD. It was 529 years after this that Shihab ad-Din Ghori conquered all of northern Bharat. But neither he nor his followers were of Arab origin. The failure of the Arabs to capture Bharatvarsha was matched by the failure of the Turks, founders of Ghazni. Those who finally wrested the kingdom of northern Bharat from Prithviraj, Jaichandra, and the Senas were Pathans or Afghans. In other words, the Pathans achieved their conquest 529 years after the Arabs invaded India, and 213 years after the Turkish did the same. The Pathans had not made as much progress or amassed as much power and influence as the Arabs or Turks, they merely completed what their predecessors had begun when invading Bharatvarsha. It was through the combined efforts of these three nationalities, the Arabs, the Turks, and the Pathans, that Bharat lost its independence over a period of five hundred years.[3]

This is the testimony of Muslim witnesses to history. It is also essential to remember that by the time they confronted the Hindus, the latter were already in a state of decline, with their sovereignty waning. There can be little doubt that the Hindus who lived before the age of Christ had far greater power. That was the era when the Greeks had their encounters with the Hindus. Second to none when it came to martial prowess, they were nevertheless full of praise for the courage and military skills of the people of Bharatvarsha. In their accounts of the Macedonian conquests, they stated repeatedly that they had not come across another nation in Asia as adept at warcraft as Bharat, and that their casualties at the hands of the Hindus were higher than was the case with any other nation. Anyone harboring any doubts about the abilities of the people of ancient Bharatvarsha on the battlefield need only read what the Greeks have written about it.

The land of Bharat, endowed with all manner of wealth, was the object of naked greed for many a kingdom. This is the reason various nations have attempted at various times in history to enter Bharat through the mountain gateway in the northwest and conquer the realm. From Persians to Greeks, from Scythians to Huns, from Arabs to Turks, all of them occupied small tracts of land on the banks of the Indus for short periods of time before being forced out again. Until the fifteenth century, there was no other nationality on Earth, and probably never had been, which had repelled attacks from every other mighty nation. There is no doubt that it was the might of the Hindus that enabled them to protect their own successful existence—no other reason can be discerned.

Despite such plentiful evidence, we are told constantly that Hindus have always been incapable of warfare. To the near-sighted there are three reasons for this eternal blot on the reputation of Bharatvarsha.

First, Hindus have no ancient history of their own. Who will sing your praises if not you yourself? It is in the nature of humans not to accord any importance to one who does not identify himself as a great man. When has one nation ever extolled the virtues of another? The proof of the martial prowess of Romans is in histories written by Romans. We learn of the heroic exploits of Greeks on the battlefields from Greek texts. That Muslims are adept at warfare is also something we have come to know by believing their own statements. Hindus alone have no glory to lay claim to in this matter, because there were no Hindu witnesses to it.

The second reason: Only those nations that have been desirous of usurping other kingdoms have come to be known as warlike. Those who have been content to defend themselves, without seeking to annex other people's lands, have never achieved the glory of being heroes. Heroism and righteousness do not usually coexist. Even at present the term "decent man" refers to incompetent people of a pusillanimous nature. "Hari is a decent man" means Hari is a bungling fool.

We do not claim that Hindus were completely bereft of the desire for acquiring the kingdoms of others. They could not be accused of never attacking one another. However, during the reign of the Hindus, Bharat-varsha was divided into many small realms. But Bharat is so extensive that none of the kings of these tiny realms desired to extend their reign far beyond their own borders. No Hindu king had ever succeeded in includ-ing all of Bharat in his empire. Moreover, Hindus hated people of other faiths so very much that there was no possibility of their harboring the incli-nation to rule over them. On the contrary, sallying forth to conquer such kingdoms would have meant risking the extinction of their own faith and nationality. Therefore, despite having the means to do so, there was no pos-sibility that Hindus would venture beyond Bharatvarsha to attack other kingdoms. It is true that much of the present-day kingdom of Kabul was in the past part of a Hindu state, but then the region was at that time consid-ered to be a part of Bharatvarsha.

The third reason for the shame of ancient Hindus is this: They have long been under subjugation. What claim to heroic glory can a nation make when it has been under a yoke for centuries? But the diminished valor of present-day Hindus cannot be wielded as a reason to accuse their ancient forefa-thers of cowardice. It has been observed in many countries that their ancient and the modern people do not resemble each other greatly in nature. Like Bharatvarsha, Italy and Greece are also examples of this. Just as it would be unjust to conclude from the characteristics of medieval Italians and present-day Greeks that ancient Romans and ancient Greeks were cowards, so too would it be unfair to use the present state of subjugation of the peo-ple of Bharatvarsha as proof of the weakness of ancient Hindus.

Nor do we aver that the people of modern Bharatvarsha are timid and therefore languishing under the rule of a foreign power. There are other rea-sons for this. Here we shall present two of them in some detail.

First, the people of Bharatvarsha are by nature devoid of the desire for independence. Let people of our own nationality and race rule us, but we shall never be subjugated by other nations—this is not a credo for the inhab-itants of Bharat. They do not hold dear the notion that being ruled by rep-resentatives of their own nationality is more beneficial or greater reason for happiness, or that being ruled by the scepter of monarchs of other nationalities is distressing. They may have an inkling that independence is preferable to being ruled by others, but it is no more than an inkling, without being converted into actual desire. We may be aware of the value of many qualities without necessarily experiencing a need to emulate them. Is there anyone who does not praise Harishchandra's altruism or Curtius's patriotism? But how many of us are prepared to sacrifice everything, as Harishchandra did, or lay down our own lives, as Curtius did? The love for independence has been converted into a virile desire among ancient and modern European nations. They believe that it is one's duty to give up everything, including one's life, before one surrenders one's freedom. But this is not the case with Hindus, who prefer to think, "Let he who wants become king; it is no business of ours." A king of one's own nationality is no different from a king from a foreign land. As long as they are good rulers, it makes no difference which nation they belong to. Is there any assurance that a king from one's own nation will be a good ruler, but a king from a different nation will not? If there is no such assurance, why must we lay down our lives for a king of our own nationality? The kingdom belongs to the king; let him defend it himself if he is able. We are indifferent, for no one will bequeath a portion of their riches to us. Let he who wants become king, we shall not raise a finger on behalf of either the defender or the aggressor.[4]

Today, educated as we have been by the freedom-minded British, we can see the errors in all these suppositions. But these proclivities are not unnatural, nor are the errors easily discernible. Some nationalities are by nature inclined toward independence, while others, despite being civilized, have no particular faith in it. Many things are desirable in this world, but not everyone pursues each of them in equal measure. Wealth and fame are both desirable, but we usually find that while one individual is engaged in amassing wealth and ignoring fame, another wishes for nothing but fame, caring little for wealth. One person is so intent on becoming rich that his reputation suffers on account of his parsimony and avarice, while another does not think twice before extinguishing his wealth to acquire fame though his magnanimity. It is no easy matter to decide which of these is right. At least it is certain that neither of them is going against their nature. In the same way, the Greeks held independence dear to their hearts, while it mattered little to the Hindus, who were partial to the pleasures of a peaceful life. This is merely a matter of diversity in national character, not a cause for astonishment.

But many people think otherwise. They conclude from the Hindus' disinclination for gaining independence that Hindus are weak, cowardly on the battlefield, and incapable of wresting freedom. They forget that Hindus have never been desirous or diligent in pursuing independence. Either of these characteristics would have proven beneficial.

We do not mean to suggest that this disdain for independence is a trait of the modern Hindu alone, for it appears to be an eternal characteristic of Hindus. Those who surmise that the Hindus have lost their desire for independence because of seven centuries of subjugation are incorrect. There is nothing to be found in Sanskrit literature that will enable ancient Hindus to be identified as people striving to live in a state of independence. There are no paeans to freedom in the ancient Puranas or poetry or drama. With the exception of Mewar, there is no record of a Hindu society engaged in any effort whatsoever to secure independence. There are copious references to the endeavors of kings to protect their realm and riches, to the valor of the courageous, to the battlefield exploits of the Kshatriyas. But the aspiration to be independent is not among them. Freedom and independence are foreign ideas. If one were to investigate the reason for this characteristic disregard for independence, the causes will not prove to be out of reach. A minor reason was the fertility of the soil and the excessively hot climate of Bharatvarsha. With bountiful harvests and a profusion of all manner of resources, living was not a matter of great effort. No one had to toil very hard, and there was plentiful leisure. Being spared arduous physical work, people found their minds turning inward naturally, with an abundance of both cogitation and meditation. One outcome of this was the development of a poetic sensibility and deep knowledge. This is why the Hindus became the finest poets and philosophers in the world in a very short time. But the second consequence of this introspective nature was a lack of faith in external happiness, which in turn inevitably gave birth to inactivity. The lack of interest in independence was but one of the manifestations of this inactivity. This disinclination to act is evident in both the religion and the philosophy of the Aryans. Whether it was in the Vedic or the Buddhist religions or in the philosophy of the Puranas, this quality is always welcomed. The philosophy of the Vedanta and Samkhya were born from the Vedas, and in them deliverance lay in the cessation of physical pleasures. Shedding desires was, therefore, virtuous. The essence of Buddhism said that liberation came in the same way.

One may ask at this juncture why the Hindus made the effort to keep foreign nations from taking away their independence over the long period of fifteen hundred years if indeed they were so disdainful of the state of freedom. The invaders cannot have been repelled easily—it must have needed considerable hardship on the part of the defenders. Why did the Hindus endure so much hardship for a pleasure they had no interest in?

The answer to this is that there is no evidence that the Hindus as a nation had to go to great lengths to turn away the Greek, Scythian, and other invaders. The Hindu rulers were intent on protecting their kingdoms and riches, and the soldiers they had engaged went to war for this. Whenever possible, these forces defeated the enemy, which automatically preserved the independence of the kingdom. But there is no evidence anywhere that the general populace was also inspired to declare, "We shall not permit anyone from another nation to rule over ours." The contrary, in fact, is considered to be the truth. Whenever a Hindu king or Hindu general was killed on the battlefield because of the rage of the gods of war, the Hindu soldiers promptly gave up and fled, without regrouping. Their reasoning: Whom would they fight for now? When the king became inactive in the task of protecting his kingdom, either because of death or for some other reason, the Hindus stopped waging war at once. No one took the king's place in an attempt to preserve the independence of the kingdom—no initiative was taken by any member of society to protect the undefended realm. And whenever, because fate so decreed, a Greek or Persian or Scythian or Baloch leader defeated the ruler of some fragment of Bharatvarsha somewhere and ascended the throne, the subjects of the kingdom honored him as their new lord with no reservation, without any objection to the usurpation of their realm. For three thousand years, everyone has engaged in conflict with everyone else—one Aryan race with another, Aryans with non-Aryans, Magadha with Kannauj, Kannauj with Delhi, Delhi with Lahore, Hindus with Pathans, Pathans with Mughals, Mughals with the British—to incinerate Bharatvarsha in the flames of war. But all of these were battles between kings—ordinary Hindus never fought those wars on anyone's behalf. The kingdoms of Bharatvarsha have been conquered by different nations, but it can never be said that another has conquered the Hindu society, because Hindu society has never entered into a war with another nation.

This line of thought brings us to the second reason for the long-standing subjugation of the Hindus. To wit, the lack of unity in Hindu society, the

lack of the establishment of a Hindu nation, the lack of the desire to ame-
liorate the lot of a nation—call it what you will. We shall explain in some
detail. I am a Hindu, so are you, so is he and he and he, and so are millions
of others. Whatever is most beneficial to these millions of Hindus is what
is beneficial to me. What is not beneficial to them is not beneficial to me
either. Therefore, it is my duty to do whatever will ensure the well-being of
millions of Hindus. And it is my duty to eschew whatever causes them harm.
And just as this is my duty, so too is it your duty, and his and his and his,
and that of millions of Hindus. And if the task of all Hindus is the same, then
it is the duty of all Hindus to work in unison, with a single goal. This realization is but one part of building a nation—no more than half. There are
many nationalities in the world besides Hindus, but their well-being
cannot ensure that of ours too. In many cases, their benefits may accrue to
our detriment. And in such cases, we must act in a way that does not lead
to their benefit. If this means oppressing other nations, we must do it. Con-
versely, just as whatever is beneficial to them may be harmful to us, so too
might our well-being lead to harm for them. But we shall not desist from
improving our own lot for this reason. If we have to ensure our well-being
by causing harm to other nationalities, that is what we must do. This is the
other half of what must be done to establish our nation.

We can see that such a mentality cannot be acknowledged as a pure,
innocent one. It has a grave and damnable aberration, which leads people
to the erroneous conclusion that the betterment of other nationalities can
only mean harm to one's own, and that harm to other nationalities must
necessarily lead to the betterment of one's own. Europeans have suffered
greatly as a result of this perverted belief, with Europe being destroyed by
the flames of war more than once.

Whether a strong sense of nationality is good or evil, nations that adopt
it tend to become more powerful than others. This awareness is particularly visible in Europe today, and several violent revolutions are taking place
on the continent under its influence. It has turned Italy into a single, united
nation, and it has enabled the creation of a mighty new German empire.
There is no telling what else it might succeed in creating.

We do not claim that this sense of nationality never existed in Bharatvarsha. European scholars have concluded that the Aryans were not always
inhabitants of Bharat, that they arrived here from elsewhere and conquered

the land. The Vedas were composed at the time of the first Aryan conquest, which is referred to by scholars as the Vedic period. That the motivation of establishing a nation was strong in the Vedic period and immediately afterward is evident from many of the Vedic texts. The manner in which the Brahmins, who were at the time the controlling group, laid down rules for society also points to a similar desire. The enormous differences codified between the Aryan castes and the Shudras came about for this reason. But as the Aryans dispersed across the land, nationhood was no longer a consideration. Different groups of Aryans captured different regions of Bharatvarsha, which was thus fragmented into numerous societies. Distinctions in social mores, languages, rituals, and all modes of living eventually turned into distinctions between nationalities. From the Baloch to Poundra, from Kashmir to the kingdoms of the Cholas and the Pandya, Bharatvarsha was, like a beehive, filled with a multitude of nations and of societies. Eventually, a new religion was born of the hands of Shakya, the prince of Kapilavastu, and the distinction of religion was added to all the other distinctions. Separate kingdoms, separate languages, separate rulers, separate religions: Where was the possibility of being a single nation anymore? Like fish in an ocean, the people of Bharatvarsha lost their unity. Then the Muslims arrived, multiplying rapidly. Over the years newer communities of Muslims began to arrive from the other side of the mountain ranges, like a succession of waves upon a shore. The people of Bharatvarsha began to convert to Islam in the thousands, either in hope of royal favors or in fear of the king's tyranny. As a result, societies turned into a mixture of Hindus and Muslims. Hindus, Muslims, Mughals, Pathans, Rajputs, Marathas—all began to work together. Where was the question of national unity? What national identity remained possible?

Our Bharatvarsha is home to many nationalities, with distinctions in terms of domicile, language, genealogy, and religion. Bengalis, Punjabis, Telugus, Marathas, Rajputs, Jats, Hindus, Muslims—which of them will unite with one another? When there is religious unity the lineages are different, when lineages match the languages do not, when the languages are the same the domiciles vary. Rajputs and Jats have the same religion but different lineages and are therefore different nationalities. Bengalis and Biharis have a common lineage but are separate nationalities by virtue of language. Maithilis and Kannaujis have the same language but belong to different regions. That is not all. Even those who share the same religion, language, genealogy, and region are not united as a nation. Bengalis do not have the unity of a Bengali nation; Sikhs do not have the unity of a Sikh nation. There is a specific reason for this. When different nationalities become part of a single empire for a very long time, their sense of nationality disappears gradually. Just as you can no longer tell the waters of one river apart from another once they have both flown into the ocean, so too is the case with different nationalities in a single empire. The distinctions between them disappear, but they do not become united. The different nations that became part of the Roman Empire faced these circumstances, as did Hindus. And so the idea of establishing a nation has long disappeared in Bharatvarsha. And because it has disappeared, Hindu society has never accomplished anything as a nation. In its absence, kings of all nationalities have been crowned in Hindu kingdoms, with Hindus raising not a finger to maintain their independence.

Only twice, in recorded history, did Hindus rise as a nation. Once, when Shivaji read the mantra in Maharashtra, and the lion's roar aroused all the people in the region. That was when Marathas became brothers to one another and created the magical power by which the hitherto undefeated Mughal Empire was forced to retreat. The eternally victorious Muslims were defeated by the Hindus. All of Bharatvarsha bowed to Maharashtra. Even today British rule over Bharatvarsha is not absolute; they have to share it with the Marathas. The second time, the magician was Ranjit Singh, who wrought the magic of the Khalsa. As the identity of a nation grew, the Hindus even captured a portion of the Pathans' own land. The fearless British quaked at the roar of the Khalsa, but fortunately for them, an abler magician in the form of Dalhousie dismantled the Khalsa magic. But Ramnagar and Chillianwala were written into history.

If the rise of the idea of a nation in only a part of Bharatvarsha could have achieved so much, what could not have been possible if all of Bharatvarsha had united as a single nation?

The British are our beneficiaries. They are teaching us a new vocabulary, they are informing us of things we knew nothing about, they are showing us, telling us, explaining to us things we have never seen or heard or understood. They are demonstrating to us how to walk on a path we have never walked before. Many of these things we are learning are priceless. I have referred in this essay to two of the priceless jewels we have acquired in this manner: a love for freedom and the establishment of a nation. The Hindus did not know what these meant.

THE RUIN OF THE NATIVE AMERICANS, 1889
Pandita Ramabai [Ramabai Sarasvati]

... Braggarts, cheats, close-fisted men, without spending even a copper of their own money, bestow favors and beneficence, merely through words or by looting the goods of others. If the actions of such men are to be described, it is the custom among us to call it "feigning generosity with another's wealth." A huge event that serves as an incomparable example of such feigned generosity has come to pass in European history. This event has a very immediate connection to us and to our Native American brethren, denizens of the Americas, hence it must be told to you. . . .

[This] superficial act was committed by a Pope*ji* of Rome, as resolute and learned men like Columbus set out to voyage the world by sea and to discover new wealthy lands. In the fifteenth century, Spain and Portugal were followers of the pope, favored by the pope's indulgence. In 1493 the Reverend Pope*ji*, Alexander VI by name, was very pleased to give his favorite disciples two great boons. The pope, promulgating a decree known as a "Bull," declared that all new countries or islands the two governments of Spain and Portugal might discover would be under the ownership of those rulers. In order to avoid conflict between the two, he drew an imaginary line from north to south in the middle of the Atlantic ocean and stipulated that those continents or islands like America which had been found or would be found in the future in the Western hemisphere would be under the possession by the king of Spain; and Africa, India, and their neighboring islands in the Eastern hemisphere, to the right of the aforementioned line, were to be owned by the king of Portugal. Africa, America, India, and their neighboring islands—what were they to the pope, the land of his fathers? Where did the pope the right to bestow it upon the kings of Portugal? But there is no saying what hypocritical and heretic persons will do. Hence, I feel like the pope's actions merit the name "feigning generosity with another's wealth."

... At the time the Europeans went to the Americas, and began to mine the gold there and bring back men they captured, the native people were living in a state of ignorance, as has been described above. They did not know at all how to use deadly weapons such as ammunition, cannons, and guns, or what they were.... In our *Puranas* we hear stories of miraculous and invincible weapons such as the missiles of Agni (Fire), Indra (the Lightning Bolt), and Vayu (Wind) but we do not know what these weapons are, what they look like, how to use them. In such a case, if someone who knew these weapons came to our country and it took his fancy to conquer us, he would be able to do so with ease. Even a hundred thousand people, should they be ignorant of such weapons, would not be able to last in front of him; not only that, but ignorant people will conclude that by having such marvelous knowledge, he must be a superior being to ourselves, and divine, and thereupon they will begin to needlessly fear him. The poor Native Americans were in the same condition. It is not that they were weaker than the Europeans, or that they did not like liberty, and when the Europeans began to meddle with their freedom, it was not that the Native Americans did not resist it. But they were ignorant, naïve, and credulous. Fearing omens and shadowy nothings, they sometimes did not go against their enemies. At other times, they were frightened upon seeing the enemies' guns, cannons, other firearms, and horses.

What could the poor folks even do? Even if a thousand men unite and are prepared to fight the enemy, if your lone enemy showers you with fire and fiery bullets, you would not be able to stand your ground; for you do not have the appropriate weapons to contend with him. In such a situation, it is no big surprise that five or ten thousand Europeans managed to raze hundreds of thousands of Indians. Their doing this is simply the same as a strong, armed man cutting off the heads of hundreds of thousands of orphaned, unarmed tender babies. No one would call this act one of true bravery. If these Europeans had laid down their firearms and won them at wrestling or in a battle using used bow and arrows, flint-tipped knives, and bone-tipped lances like they did, that would have proved them truly warrior-like. But it gives one great sadness to think that those who called themselves godly and went forth to educate the ignorant, to show those who were falling into hell the path to heaven, ended up destroying the poor innocent Indians by relying on bad tactics such as deceit, trickery, cruelty, and false speech, at every step of the way.

Now it is not my argument that the Native Americans were without fault from the beginning to the end, but they emphatically never put themselves in the Europeans' way. They never set out on trickery. On the contrary when the Europeans first came to their land, believing them to be "Children of the Sun," they welcomed them with great respect. They tried to please them by offering them gifts of gold, fruits, and so on, according to their capacity. Even then these White Gods were not satisfied, and, finding great treasure there, began to extract as much as they could from the Indians to their detriment. Is there any man on Earth who would not resist such an all-devouring God? I cannot blame them for trying to protect their rights in any fashion. Their misfortune was their ignorance. The means of dispelling this ignorance were not in their compass at the time. A man who, having all the means to get rid of his ignorance, does not do so is undoubtedly to blame for that. But if he did not do so because he lacks the tools, what is the poor man's fault? If one reads the history of the Indians, it becomes clear that ignorance (of which naivete, credulity, the fear of omens, the fear of ghosts and spirits, and so on form a part) is one of the chief reasons for their ruin.

The proverb goes that when two men fight, it is the third who profits. Malice among people is ruinous to large and small households, to society and to country. In truth the root of malice is ignorance. When people have a mutual misunderstanding due to some trifling reason, there malice is begat. Once malice takes root, there are quarrels aplenty. People consider one another enemies because of quarrels, and they try to harm their enemies by all means. If the enemy is strong, then it feels like an outsider's help might be considered necessary to harm him. And when a third enters a quarrel, he achieves his ends by making the fighting parties into puppets in his own ends. And so it turns out that he gains, while all others lose. It is bad for any family or country to have feuds among themselves. Due to the contentious disputes among our countrymen, foreigners could gain ingress and we lost our independence, this much is evident to every person that reads the history of Hindustan. Our Native American brethren met the same fate. While they were fighting among themselves, the White people gained ground. Of those, the weak ones who had conflicts with stronger groups of Native Americans thought of taking the help of the White outsiders to defeat strong enemies of their own races. They brought White people to their own countries and gave them whatever help they required. As a result, while their own enemies were destroyed, they themselves did not reap the benefits and instead incurred a heavy loss. The Whites, after defeating their enemies, forcefully kicked them out of their countries—and the White lords ensconced themselves as the sole sovereigns of that country! Thus it becomes apparent that both the weak Indians who helped the Whites destroy enemies of their own race and similarly ignoble persons in our own country ultimately hurt their own people, of their own make and blood, with their actions.

The Europeans of the Spaniards, Portuguese, French, English, and Dutch races seized the opportunities described above, and with different means wrested away the motherland of the Native Americans from them; and setting up new colonies, they established their own kingdoms. Today the Native Americans are scattered all over America like the shards of a shattered glass bowl. To eat what is provided by White men that rule the land; to drink water with their permission; to mutely pass their time on Earth; to be hunted by White men like the birds and beasts of the forests—this has become the only purpose of the Native American's life.

STRENGTH OF THE BRITISH, 1897
Muhammad Beg

On an Indian, the first sight of British muscle and bone, creates a profound impression. He cannot but compare it, in his own mind, with the poor physique of his own countrymen and conceive how much this superior physique counts for all that is great and good in the British. The contrast between Indians and British is very striking, not simply in colour, or stature and strength, it is equally striking in the active energetic habits of the latter, as compared with the slow, lazy, don't-care sort of appearance in this country. It is astonishing to see how some of the most corpulent and unwieldy men in London, could be as active and quick of movement as the thinnest young men imaginable. None is lazy, none is indolent, none does his work in a half-hearted, slipshod or slovenly sort of way, as is so very general in India, but everything is in full swing, during the working hours, and everybody is doing his very best, without sparing or stinting his energies. Judging from the life they live, no matter what the cause is, one would conclude that the end of life in the West is work, while the end of life in the East seems to be an easy-chair. *Here, indolence; there, activity*, is the prominent national characteristic.

Above all, the discipline and system one sees in the very London crowds, and in the life of the English, is something wonderful. It is a problem how all that has come to the nation in general, and what peculiar training it is that has made them all so compact, solid and united, that the ordinary people of London could, in times of emergency, do as well as, if not better than the forces of our Nawabs and Maharajahs. Altogether the British are a peculiar race, of peculiar origin. If every Briton is only compelled to bear arms for a period, and to undergo a course of military discipline, it would be hard to conceive their concrete, national strength. Without training of any sort, it looks from its build and make a nation of soldiers.

I had the good fortune to be present at the Aldershot parade of 30,000 young British soldiers, including regiments of Horse-Guards and Life-Guards. I have not seen in my life anything so perfect and beautiful as this organisation of Horse-Guards and Life-Guards. I cannot imagine for strength or stature, men better than those composing these regiments, which seem to consist of the pick and flower of the Army; nor can I picture to myself stronger or more graceful animals, than their horses. And the same, with reference to their arms. They left, in every principle and detail, nothing to be desired. . . . The parade was the grandest I saw, and it was the very picture of British might.

From Aden to London, one sees how the navy is working. The British forts and fortifications, and the men-of-war, one sees on the voyage to England, are quite a novel experience to an Indian. The British have made the sea their home. They can do everything on sea, quite as well as, if not better than, what any nation can do on land. It struck me how closely superior strength is associated with an idea of permanency. Whatever is weak, is a reminder of the transient nature of our existence, whereas, whatever is strong, is just the reverse. The impression British strength makes on one's mind, both on land and sea, evokes the expression "What wonderful people these, who can conquer them?"

We also saw the Navy Review. We were taken in the *Campania*. The Prince of Wales received the royal salute. There were five lines of men-of-war, each five miles long, making a total of 25 miles in length. There were men-of-war possessing guns weighing 110 tons each. The royal salute of 160 men-of-war, nine-tenths of which were ours, rent the air and made it literally tremble.

It looks as if the whole of England is a vast army: for what man is there who is not strong? What man is there who does not know the use of arms? What man is there who cannot ride? What man is there who will not, or cannot, if occasion needs, fight? . . . I should be the last to flatter any individual or nation: and when I say that the British Army and Navy is a marvel of strength, organisation and discipline, that might well infuse into other nations "the desire as well as despair" of competing with the British, I am stating what I feel. England has got the wealth of men, arms, ammunition, transport, and above all, money,—the indispensable fuel to work everything with—to so remarkable a degree of *conserved* and *tested* perfection, that all that one could do by way of describing it falls short of its desert. . . .

WHAT CAN ENGLAND TEACH US?, 1897
Indo-Anglian [Baman Das Basu]

Professor Max Müller in his Lectures on "India, What Can It Teach Us?" has eloquently described all that India can teach the Christian nations of Europe. But no one has fully dwelt on what England can teach us—Indians.

The first and the greatest lesson which we should learn from Englishmen is their collective selfishness as a nation. Englishmen are very selfish. It is not the individual selfishness, but it is the national or what they call enlightened selfishness that we have to learn from the Christian natives of England. No one has ever accused the English of not being selfish. Even they themselves have acknowledged this. Indians, on the other hand, collectively are not selfish. There are, of course, selfish individuals. But selfishness is not a collective virtue or vice of Indians.

Again, Indians are given to contemplate on the world to come rather than to mind the affairs to this world. Natives of England, on the other hand, employ all their energies and thoughts to improve their position in this world. Here, we think, Indians could borrow with advantage a page from the lives of English people. The deep spiritual nature of Indians should be strongly tinctured with the secular script of the Christian West. Then and then only they will be able to maintain their position in this world.

Closely allied to the national selfishness and worldliness of the English, is their patriotism. The Sanskrit language has no word corresponding to patriotism. Of course, we exclude from consideration words coined in recent times. The want of the spirit of patriotism amongst Indians has been assigned to their system of village communities. But it appears to us that the want of patriotism was due to there never having been so keen a struggle for existence in ancient times in India as there is now. Schiller has truly observed that "the edifice of the world is only sustained by the impulse of hunger and love."[5] It is this want of the impulse of hunger which accounts for the want of patriotism in ancient India. On the other hand, this impulse of love, not only for human beings, but for the whole animate creation, so vigorously preached by Buddha and his disciples, stood in the way of the growth of patriotism in the Western sense. For, *this* patriotism is, after all, the selfishness one feels for one's own nation. To do a good turn to his own nation, a Western patriot does not hesitate to cut the throats of another people. According to English notions of patriotism, Clive was a patriot, Warren Hastings was a patriot, and Lord Dalhousie was a patriot, because all of them enriched their own nations at the expense of another people.

It is highly necessary for Indians to learn patriotism from the Christian nations of the West; for now, the old times are gone, old manners are changed. In the struggle for existence, which is now going on in the world, Indians are liable to be exterminated if they do not cultivate the spirit of patriotism. This will be a stimulus to improve their present pitiable and miserable condition. "Love of country," writes Dean Ramsay,

> *must* draw forth good feeling in men's minds, as it will tend to make them cherish a desire for its welfare and improvement. To claim kindred with the honorable and high-minded, as in some degree allied with them, must imply at least an *appreciation* of great and good qualities. . . . This is surely a spirit to be cultivated in a world like this;—in a world where we find so many causes arising that produce bitter animosities and violent contentions; in a world where we find even the stronger ties of natural affection broken amidst the jealousies and alienations of men's hearts. The love of country, then, we would advocate, not as a matter of pride, or as a mere sentiment, but as a *principle*, of which the tendencies are decidedly favourable to benevolent and virtuous emotions. We have no hesitation in advocating the cause, even at the risk of incurring thereby the charge of being "*national*," which this declaration may bring upon us.[6]

Indians then stand sorely in need of cultivating this spirit of patriotism, *minus* the robbing instinct. This is perhaps the greatest lesson which England can teach us.

Hero-worship is another great lesson which we ought to learn from England. The English are a nation of hero-worshippers. They worship their great men while alive, and cherish their memories when dead. We Indians do not know how to honour our great men. In his work on "Past and Present," Carlyle defines

hero-worship to be the summary, ultimate essence, and supreme practical perfection of all manner of worship and true worships and noblenesses whatsoever. . . . Hero-worship, done differently in every different epoch of the world is the soul of all social business among men; that the doing of it well, or the doing of it ill, measures accurately what degree of well-being or of ill-being there is in the world's affairs.[7]

"Great men," again to quote the same author, "were the leaders of men; the modelers, the patterns, and in a wide sense creators, of whatever the general mass of men contrived to do or to attain. . . . We cannot look, however imperfectly, upon a great man, without gaining something by him."[8]

In England, memorials or even statues are raised to men having any pretension to distinction. But what have we done to keep green the memories of our great men? Is it not a matter of regret that we have done nothing to honor our departed great? Modern India has not produced a greater man than Rajah Ram Mohan Roy. It ought to make Indians blush that they have not tried to perpetuate his memory in any suitable shape.

England is the richest country in the world. Her material prosperity is due to the industries and manufactures carried on in that country, her foreign trade, and above all to the enterprising spirit of the English people. India, on the other hand, is the poorest country in the world. India abounds in mineral and vegetable resources, but for want of sufficient capital, they cannot be developed and exploited. Indians should try to make their country rich. There is much truth in the complaint that the present poverty in India is to a great extent due to her connection with England, for England has crushed those industries for which India was at one time famous.

Again, Indian capitalists do not venture to invest their money in factories and other industrial concerns, because they see how the Christian philanthropists of Manchester and Dundee are trying their best to ruin the rising cotton and jute industries of India. These Christian philanthropists do succeed (as they have done in the past) in their attempt to ruin Indian industries. Lord Lawrence wrote: "The difficulty in the way of the Government of India acting fairly in these matters is immense. If anything is done or attempted to be done to help the natives, a general howl is raised, which reverberates in England, and finds sympathy and support there."[9]

Englishmen, as Napoleon observed, are a nation of shopkeepers. Is it conceivable that they will cut their own throats by encouraging Indians to manufacture their own cloths and other articles of necessity and luxury? Let those Christian missionaries and Anglo-Indians who are never tired of taunting Indians with want of enterprising spirit and so on, ponder over the matter and say if India has any fair chance of getting rich by her industries and factories? However, Indians should not lose heart. If patriotism means anything, they should try to use country made articles and boycott foreign goods.

From a worldly-wise nation like the English, one can no more expect to learn lessons in honesty and veracity than from the Bunyan's great hero, the Worldly-wise Man. But of whatever failings the English may be guilty in their dealings with other people, amongst themselves they are angels. Let us try to emulate this trait in their character. Let us stand shoulder to shoulder with our Indian fellow-countrymen, do everything that lies in our power to help the cause of national progress and not cut each other's throats.

These are some of the lessons which we should try to learn from the English.

NOTES

"Indian Views of England" originally appeared as Nagendra Nath Ghose, *Indian Views of England* (Calcutta: Thacker, Spink, 1877). "The Shame of Bharat" was originally published in 1879. It was subsequently republished as Bankim Chandra Chatterjee, "Bharat Kalanka," in *Bankim Rachnabali*, vol. 2, ed. Jogesh Chandra Bagal (Calcutta: Mahandranath Dutta, 1954). Translated here by Arunava Sinha. "The Ruin of the Native Americans" originally appeared as Pandita Ramabai [Ramabai Sarasvati], *Yunaited Stetsci Lokasthi ani Pravasavrtta* [The condition of the peoples of the United States] (Mumbai: Nirnaysagar, 1889), 13–41. Translated here by Sravya Darbhamulla. "Strength of the British" was first published in English as Subedar Muhammad Beg, "Strength of the British," in *My Jubilee Visit to London* (Bombay: Thacker, 1899), chap. 15, pp. 52–56. "What Can England Teach Us?" was originally published in 1897. It was subsequently republished as Indo-Anglian [Baman Das Basu], "What Can England Teach Us," *Modern Review* 3, no. 2 (1908): 158–60.

1. Henry Sumner Maine, *The Effects of Observation of India on Modern European Thought* (London: John Murray, 1875).

2. Maine, 17.

3. Author's Note: The Arabs and Turks had annexed small portions of western Bharatvarsha.

4. Author's Note: We do not claim that there was never a race in Bharatvarsha that did not desire to be independent. Those who have read the marvelous accounts about the Rajputs of Mewar in [James] Tod's *Annals* are aware that there has not been another race in the world more determined to remain independent than the kings of Mewar. The outcome of this love for freedom has been exemplary. Despite being a relatively small state, Mewar has flown a Hindu flag although surrounded on all sides by a Muslim empire. Not even the might of Emperor Akbar could vanquish Mewar. Even today, the royal family of Udaipur is considered one of the oldest in the world. But those days are gone from our lives, and what we have said above is applicable to Hindus in general.

5. Friedrich Schiller, "Die Weltweisen," in *The Poems of Schiller*, ed. and trans. Henry D. Wireman (Philadelphia: Kohler, 1879), 310–13.

6. E. B. Ramsay, *Reminiscences of Scottish Life and Character* (Edinburgh: Edmonston and Douglas, 1872), 256–57.

7. Thomas Carlyle, *Past and Present* (New York: Wiley and Putnam, 1847), 33.

8. Thomas Carlyle, *On Heroes, Hero-Worship, and the Heroic in History* (London: Chapman and Hall, 1840), 3.

9. R. Bosworth Smith, *Life of Lord Lawrence* (New York: Scribner's, 1883), 2:478.

Chapter Nine

TO TEACH THE WEST

ASIA'S MESSAGE TO EUROPE, 1883
Keshub Chunder Sen

Whence this plaintive and mournful cry, which so profoundly distresses the patriot's breast? It seems that a whole continent is writhing in agony beneath the lash of oppression and sending forth from the depths of its heart a deep wail of woe. . . . And what is the burden of her complaint? The desperate onslaughts of Europe's haughty civilization, she says, have brought sorrow into her heart, ignominy on her fair name, and death to her cherished institutions. Many there are in Europe who hold that all beyond the Ural, to the remotest shores of the Pacific, is afflicted with moral leprosy. . . . The entire continent is given to ignorance and barbarism and heathenism; and nothing good, it is said, can come out of this accursed land. Swayed by these considerations and actuated by these feelings, Europe has for many long years been fighting and warring with Asia, and, like a sworn foe, carrying on depredations into the uttermost parts of the East. Most sanguinary and deadly has this war been, and verily it has no parallel in the annals of the world. It has perpetrated frightful havoc among the nations of the East, sweeping off like a deluge their ancient glory and greatness. . . . Before the formidable artillery of Europe's aggressive civilization the scriptures and prophets, the language and literature of the East, nay her customs and manners, her social and domestic institutions, and her very industries have undergone a cruel slaughter. . . .

This voice of rebuke and remonstrance I raise before you is not the voice of base ingratitude. For all the good Europe has done, for all the material and moral benefits she has conferred, we in Asia feel profoundly grateful. Her science and literature, her commerce and trade, her politics and religion have saved us from ignorance and error, and given us light and liberty and joy, and have laid all Asia under lasting obligations. But Europe, thou holdest in one hand life and in another death. Thy civilization has proved a blessing, but inasmuch as it utterly exterminates our nationality, and seeks to destroy and Europeanize all that is in the East, it is a curse. Therefore will I vindicate Asia. Yes I, for I am a child of Asia; her sorrows are my sorrows, her joys my joys. These lips shall plead for Asia. . . .

Is not Asia the birthplace of great prophets and saints? . . . In this one place you could count all the leading prophets and all the greatest religious geniuses of the world. No great prophet was born outside the boundaries of Asia. Is not this a noteworthy fact? . . . It is not the exclusive seat of any single system of faith. It is not the exclusive property of any particular sect. Jews, Christians and Mohammedans, Hindus, Buddhists and Parsis, all recognise in Asia their common home. The spirit of Asia is cosmopolitan, catholic, and comprehensive, not partial, one-sided or sectarian. Not even her worst enemies can predicate narrow exclusivism of Asia. She has cradled and nursed and suckled all the great Churches of the East and the West. . . . How from one heart grew such great and glorious geniuses as Jesus and Buddha, Zoroaster and Confucius, must strike every thoughtful man with astonishment. How in the same land flourished pantheism, polytheism and monotheism; communion, asceticism, rationalism, ritualism, quietism and the most transcendental spiritualism; how on the same soil grew such divergent creeds as Hinduism and Buddhism, Judaism and Christianity, Mohammedanism and Zoroastrianism, Confucianism and Sikhism, must remain an abiding marvel in all ages. All, all the great religions are mine, saith Asia, and their founders are all my children. . . . Can I be a sectarian? As a Bengali I might; as an Indian I might; but as an Asiatic I cannot, I dare not be a sectarian. There are around me so many master minds that demand my reverential allegiance, so many types and aspects of faith and character which claim my sympathy, that I must take a broad and eclectic position, and disclaim even the semblance of narrow sectarianism.

Europe, I charge thee to be unsectarian. Asia's first message to Western nations is—put the sword of sectarianism adroitly into the sheath. Let there be no more sectarianism. . . . It is an abomination in the sight of the Lord. It is made up of envy, jealousy, pride, anger, resentment, and vindictiveness. It excites and inflames the worst passions of the heart. It makes a brother stand against a brother, a sister against a sister. . . . Woe unto sectarianism! In the depths of carnality it has immersed the world. Look at your own hearts, and let them testify. Has not sectarianism blackened and embittered the heart every time it has held us in its deadly coil and poured into us its fatal venom? . . .

Sectarianism is not only carnal, it is also unscientific. . . . In science there cannot be sects or divisions, schisms or enmities. Is there one astronomy for the East and another for the West? Are there different anatomies in different climes and ages? Is there an Asiatic optics as distinguished from European optics? Is there such a thing as Jewish zoology and Mohammedan geometry? . . . There can be but one science; it recognises neither caste nor colour nor nationality. . . . Europe, the world has given thee credit for thy devotion to science. Thou hast unraveled the deepest mysteries of the physical world with the light of science; amidst hopeless confusion, perplexing contradictions, and the gravest anomalies thou hast found unity, order, and law. Why wilt thou not then recognise and uphold the scientific unity and harmony which underlies the many systems of faith prevalent in the world? As a votary of science thou canst not surely revel in multiplicity. . . .

Asia does not boast of science. She is innocent of the great discoveries and achievements of modern science, which have made Europe so great. Yet she has spontaneously and instinctively realized the synthesis of church unity. Without learning, without philosophy, without erudition, Asia jumped under a sort of natural impulse into the unsectarian eclecticism of faith. Instinct, not learning, has made her catholic in her faith. What Asia has done intuitively, Europe will do reflectively. The West will have to verify theologically what the East has realized in religious consciousness. The great scholars of Europe will be called upon to vindicate and verify, upon philosophical ground, the scientific unity of all the great religions which Asia has founded and shaped with all the simplicity and freshness of natural inspiration, and with all the wonderful versatility and the infinite resources of her inventive genius. Thus shall Europe and Asia be drawn towards each other in unsectarian fellowship, and thus shall they recognise, each in her own way, an essential unity and harmony amid the multiplicity of churches and sects.

But perhaps it will be said that sectarianism may be opposed to science, but surely it is not opposed to nature. The objector may argue—behold endless varieties and diversities innumerable in the amplitudes of nature. There is no uniformity, but diversity everywhere. Why shall we then give up our differences, and reduce all sects to the dead level of uniformity? Let me assure you that by unity I do not mean uniformity. Uniformity is the death of nature; it is the death of the soul. Where life is there must be variety. What nature proclaims, what Asia demands, is unity in variety. Great is Europe, let her flourish. Great too is Asia, let her prosper. We want not their annihilation but unification. Let all sects retain their distinctive peculiarities, and yet let them unite in fraternal alliance. The unity I contend for is the unity of music. For in music, though there are hundreds of diverse shapes producing various sounds, yet there is sweet harmony among them. . . .

One more illustration. . . . In the State, more than in anything else, you see the perfection of that principle of unity which we contend for. In a free government, established upon constitutional principles, you see unity in the most perfect form of outward organization. How many individuals, how many races, tribes and nationalities are comprised in a State! Their habits and tastes and proclivities, how different and even antagonistic! We see a heterogeneous mass of ill-adjusted and ill-assorted individualities, ready at any moment to clash and knock each other into death and annihilation. An extended empire, a vast republic, with its million units, sleeps over a volcano, and danger, is always imminent. What is it, I ask, that holds these units together, and prevents their inflammable antipathies from bursting into a catastrophe? A mysterious ruling power holds these millions of souls in its clutches, and the irresistible magic of law maintains order and discipline among them. We wonder how harmony prevails over this wide extent of territory, how peace reigns amid such endless varieties. What is law? What is government? At best an invisible power, almost shadowy and intangible. Yet tremendous is its authority, before which even mighty heroes bow and crowned heads offer ready obeisance. The State is a vast and complicated machinery, in which numberless wheels of various sizes and shapes are ever moving, each in its proper place, and working harmoniously towards a common end. This is the perfection of consolidated fellowship.

Here is no sectarianism, no exclusiveness, no attempt to ignore or destroy each other. . . .

And when many such Governments administer their respective affairs side by side, there springs up an international amity and harmony in which the life and growth of each find a mighty safeguard. What a wonderful thing is "balance of power" in the civilized world! This political equipoise, this equilibrium of national agencies and forces is indeed a marvel. How it protects the weakest and gives security to the least! Look at Europe. The nations differ, and their antipathies are unmistakable; and yet they live, move and have their being in mutual recognition, and in the subordination of their respective interests to common welfare. They may dislike each other in many things, but none can kill a disagreeable neighbour. Can England demolish Germany? Will Germany kill France? Is it possible that Russia will slay Turkey, and obliterate it from the map of Europe? Such things may be desired and even longed for, but they are not possible in the economy of Providence, so long as each nation has a particular mission to fulfil. Each nation may endeavor to swallow and absorb the rest but Heaven sets its face against such monstrous and selfish ambition. England may wish that all Europe should be Anglicized, France may wish to make all Europe French, and Germany German; America may desire to see the whole world Americanized. But Providence favours not such fatal fancies and annihilating propensities of any single Power. Heaven abhors monopoly and vouchsafes unto each individual and nation freedom of action and diversities of operation, so that each may grow with all the freshness and variety of natural growth. . . .

Do the interests of the individual suffer because of his association with other individuals? Does the village community get impoverished in its resources and strength because it enters into fellowship with other villages? . . . Civilization has proved that man does not become less affectionate to his own kinsfolk by extending his love to the outside world, that no nation made itself poor or unhappy by going out to serve other nations. . . . There is a natural and an irresistible tendency in man's progressive nature towards social fellowship. Everywhere you see this unmistakable tendency on the part of individuals to form groups and settle in communities. In all ages and climes humanity is rushing, like an impetuous current, towards a community. Nature interdicts selfish solitary existence. She is always pulling the animal man out of his den and educating him into true social

manhood. In fact, barbarism means life in the individual while civilization signifies life in the community. What is narrow and selfish belongs
to barbarism, while civilization is identified with what is broad and
world-wide. . . . The history of civilization is the history of the construction of communities and the growth of nationalities in different parts of
the world. . . .

Come, then, Europe, let us shake hands with each other with the utmost
cordiality. Let us bury all our hostilities and enmities, and plant the sacred
olive on their grave. Heaven demands reconciliation, let the earth obey. Let
us avail ourselves of all opportunities which God's merciful Providence
vouchsafes unto us to cement the ties of international fellowship. I am proud
to regard myself as a loyal subject of Queen Victoria, and I rejoice to see
under her triumphant banner the union of India and England, of the East
and the West. . . . Every evening party and friendly reunion, where Asiatics and Europeans meet in social fellowship, is to me a religious gathering,
destined to further the purposes of God. These little groups, one here and
one there, scattered all over the country are but the upheavings of that tide
of racial amalgamation which is going on everywhere. Whether it is politics
or trade, pleasure or business, that brings the European and the Asiatic races
together, I see only the gradual formation of a diversified congregation. . . .
Everything seems to hasten the day of reconciliation. After war comes
peace; after centuries of separation comes sweet reconciliation. . . .

INDIA'S MISSION AMONG NATIONS, 1893
Annie Besant

Every person, every race, every nation, has its own particular keynote which
it brings to the general chord of life and of humanity. Life is not a mono-
tone but a many-stringed harmony, and to this harmony is contributed a
distinctive note by each people that becomes a marked nationality. Thus
Rome struck the note of civic greatness, devotion to the State as the ideal
of the citizen, conquest for the glory of the State as the national duty; Greece
struck the note of intellectual greatness, enriching the art and the literature of the world with priceless treasures, and impressing even on her
conquerors the stamp of her intellectual royalty. And India, rising high
above them both, struck the note of spiritual greatness, of pure devotion to
a spiritual ideal, of worship that asked only to become what it adored, of

the gathering of spiritual knowledge. The three nations may stand as types: of humanity physical, humanity psychical, humanity spiritual, and while the two that represented the transitory body and the transitory mind have perished, leaving only their history, the one that represented and represents the immortal spirit remains, for, as Sri Krishna says, the spirit is "unborn, constant, eternal and ancient, nor does it perish in the perishing body." India's body may perish as a body politic, but her eternal spirit remains, the spirit that has made *Aryavarta* the cradle of religions and her scriptures the fountainhead of all the scriptures of later faiths.

This spirituality of India has, then, been her contribution to the world's progress. . . . And it is the perpetual affirmation of spirituality as the highest good that is India's mission to the world. As her past glory resulted from her spiritual knowledge and devotion, so must her future be based on the revival and re-proclamation of the same. Her genius is for religion and not for politics, and her most gifted children are needed as spiritual teachers, not as competing candidates in the political arena. Let lesser nations and lesser men fight for conquest, for place and for power; these gimcracks are toys for children, and the children should be left to quarrel over them. India is the one country in the world in which it is still easy to be religious, in which the atmosphere of the land and the psychic currents are not yet wholly penetrated with materiality. If religion perish here, it will perish everywhere, and in India's hand is laid the sacred charge of keeping alight the torch of spirit amid the fogs and storms of increasing materialism. If that torch drops from her hands, its flame will be trampled out by the feet of hurrying multitudes, eager for worldly good, and India, bereft of spirituality, will have no future, but will pass on into the darkness, as Greece and Rome have passed.

INTERNATIONAL ETHICS, 1899
Swami Abhedananda [Kaliprasad Chandra]

I come from a country which has loved and worshipped peace since the prehistoric times. . . . But the result of this love of peace is known to you all. There is no country in the world that has suffered so much from foreign invasions as India. If we want to love peace and if we want to carry it out into our daily life, we shall have to find the necessary environments for growth of peace in a nation. India did not find such environment. She has been attacked from ancient times, first by the Greeks, then by the Scythians, then by the Mongolians, then by the Tartars, then by the Mohammedans, and lastly by the Christians.

What is India to-day? Worse than Cuba in some districts. India has no liberty of expressing her political views, no liberty of the press. Overtaxed and oppressed in various ways, she has lost her commerce, her trade and her arts, and last of all her freedom. India will regain peace, not by bloodshed, but through conflict. By conflict I do not mean the shedding of blood, but that kind of war which is intimately connected with all our life. We are struggling all the time. We are fighting with the obstacles that are trying to prevent us from attaining to freedom. We shall have to fight, first of all, with our superstition, then with our prejudice, then with our national customs, which have been handed down from our forefathers and ancestors; and through this struggle we shall at last attain to freedom.... That freedom does not mean one-sided freedom, but it means political freedom, social freedom and last of all, religious freedom.... Let us be ready to fight with our superstition, to fight with our ignorance. Let us be ready to fight with the lower nature, and then to raise ourselves on the higher platform. Our lower nature prevents us from reaching that liberation and elevation of the soul, which is the end and aim of each individual as well as of each nation. That freedom can only come when we conquer the lower nature which expresses itself as selfishness. Selfishness is the expression of our lower nature, of our animal nature; and we shall have to fight with that animal nature. We shall have to become unselfish in all our acts both social and spiritual.

How can we attain to that unselfishness? How can we attain to that freedom? Not by bloodshed, but by understanding the principle of nature. By the principle of nature I mean the great plan, the grand truth, which is manifested in every department of nature; and that truth is "Unity in Variety." If we can understand this law, this plan of nature, and if we observe it in our everyday life then we shall be unselfish, then we shall be able to recognise the rights of others, then we shall be friendly to others, and help others as we help ourselves. The basis of international ethics does not depend on the statement of certain dogmas which have been handed down to us through preachers of through books, but on the recognition of Unity in Variety—the recognition of oneness in spirit. We are all on in Spirit (or *Atma*).

Not only are we brothers but we are one with others as with ourselves. Brotherhood is the second stage in the perception of this unity, and oneness is the highest. This plan of nature "Unity in Variety," is manifested physically, mentally and spiritually. As by studying physical nature we come to the conclusion that all the various forces of nature are nothing but the different expressions of one eternal energy—that energy you may call by any name you like: scientists call it energy, but religionists call it the will of God; as by studying Biology we come to know that there is one life principle which is manifesting itself in nature from the lowest amoeba up to the highest man—the difference is not of kind, but of degree; as by that comparative study of Anatomy we come to understand the unity of species—so by studying philosophy, by studying our own inner nature, we come to the conclusion that there is but one mind manifesting itself in the universe. When that mind manifests itself through this body, it becomes my mind, and when it manifests itself through your body, it becomes your mind.

Similarly, when we study the religions of different nations, of different peoples, we come to the conclusion that there is one universal spirit (*Atma*) which manifests through various forms. Some call it God, some call it Father in heaven, some call it Allah, some call it Brahman. The difference is in the name only. As the same substance water, is called by various names by various people who inhabit different countries,—some call it *water*, some *aqua*, some *eau*, some *waster*, some *pani*, some *vari*, some *jalam* and so forth, but the substance is the same—similarly that one spirit which you may call by any name you like, is manifesting itself in and through us and in and through each individual soul, . . . when we recognise that, we cannot be unkind to any living creature, we cannot shed the blood of any living creature, but then we realise the spirit which Christ had, when he said, "Love thy neighbour as thyself." The explanation of that highest ethical law we do not find in the Testaments. By reading the Testaments, we do not understand the reason why we shall love our neighbours as ourselves, and not kill them. That explanation was given in Vedas by the ancient Rishis or seers of truth, as they are called, who lived in the prehistoric times during the Vedic period in India. They understood that and explained it through that eternal law of nature, "Unity in Variety." They said, we should love our neighbours as ourselves, because we are one in spirit. We are our neighbours. As we love ourselves, we must love our neighbours in the same way, because we are our neighbours.

This grand truth of "Unity in Variety" was applied by the sages of India in the religious line of thought. They understood that this "Unity in Variety" is also expressed in the spiritual nature. So they did not found their religion on certain dogmas or the sayings of certain prophets, but they founded their religion on the spiritual laws of nature on the "Unity in Variety." They said that each individual must have his or her own religion—a religion which suits him or her. Those who try to force one line of thought on all men, women, and children, of all countries and of all nations, do not recognise this law of "Unity in Variety," and consequently, they act against the law of nature. But those who recognise this law, become conscious of the fact, that one spirit is manifesting itself through each individual soul, and therefore they recognise the rights of all. . . .

The religion of the Hindus is not built around a particular person like Jesus or Buddha, but it is entirely based on this principle of oneness which was expressed in *Rig Veda* by the well-known passage: "That which exists is one. Men call it by various names." Their religion does not depend upon any particular book, but on the truth which underlies the sayings of all the great teachers that flourished in different parts of the world at different times. A Christian missionary comes to India and preaches: "Look at the teachings of Jesus—the Sermon on the Mount—how ethical, how glorious, how beautiful are they! He is the saviour. If you do not believe in Jesus you will be damned forever." But a Hindu says to the missionary, "Have you read the *Bhagavad Gita* which has been translated into English by Oriental scholars?" Our missionary friend says, "No." Then our Hindu friend says: "Go and read it; and you will find the same ideas expressed, only in different words." But he does not believe in that. He says: "No, your prophets were false prophets, they did not understand the laws of nature, nor religion." He does not believe in anything which did not come through Christ. If they came through Christ, they were all right, because our missionary friends believe in Christ alone, not in any other prophet.

The other day, I went to hear Dr. Barrows, who was the Secretary of the Parliament of Religions in Chicago, and who, after travelling for three months in India, returned to America, and gave a course of lectures in the Union Theological Seminary. He said that the Hindus have no morality, no ethics, no philosophy, no religion; if they have got anything they have got it from the Christian missionaries. This will give you an idea of the spirit of the Christian missionaries. Their eyes are blinded by superstition and bigotry, consequently they do not see good in others. These missionaries come to teach us what you are trying to forget. They do not know that what Jesus taught the Jews, was known and practiced by the Hindus long before his birth. And even to-day the Hindus are practically better followers of the teachings of Jesus than those who profess Christianity. The ethical and spiritual teachings of Jesus are the same as the ethical and spiritual teachings of the Hindu prophets. The missionaries do not realise this and so they find fault with the Hindus and deny their prophets.

This non-recognition of the rights of others whether in the religious or secular domain, this non-recognition of the eternal law of "Unity in Variety"—is the cause of all evil, of all international conflicts, of all war and persecution—social, political and religious. So the moment we come to know this law, the moment we realise that we are all one in spirit with the Father in heaven, we become kind to all, we love all living creatures and attain to freedom and peace, which are the end and aim of all religions, and of nations.

NOTES

"Asia's Message to Europe" was delivered as a lecture on January 20, 1883. It was subsequently published as Keshub Chunder Sen, *Asia's Message to Europe* (Calcutta: R. S. Bhatta, 1883). "India's Mission Among Nations" was delivered as a lecture on November 6, 1893. It was subsequently reprinted as Annie Besant, "India's Mission Among Nations," in *The Birth of New India* (Madras: Theosophical, 1917), 85–86. "International Ethics" originally appeared as Swami Abhedananda [Kaliprasad Chandra], "International Ethics," *Prabuddha Bharata* 4, no. 30 (1899): 9–12.

FURTHER READING

1. ENGLISH EDUCATION

Bhai, Narayan. "On the Comparative Advantages of Native Education Through the Vernacular Medium, or Through the Vernacular and English." In *Two Hindus on English Education, &c., Being Prize Essays*, 1–54. Bombay: Bombay Gazette Press, 1852.

Brahma-Samaj. *An Appeal to the British Nation for the Promotion of Education in India.* Calcutta: C. H. Manuel, 1861.

Cursetjee, Manockjee. "On the Moral Regeneration of the Natives of India." In *A Few Passing Ideas for the Benefit of India and Indians*, pt. 3, pp. 48–69. London: Emily Faithfull, 1862.

Datta, Babu Manmatha Nath. "Raja Ram Mohun Roy." *Indian Magazine and Review* 27, no. 312 (December 1896): 647–49.

"Early Native Education Under British Auspices." *Mookerjee's Magazine* 1 (November 1872): 233–45.

"Government Education." *Calcutta Review* 37, no. 74 (December 1861): 194–224.

"Hindoo Intellect." *Calcutta University Magazine* 1, no. 2 (August 1864): 25–29.

A Hindustani. "Compliments Paid to Government Education." *Bengal Magazine* 4 (December 1875): 227–34.

Mahmood, Syed. *A History of English Education in India.* Aligarh: M. A. O. College, 1895.

Mookerjee, Mohindro Nauth. *The Effects of English Education Upon the Native Mind, Observed in a Moral, Social, Physical and Religious Point of View.* Serampore: Tomohur Press, 1871.

The Relation of Government to the Higher Education from the Hindu Point of View. Madras: Scottish Press, 1882.

Roy, Rammohun. "A Letter to Lord Amherst on English Education." In *The English Works of Raja Rammohun Roy*, 469–74. Allahabad: Panini Office, 1906.

Satthianadhan, Samuel. "What Has English Education Done for India?" *Indian Magazine and Review* 27, no. 311 (November 1896): 571–85.

Sen, Bireswar. *Influence of English Education: Bengal and the N. W. Provinces*. Benares: P. C. Chowdry, 1876.

Sen, C. C. *A Discourse on Education, Being the Substance of the Inaugural Address Delivered at the Students Association, Jessore*. Calcutta: Bhoobun Mohun Ghose, 1880.

"Western Influence." *Journal of the National Indian Association* 6, no. 63 (March 1876): 85–86.

2. CROSSING THE SEAS

Bahadur, Rajah Inder Karan. *Do the Hindu Shastras Prohibit Sea-Voyages*. Poona: Arya-Bhushana Press, 1899.

A Brahmin Liberal. "Crossing the Sea for Hindus (II)." *Journal of the National Indian Association*, no. 162 (June 1884): 278–80.

British Indian Association North-Western Provinces. *Supplement to Bye-Laws of the British Indian Association, N. W. P., Relative to the Department for Encouraging Travel to Europe*. Aligarh: The Institute Press, 1869.

Damodar, Bhaskar. "On the Advantages That Would Result to India by the Establishment of a *Serai* or Public Bungalow in London." In *Two Hindus on English Education, &c., Being Prize Essays*, 55–71. Bombay: Bombay Gazette Press, 1852.

Dar, Bishan Narayan. "Foreign Travel." In *Indian Social Reform*, edited by C. Yajnesvara Chintamani, 188–229. Madras: Minerva Press, 1901.

Ghose, N. N. "Preface." In *A Visit to Europe*, by T. N. Mukharji, vii–xii. Calcutta: W. Newman, 1889.

Gopalacharlu, S. E. "Sea-Voyages by Hindus (II): Is Sea-Travel Prohibited to Brahmins?" *Imperial and Asiatic Quarterly Review* 4, no. 8 (October 1892): 300–10.

"Hindu Voyages and Colonisation." *Kayastha Samachar* 1, nos. 9 and 10 (March and April 1900): 154–58.

Hobhouse, Mary. "Further Sketches by an Indian Pen." *Indian Magazine* 21, no. 231 (March 1890): 139–49.

——. "London Sketched by an Indian Pen." *Indian Magazine* 21, no. 230 (February 1890): 61–73.

Krishna, A. Ram. "The Sea as a Profession for Educated Natives." *Journal of the National Indian Association*, no. 166 (October 1884): 452–57.

"List of Indian Gentlemen and Ladies in the West." *Indian Magazine and Review* 25 (January 1900): 11–19.

Misra, Uma Sankar. "How It Strikes an Indian." In *Political Social and Literary Papers*, 103–24. Benares: Chandraprabha Press, 1890.

Mookherjea, Devendra Nath. "Hinder Samudra Yatra or Sea Voyages by Hindus." *Calcutta Review* 96, no. 191 (January 1893): lxii–lxiii.

Prayaschitta—Hindu Methods Prescribed by the Dharma Sastras; Prayaschittas Required for Sea-Voyages and Taking Tea with Europeans; the Hypocrisy Thus Produced; the

True Prayaschitta. Price Papers on Indian Reform 42. Madras: Christian Literature Society, 1895.

"The Restrictions Against Sea Voyage." *Indian Appeal* 2, no. 14 (October 1890): 142–43.

3. THE GREAT GAME

"21 Per Cent. Growth of Indian Military Expenditure in 20 Years!!" *Indian Leaflets No. 9.* Calcutta, 1885.

"The Afghan Imbroglio: Who Is to Pay for It." *Quarterly Journal of the Poona Sarvajanik Sabha* 1, no. 3 (January 1879): 1–17.

Ali, Muhammad Mahfuz. *The Truth About Russia and England: From a Native's Point of View.* Lucknow: R. Craven, 1886.

"The Appalling Costliness of the Indian Army." *Indian Leaflets No. 11.* Calcutta, 1885.

"The Armies of the Native States." *Quarterly Journal of the Poona Sarvajanik Sabha* 1, no. 4 (April 1879): 1–23.

Banerjea, Surendra Nath. "The Meeting in South London." In *Speeches by Babu Surendra Nath Banerjea, 1886–1890,* edited by Raj Jogeshur Mitter, vol. 3, 139–48. Calcutta: K. N. Mitra, 1890.

Bombay Branch of the East India Association. "Petition to House of Commons Relative to the Egyptian War Expenses." *Journal of the East India Association* 15 (February 1883): 86–88.

Bosu, Srish Chandra. "Afghan War Contribution." In *Public Speeches of Babu Srish Chandra Bosu Sarvadhicari,* 14–18. Calcutta: Peary Mohan Mookherjee, 1897.

"The Central Asian Question." *Quarterly Journal of the Poona Sarvajanik Sabha* 4, no. 3 (January 1882): 1–20.

"The Cost of the Afghan War." *Oriental Miscellany* 3, no. 24 (March 1881): 118–19.

"Cost of the Burmah Expedition." *Voice of India* 4, no. 3 (March 1886): 142–50.

Davar, Dinsha D. "England and Russia." *Journal of the East India Association* 13 (June 1880): 22–47.

Dutt, Romesh C. "Liberalism and Peace." In *Speeches and Papers on Indian Questions, 1897 to 1900,* 28–32. Calcutta: Elm Press, 1902.

"The Egyptian Difficulty." *Hindu Reformer and Politician* 1 (1882): 247–52.

Framjee, Dosabhay. *A Lecture on the Freedom and Blessings of the British Government Contrasted with the Tyranny and Oppression of Russia.* Bombay: Duftur Ashkara Press, 1856.

Ghose, Lalmohun. "Anniversary Meeting of the Women's Peace and Arbitration Auxiliary of the London Peace Society." In *Speeches by Lalmohun Ghose,* edited by Asutosh Banerji. Calcutta: Thacker, Spink, 1880.

Indian National Congress. "Seventh Resolution Asking for an Equitable Contribution by England Towards the Military Expenditure of India." In *Report of the Eighth Indian National Congress, Held at Allahabad, on the 28th, 29th, and 30th of December 1892,* 82–87.

J. C. "Central Asia and India." *National Magazine* 1, no. 6 (December 1887): 201–5.

Joshi, G. V. "A Fresh Military Charge on Indian Revenues." In *Writings and Speeches of Hon. Rao Bahadur G. V. Joshi,* 1125–28. Poona: Arya Bhushan Press, 1912.

——. "Ways and Means of Meeting the Additional Army Expenditure." *Quarterly Journal of the Poona Sarvajanik Sabha* 8, no. 4 (April 1886): 1–30.

"Kashmir and the Foreign Policy by the Government of India." *National Magazine* 7, no. 5 (May 1893): 181–89.

Khan, Hamid Ali. *The Bulwark for India*. London: Empire Printing and Publishing, 1885.

Mehta, Pherozeshah. "Speech on the Arms Act." In *Speeches and Writings of the Honourable Sir Pherozeshah M. Mehta*, edited by C. Y. Chintamani, 263–64 (Allahabad: The Indian Press, 1905).

"Memorial to the Right Honourable William Ewart Gladstone Relative to the Afghan War." *Journal of the East India Association* 13 (January 1881): 146–57.

"Military Expenditure." *Indian Appeal* 4, no. 24 (April 1892): 287–89.

"Military Expenses." *Indian Economist* 1 (December 1869): 146–47.

Mookerjee, Satya Chandra. "The North-West Frontier of India." *National Magazine* 7, no. 5 (May 1893): 177–80.

"A Native on Russia and England." *English Opinion on India* 1, no. 1 (February 1887): 9–13.

"The Native States of India and Their Armies." *Quarterly Journal of the Poona Sarvajanik Sabha* 7, no. 3 (January 1885): 23–67.

Pal, Kristo Das. "Military Expenditure." In *Speeches and Minutes of the Hon'ble Kristo Das Pal, Rai Bahadur, 1867–81*, edited by Ram Chandra, 286–97. Calcutta: B. H. Banerjea and Co., 1882.

"Russian Advance in Central Asia." *Voice of India* 2, no. 6 (March 1884): 221–23.

"The Russian Bugbear." *Native Opinion*, 5, no. 27 (July, 1868): 5.

"'Russia's Policy,' Extract from a Leader of the 'Hindoo Patriot,' November 20, 1876." In *Indian Speeches and Documents on British Rule, 1821–1918*, edited by J. K. Majumdar, 109–11. Calcutta: Longmans, Green, 1937.

Vicarious. "Facts About Russia." *National Magazine* 2, no. 1 (January 1888): 18–26.

4. THE EASTERN QUESTION

Ahmad, Rafiuddin. "The Eastern Question." *Nineteenth Century* 38, no. 226 (December 1895): 1008–14.

——. "England in Relation to Mahomedan States." *National Review* 21, no. 122 (1893).

——. "In Defence of Islam." *Fortnightly Review* 59, no. 349 (January 1896): 165–76.

——. "Is the British 'Raj' in Danger?" *Nineteenth Century* 42, no. 247 (September 1897): 493–500.

Ali, Ameer. "Islam and Canon MacColl." *Nineteenth Century* 38, no. 225 (November 1895): 778–85.

——. "Islam and Its Critics." *Nineteenth Century* 38, no. 223 (1895).

Ali, Cheragh. *The Proposed Political, Legal, and Social Reforms of the Ottoman Empire and Other Mohammadan States*. Bombay: Education Society's Press, 1883.

"Further Outrages in Turkey—Massacre of Eight Hundred Christians." *Journal of the Maha Bodhi Society* 4, no. 9 (January 1896): 69.

"Great Britain and Turkey." *Muhammadan Observer and Moslem Chronicle* 23, no. 37 (October 1895): 438.

Jung, Salar. "Europe Revisited (I)." *Nineteenth Century* 22, no. 126 (August): 165–73.

Karanvi, L. "The Sultan and the Indian Moslem." *Muhammadan Observer and Moslem Chronicle* 25, no. 19 (May 1897): 812.

Long, James. "The Eastern Question in Its Anglo-Indian Aspect." *Journal of the East India Association* 10 (May 1877).

"Muhammadin Demonstration in Bombay in Honour of the Sultan's Victory." *Muhammadan Observer and Moslem Chronicle* 25, no. 20 (May 1897): 821.

"Sir Salar Jung on the Eastern Question." *Voice of India* 5 (1887): 590–91.

"A Student of History." "Turkey and the Moslem of India." *Muhammadan Observer and Moslem Chronicle* 25, no. 21 (May 1897): 843.

"The Sultan and the Indian Mussalman." *Muhammadan Observer and Moslem Chronicle* 29, no. 9 (March 1899): 137.

5. FREE TRADE

Dutt, Romesh Chunder. *The Economic History of India Under Early British Rule.* London: Kegal Paul, Trench, Trübner, 1902.

A Fairheart. "To the Editor of the Bombay Gazette." *Bombay Gazette*, July 19, 1841, 62–63.

A Hindoo [Tarkhadkar, Bhaskar Pandurang]. "Letter No. IV." *Bombay Gazette*, August 20, 1841, 174–75.

Jackson, R. Raynsford. *India and Lancashire: An Answer to Recent Arguments Advanced Against the Proposed Repeal of the Indian Import Duties on Cotton Goods and Yarns.* Blackburn: J. G. and J. Toulmin, 1877.

"Manchester's Triumph." *Indian Appeal* 2, no. 4 (April 1890): 52–54.

Mudholkar, R. N. "The Economic Condition of the People of India." In *Indian Politics*, edited by Womesh C. Bonnerjee, 33–48. Madras: G. A. Natesan, 1898.

Mullick, Kissen Mohun. *Brief History of Bengal Commerce.* Calcutta: Hindoo Patriot Press, 1871.

Philanthropy. "To the Editor of the Bombay Gazette." *Bombay Gazette*, July 7, 1841, 22–23.

Ranade, Mahadev Govind. "Indian Political Economy." *Quarterly Journal of the Poona Sarvajanik Sabha* 15, no. 2 (1892).

Ray, Prithwis Chandra. "Free Trade vs. Protection, or India's Case Against Free Trade." In *The Poverty Problem in India*, 1–71. Calcutta: Thacker, 1895.

Shapoorjee Bengallee, Sorabjee. "Letter to Lord Lytton on the Import Duties." In *The Life of Sorabjee Shapoorjee Bengallee, C. I. E.*, edited by Nowrozjee Sorabji Bengallee, 328–39. Bombay: Times of India Press, 1893.

Telang, Kashninath Trimbak. "Free Trade and Protection from an Indian Point of View." In *Selected Writings and Speeches.* Bombay: K. R. Mitra, 1888.

6. RACISM

Ghose, Lalmohun. "Speech on South African Policy." In *Speeches by Lalmohun Ghose*, edited by Ashutosh Banerji, 56–65. Calcutta, 1883.

"The Grievances of the British Indians in South Africa." *Madras Review* 2, no. 7 (November 1896): 401–19.

"Indian Coolies in British Guiana." *Indian Magazine and Review* 24, no. 275 (November 1893): 562–68.

Mehta, Pherozeshah. "British Indians in South Africa." In *Speeches and Writings of the Honourable Sir Pherozeshah M. Mehta*, edited by C. Y. Chintamani, 517–25. Allahabad: The Indian Press, 1905.

——. "Indians in South Africa." In *Some Unpublished and Later Speeches and Writings of Sir Pherozeshah Mehta*, edited by J. R. B. Jeejeebhoy, 96. Bombay: The Commercial Press, 1918.

Mitra, J. N. "Mauritius and Its Indian Emigrants." *Wealth of India* 1 (February 1897): 45–51.

Pillai, G. Parameswaran. "The Status of British Indians Abroad." In *Indian Politics*, edited by Womesh C. Bonnerjee, 168–80. Madras: G. A. Natesan, 1898.

7. THE OPIUM TRADE

"The Anti-Opium Crisis." *Indian Appeal* 3, no. 22 (June 1891): 257–61.

Dane, R. M. "Historical Memorandum." In *Report of the Royal Commission on Opium*, vol. 7. London: Her Majesty's Stationery Office, 1895.

A Hindustani. "Lord George Hamilton on Opium." *Bengal Magazine* 4 (August 1875).

Lyall, James B. "Note on the History of Opium in India and of the Trade in It with China." In *Report of the Royal Commission on Opium*, vol. 7. London: Her Majesty's Stationery Office, 1895.

Naoroji, Dadabhai. "India and the Opium Question." In *Essays, Speeches, Addresses, and Writings of the Honorable Dadabhai Naoroji*, edited by Chunilal L. Parekh, 363–66. Bombay: Caxton, 1887.

"Opium Cultivation and Its Traffic." *Indian Appeal* 4, no. 23 (January 1892): 280–85.

Ram, B. Jaishi. "Opium Question from an Indian Point of View." *India* 3, no. 33 (August 1892).

Shah, Syed A. M. "Opium and Its Effects: A Muhammadan Critic on the Traffic." *India* 3, no. 31 (June 1892).

Turner, Frederick Storrs. *British Opium Policy and Its Results to India and China*. London: Samson Low, Marston, Searle and Rivington, 1876.

Wedderburn, William. "India and the Opium Question." In *Speeches by Sir William Wedderburn*, edited by Raj Jogeshur Mitter. Calcutta: S. C. Basu, 1899.

8. TO LEARN FROM THE WEST

A. "The Secrets Which Give to Nations Giant Strength." *Indian Student* 1 (May 1869).

Basak, Radhanath. "Prospects and Duties of Nations." *Bengal Magazine* 5 (January 1877).

Bose, Ram Chandra. "Modern Civilization." *Bengal Magazine* 10, no. 117 (1882).

Cowasjee, Bowmanjee Cursetjee. "On the Qualities of a Nation: Abnegation, and Conscientious Recognition of Duty." In *On British Administration in India*, 33–36. Bombay: Times of India Steam Press, 1876.

"Decline of the Early Greatness of India." *Bengal Magazine* 5 (September 1876): 74–78.

Ghose, Shishir Kumar. "The Perpetual Slavery of India." In *Pictures of Indian Life*, 157–210. Madras: Ganesh and Co., 1917.

Karunkara Menon, C. "Western Influences in India." *Madras Review* 5, no. 19 (November 1899): 373–79.

Upadhyay, Brahmabandhab. "National Greatness." In *The Writings of Brahmabandhab*, edited by Julius Lipner and George Gispert-Sauch, vol. 2, 60–70. Bangalore: United Theological College, 1991.

"Western Civilisation in the East." *Indian Appeal* 1, no. 2 (October 1889): 20–22.

9. TO TEACH THE WEST

Bose, Raj Narain. "Superiority of Hinduism to Other Existing Religions: As Viewed from the Stand-Point of Theism." *Theosophist* 3, no. 9 (June 1882): 216–17.

Fidus. "East and West." *Deccan College Quarterly* 6, no. 1 (January 1898): 1–6.

Mozoomdar, P. C. *Sketches of a Tour Round the World*. Calcutta: S. K. Lahiri, 1884.

Roy, Amrita Lal. "English Rule in India." *North American Review* 142, no. 353 (April 1886): 356–70.

Satthianadhan, Samuel. "Is India Civilized?." *Journal of the National Indian Association*, no. 127 (July 1881): 411–19.

Sen, Keshub Chunder. "Jesus Christ: Europe and Asia." In *Lectures and Tracts by Keshub Chunder Sen*, edited by Sophia Dobson Collet. London: Strahan, 1870.

——. "Speech at Finsbury Chapel at the Annual Meeting of the Peace Society." In *Keshub Chunder Sen's English Visit*, edited by Sophia Dobson Collet. London: Strahan, 1871.

Swami Vivekananda. "The Conquest of the World by Indian Thought." In *Speeches and Writings of Swami Vivekananda*. Madras: G. A. Natesan, 1899.

——. "The Ideal of a Universal Religion." In *Speeches and Writings of Swami Vivekananda*. Madras: G. A. Natesan, 1899.

"The Ways of the East." *Indian Appeal* 2, no. 6 (June 1890): 84–86.

INDEX